Geography Revision Notes for Leaving Certificate

PATRICK E. F. O'DWYER

GILL & MACMILLAN

Gill & Macmillan Ltd
Hume Avenue
Park West
Dublin 12
with associated companies throughout the world
www.gillmacmillan.ie

© Patrick E. F. O'Dwyer 1995, 2000
0 7171 3033 9
Design and print origination in Ireland by
Design Image, Dublin

CONTENTS

PREFACE

The purpose of this book is to help students cover the major sections of the Leaving Certificate geography course in a clear and concise way in the months before their examination. Each topic is structured in such a way that students can learn the information given as sample answers. Some developed points may have a multi-answer use; in order to bring this point across to students, the author has purposely repeated some developed points, for example 'Oil in Norway' and 'The importance of the sea to Norway'.

The topics chosen for study in this book were determined by the required syllabus, with particular attention paid to those areas that regularly appear in the Leaving Certificate examination. For revision and examination purposes the author felt it necessary to cover some sections of the course on a question-and-answer basis, for example 'Sketch maps from photographs' and 'The historical development of towns'.

ACKNOWLEDGMENTS

The author wishes to thank the many teachers who read the manuscript and made valuable recommendations during the course of the work. Special thanks are due to all those who assisted in the preparation of this book: Hubert Mahony, Gabrielle Noble, Design Image, and the staff at Gill & Macmillan.

For permission to reproduce photographs, acknowledgment is made to the following: Aerofilms, Barnaby's Picture Library, J. Allan Cash Photolibrary, Format Photographers, Gamma, Impact Photos, Magnum Photos, John O'Brien, Ordnance Survey Office, and the University of Cambridge Committee for Aerial Photography.

MAPS AND PHOTOGRAPHS

DRAWING SKETCH MAPS FROM AERIAL PHOTOGRAPHS

CASE STUDY 1: *Donegal Town*

▲ Fig. 1.1

Study the photograph of Donegal town. Draw a sketch map (*do not trace*) of the area shown, and on it mark and label

(*a*) the street pattern of the town

(*b*) five areas of different land use in the town

(*c*) the river.

DONEGAL: A PLANTATION TOWN

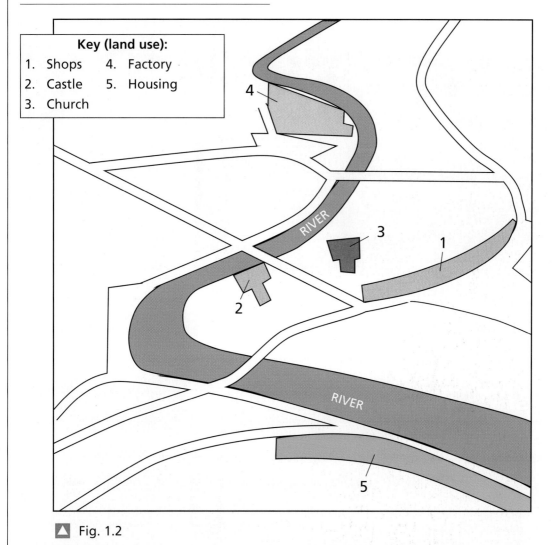

Key (land use):
1. Shops   4. Factory
2. Castle   5. Housing
3. Church

▲ Fig. 1.2

TIPS

1. Always draw a frame similar in shape to that of the map.
2. **Never** trace a map. A sketch map **must** be drawn freehand.
3. Keep the sketch size to less than half of a sheet of foolscap paper.
4. Show and name only the features that you are specifically asked for.
5. Always outline your sketch with a soft pencil. This allows you to correct errors that may arise.
6. Outline land use zones with a heavy boundary line to **limit** the area.
7. Always **mark** and **label** each land use area.
8. Use colour only if you have enough time.

CASE STUDY 2: *BALLYBUNNION*

▲ Fig. 1.3 Ballybunnion, Co. Kerry

Examine the aerial photograph. Draw a sketch map based on the photograph (you may *not* use tracing paper), and on it mark and label:
(a) two areas where coastal erosion is evident
(b) two areas where coastal deposition is evident [**only areas asked for here; if in doubt add in feature name also**]
(c) three areas of different land use that are related to the coastal location of this settlement (35 marks) [**in this case land uses must be directly related to a seaside area**]

BALLYBUNNION: A COASTAL TOWN

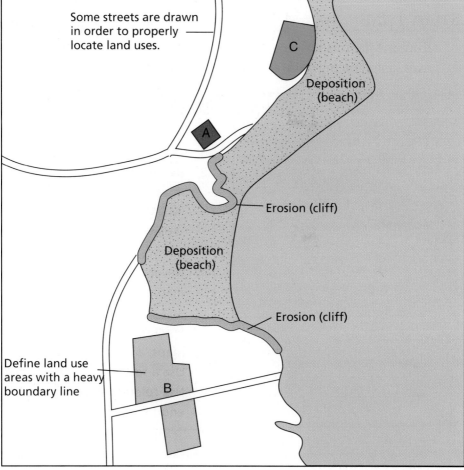

Some streets are drawn in order to properly locate land uses.

C

Deposition (beach)

A

Erosion (cliff)

Deposition (beach)

Erosion (cliff)

Define land use areas with a heavy boundary line

B

▲ Fig. 1.4

Key (land use):

A. Hotel
B. Mobile home site
C. Pitch and putt course
} These land uses are regularly found in seaside resorts.

TIPS

1. Use a key or use labelled arrows to avoid overcrowding.
2. Limit sketch size to half a foolscap page to save time.
3. Always **mark** and **label** features to be identified.

4. Carefully examine the questions asked, and include only what is asked of you. If in doubt, add one extra example.

DRAWING SKETCH MAPS FROM ORDNANCE SURVEY MAPS

CASE STUDY 1: *INISHOWEN MAP EXTRACT*

Examine the Inishowen extract (fig. 1.6) on page 7. Then draw a sketch map (*not* a tracing), and on it mark and name its physical regions.

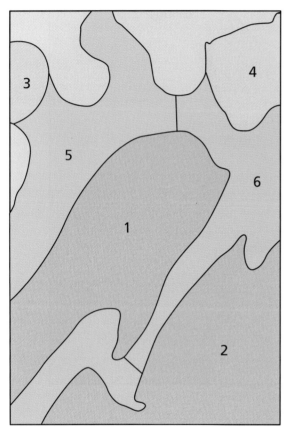

TIPS
1. Always draw a frame similar in shape to that of the map.
2. **Never** trace a map. A sketch map must be drawn freehand.
3. **'Mark'** and **'name'** (or 'label') are separate directions, and marks will be awarded for each separately.
4. Never draw a very large sketch map, as it is more difficult to draw and it takes up too much time.
5. Practise different types of sketch maps, and time yourself.
6. Use a soft lead pencil.
7. Use colour **only** if you have enough time.

▲ Fig. 1.5 Sketch map of Inishowen map extract

Key: physical regions
1. Raghtin More upland ridge } High uplands
2. Bulbin uplands
3. Dunaff uplands } Low uplands
4. Binnion uplands
5. Dunaff coastal plain
6. Basin of the Ballyhallan-Clonmany Rivers } Lowlands
7. Basin of the Owenerk River

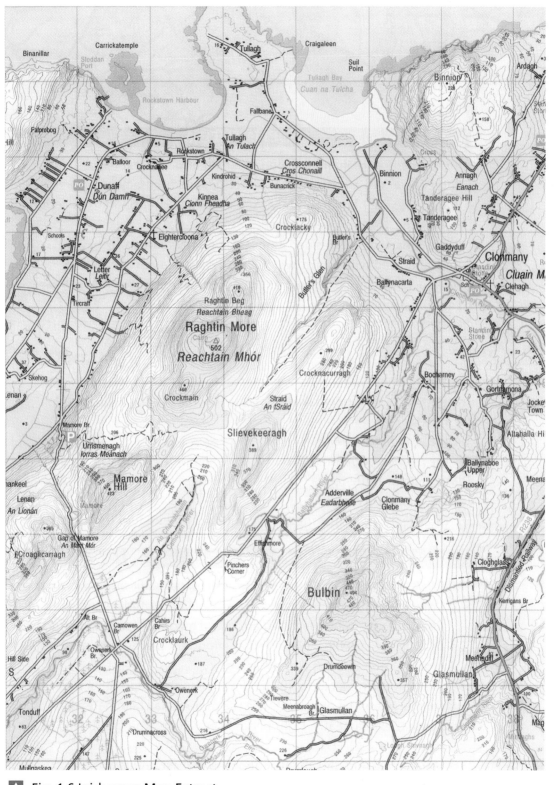

Fig. 1.6 Inishowen Map Extract

DEFINITIONS

Sketch map: a **freehand** drawing of a map or photograph.
Basin: the entire area **drained** by a river and its tributaries.
Watershed: the high ground that **separates** one river basin from another.
Plain: large, low-lying level area.
Ridge: a **narrow**, steep-sided mountain or upland area.
Highland: land with peaks **over 750 m** and large areas over 600 m.
Upland: land with peaks **over 250 m** and large areas over 180 m.
Lowland: land of altitude **between 0 m and 250 m.**

CASE STUDY 2

Examine the 1:50,000 Inishowen map extract. On a sketch map (*not* a tracing) of this region, mark and name the following:

(*a*) the coastline
(*b*) the land below 100 m
(*c*) the highest point on the map
(*d*) one major route focus
(*e*) two named rivers
(*f*) three features indicating the recreational potential of the region.

TIPS

1. Draw the frame first – same shape as map, *not* same size.
2. Draw in northings and eastings – don't measure, it takes too much time. Use *very* light lines: they are only a guide for locating features.
3. Draw in the coastline; place dots at important places (such as promontories and bays) to act as a guide.
4. Shade in the area below 100 m; draw a line that represents the 100 m contour. Don't be overexact. The use of dots may help here again. Shade the area neatly. Light pencil lines will do. You don't need to use colour.
5. Mark, name and give the height of the highest point.

6. Mark in the most important route focus, and name some routes leading into the town.
7. Draw in two rivers. Use one line for each river. Name each river.
8. Mark and name three different recreational areas (e.g. one water sports area, forest for orienteering, golf course). You may use a key to help you in this case.

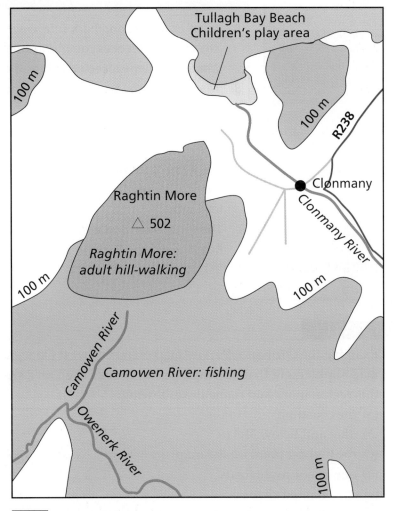

Tullagh Bay Beach
Children's play area

100 m

100 m

R238

Clonmany

Clonmany River

Raghtin More

△ 502

Raghtin More:
adult hill-walking

100 m

100 m

Camowen River

Camowen River: fishing

Owenerk River

100 m

Shaded area: >100 m

Clear area: <100 m

▲ Fig. 1.7

CASE STUDY 3

Study the Ordnance Survey map extract of Inishowen (fig. 1.6) on p. 7. With the aid of a sketch map, describe and explain how the development of the communications network is related to other features of the landscape.

THE INFLUENCE OF RELIEF ON COMMUNICATIONS

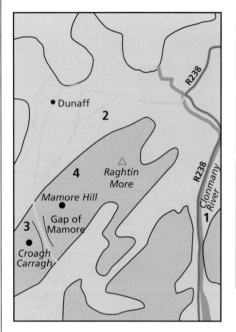

TIPS
1. In an examination, mark *four* ways in which the relief influences communications.
2. **Mark** and **name** affected routes if possible.
3. **Mark** and **name** the associated landscape features that affect the routes.

Key
1. The R238 road uses the Clonmany River valley
2. There is a high density of roads on the Dunaff lowlands
3. The third-class road uses the Gap of Mamore
4. Roads avoid the Raghtin More uplands

 Fig. 1.8

ACTIVITY

1. Examine the Ordnance Survey map extract of west Donegal in the map supplement that accompanies this book. Then on a sketch map of this region mark and name the following:
   (a) the coastline
   (b) the land below 100 m
   (c) the highest point on the map
   (d) one major route focus
   (e) two named rivers
   (f) three features indicating the recreational potential of the region.
2. Study the Ordnance Survey map extract of the Mweelrea mountains in the map supplement that accompanies this book. With the aid of a sketch map, describe and explain how the development of the communications network is related to other features of the landscape.

EXPLANATION OF EACH EXAMPLE SHOWN ON THE SKETCH MAP

1 The R238 road uses the Clonmany River valley. Statement

Development of statement

The Clonmany valley forms a natural route through a rugged upland area in the eastern portion of the map extract. The gently sloping floor of this steep-sided valley forms an ideal location for the construction of a roadway. Construction costs at such a low elevation on the valley floor, between 30 and 100 m, would be low. The valley runs in a north-south direction, providing access to Clonmany, Ballyliffin, and the northern coastline of this peninsula. In the Cloghglass region (grid ref. C 378 422) the road enters a gorge section where the valley floor is narrow and sloping northwards, while at Clonmany the valley floor is wide and level, where the R238 road keeps to its northern edge, away from the flood plain, to avoid flooding.

2 There is a high density of roads on the Dunaff lowlands. Statement

Development of statement

The Dunaff lowlands stretch from the beach at grid ref. C 310 445 to Rockstown Harbour at grid ref. C 335 485. It is gently undulating lowland at less than 40 m in altitude, with a high population density. Settlement here, as in Ireland generally, is confined to lowland areas, which provides fertile land for agriculture. The roadways run along the more elevated areas, avoiding the river lowlands, and thus form a parallel pattern. Housing is also confined to the more elevated areas. So the road pattern and the linear settlement pattern are directly related. Because so much of the surrounding land is elevated and exposed to strong ocean winds, settlement concentrates in the more habitable low-lying valleys and plains, such as the Dunaff lowlands.

3 The third-class road uses the Gap of Mamore. Statement

Development of statement

The upland areas on this map extract run north-east to south-west. Thus they form part of the Caledonian Fold mountain system, which is found in the north-west of Ireland. The Croaghcarragh-Mamore ridge forms part of this fold mountain system and forms a barrier to east-west communications between the Dunaff lowlands and the Owenerk River valley. This high upland ridge is breached by the Gap of Mamore at grid ref. C 320 430. A third-class road that joins Mamore Bridge crossroads in the Dunaff lowlands to Alt Bridge crossroads in the Owenerk River valley takes advantage of the breach. It climbs the steep ridge diagonally, using hairpin bends to reduce its gradient. A vantage point at grid ref. C 317 443 indicates the steepness of the climb above the level lowlands and the low-lying coast to the west.

4 Roads avoid the Raghtin More uplands.   Statement

Development of statement

There is an absence of roads at Raghtin More at grid ref. C 34 46. This is part of a very steep upland area, and so routes avoid it. Route construction in such areas is avoided as it would serve no immediate purpose. People avoid such areas as they are exposed to strong gales, and soils are either infertile or are limited to rock debris from frost action in winter. Even if routes were constructed here, heavy rainfall from onshore winds and night-time frost would erode the road surface in a short time. On Raghtin More, as on Slievekeerage, it is more the steepness of slope that restricts the presence of roads than the general altitude of the area.

TIPS

1. Choose *four* examples of the main theme and explain each in detail.
2. Refer to the area of map for each example chosen.
3. Examples shown on the sketch map must correspond to examples explained in the text.
4. Develop each example chosen as *statement plus development of statement*.

UNDERSTANDING THE DEVELOPMENT OF TOWNS FROM MAPS

CASE STUDY 1

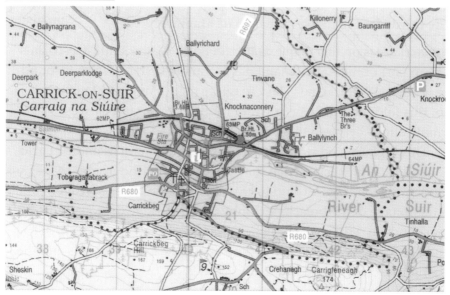

◄ Fig. 1.9 Study the map extract (fig. 1.9) and then account for the development of Carrick-on-Suir at its present location.

1 Focus of routes
Statement

Development of statement

Carrick-on-Suir is sited at a bridging point of the River Suir. As a result it has become a route focus. One national primary road (N24), five regional roads (R696, R697, R680, R676, and R677) and third-class roads all meet here. Carrick-on-Suir is a focus of routes through upland ridges to the north and south, and so it has developed as an important urban centre.

2 Market town
Statement

Development of statement

Carrick-on-Suir is situated on a wide and gently sloping lowland river valley at approximately 10 to 20 m above sea level. The area is well drained by many streams and rivers, such as the Suir, the Glen River, and the Lingaun River, all of which flow in a south-easterly direction. The valley of the Suir appears to be undulating, all of which suggests that the area is a fertile farming region. As it is also a route centre and is centrally located in a lowland region, it is probably a market town.

The presence of a railway station on the north side of the town suggests that at one time fairs may have been held in the town, with the railway carrying purchased cattle to other destinations, such as ports for export.

3 Defensive settlement
Statement

Development of statement

The name Carrick-on-Suir suggests that the town is built on a rock outcrop for defence. Carrick-on-Suir is sited on a bend of the River Suir. There is a castle on the north-eastern end of this loop. This suggests that the castle was constructed for defensive purposes, to guard the town against attack from the downstream side facing the estuary of the river. The words 'Town wall' near the castle suggest that it was a walled town, so the castle was probably built by the Normans. The presence of a castle allowed local farmers to live near and within the walled town for protection against attack by the native Irish. Thus the town's population grew in size. Because it is a bridging point of the river and also a route focus, its importance as a defensive settlement led to its development.

4 Services centre

Statement

Development of statement

The presence of a castle to the east of the town suggests that Carrick-on-Suir may have started as a defensive settlement. Today it has outgrown this early factor. The town has developed on both banks of the River Suir, suggesting that it has become a prosperous and thriving town. The many churches, the school, Garda station, fire station and information office suggest that the town offers these services and many others, making it an important centre for the local urban and rural populations.

The River Suir is wide on the downstream side of the town, which suggests that it may be a port town. Thus the river may have been an important influence on the development of the town.

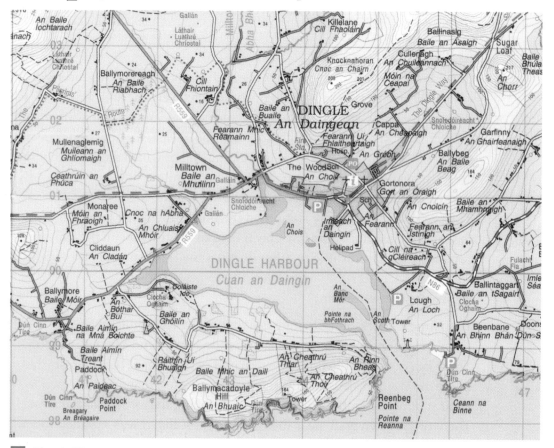

▲ Fig. 1.10

Study the map extract (fig. 1.10) and then account for the development of Dingle at its present location.

1 Focus of routes

The town of Dingle is sited at the meeting place of coastal and inland roads. Coastal routes such as the regional road R559 from Ventry and national secondary road N86, as well as coastal third-class roads, meet at Dingle. Inland routes such as the regional road R559 from Murreagh and the third-class roads from Feoghanagh and Conor Hill all take advantage of mountain passes, cols and river valleys to focus on Dingle.

2 Site

Dingle is sited on sloping land between 0 and 60 m above sea level. The town faces to the south-west, and its high, sloping site offers a view over Dingle Harbour. It is located on the south-western slopes of Ballysitteragh Mountain, which protects the town from cold northerly winds in winter. Dingle is sited on the coast and on an enclosed and sheltered harbour that is protected from ocean winds and waves by a peninsula of land to the south-west.

3 Services centre

Dingle displays a variety of services. The presence of a hospital suggests that it is the most important and centrally located urban centre in the region. There is a helipad to the south-east of the town, which offers support for hospital patients and is possibly used as an important link in marine and mountain rescue services for this rugged inland and coastal region. There is a school in the eastern part of the town, which suggests that it is an educational centre. Other services include a post office and large public car park, indicated by its associated symbol near the quayside at the southern end of the town.

4 Tourist centre

The information symbol in Dingle indicates that it is an important tourist centre. Local names such as the Dingle Way, Cosán na Naomh or Saints' Path and the Pilgrims' Route offer scenic routes for walkers. The numerous historical settlement sites, such as Dún Cinn Tíre, and monuments such as the *galláin* and *tuama meigiliteach* would offer a variety of interest for historians and tourists alike. Scenic glaciated mountain valleys and lakes such as An Loch Dubh to the north and the beach at Ventry to the west of the town offer variety for the tourist.

SETTLEMENT PATTERNS

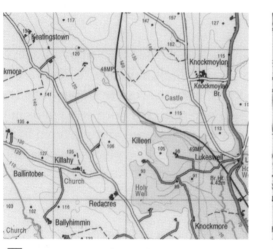

▲ Fig. 1.11. Nucleated pattern

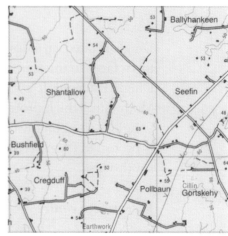

▲ Fig. 1.12. Dispersed pattern

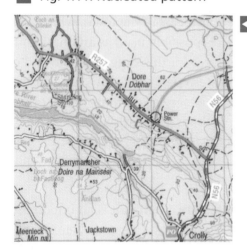

◀ Fig. 1.13. Linear pattern on roads

Rural housing

Village/town

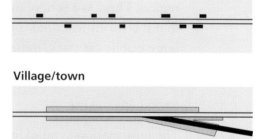

▲ Fig. 1.14

1 Linear pattern (fig. 1.13)

When buildings occur in a line, they are said to form a linear pattern.

Modern linear settlement is characterised by the erection of bungalow-type structures. These rectangular structures are reasonably priced and relatively easy to construct, and so form the most numerous type of new dwelling in rural Ireland. In rural areas an area of roughly 0.20 hectares (approx. ½ acre) is required for planning permission in order to accommodate the dwelling and sewage system. This land is generally only available and desired along roadways. It is *desired* along roadways because services such as telephone cables and water supply pipes are limited to roadside margins. It is *available* along roadways because farmers are willing only to sell narrow strips of land, which fetch a high retail price.

Linear settlement also develops along valley routes, especially on south-facing slopes, which are warmer and sheltered from cold northerly winds.

Where towns or villages develop on an important route (e.g. Droichead Nua (Newbridge) in Co. Kildare), demand for frontage on such a road is high. Shops, garages and filling stations, pubs etc. need passing traffic to fulfil their threshold needs. Buildings therefore tend to form a line on both sides of the road.

2 Dispersed pattern (fig. 1.12)

Dispersed housing

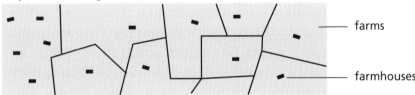

▲ Fig. 1.15

When numerous buildings are dotted over an area such as on a lowland plain they are said to form a dispersed pattern.

By the early eighteenth century the Irish and feudal land systems had started to disappear. **Commonage** (open grazing land) was enclosed with fences and hedges, and the land was redistributed among the original farmers. Farms were arranged by squaring or striping, and each tenant built a house on his newly enclosed farm. Each farmer now held a farm and farmhouse of his own and no longer held a farm in common with others. Thus a dispersed or scattered rural settlement pattern developed, which persists to the present day.

Throughout Ireland, farmhouses are widely separated from each other. Some are sited at the end of long lanes far from roads, while others have roadside sites. An overall dispersed pattern emerges in rural areas.

The density of this distribution may vary from region to region. For example, in areas where farms are large, such as in the eastern part of Ireland, houses may be widely scattered, giving low-density settlement, while in areas where farms are small, such as in the western part of Ireland, houses may be more closely spaced and give rise to high-density settlement.

3 Nucleated Pattern (fig. 1.11)

Urban – town

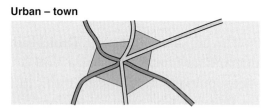

Rural – Clachán

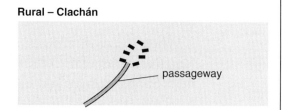

passageway

▲ Fig. 1.16

Nucleated settlements are those in which the buildings are grouped together.

In rural areas, especially in parts of the west of Ireland, unplanned clusters of farmhouses provide examples of nucleated settlements (e.g. the Ballydavid area of the Dingle peninsula). They are remnants of the **rundale** farming system (the infield around the dwellings was tilled and the outfield used as commonage). This was practised in the native Irish parts of the country. Even though many of these houses still stand, they may now be used as animal shelters or fodder stores. Few are used as dwellings.

Sometimes buildings are grouped together, such as at the foot of a hill on a dry point in a marshy area, or at a wet point in an area of porous rock, such as in the Burren in Co. Clare.

Most towns are nucleated. Towns become the focus of routes. Land at such a focus is in great demand for business, industry, and housing. Thus the land at the junction of these routes, along these routes and in the sectors between these routes is built on to provide for these demands. Buildings are grouped together, and so they are nucleated (e.g. Limerick, Nenagh).

■ Absence Pattern

Settlement is absent from elevated areas over 200 m (approx. 700 feet). Elevated areas are generally wet and are exposed to strong winds, especially in winter. Temperatures are cooler than lowland areas because of the effect of altitude, and so crop growth and crop variety are limited, while soils are thin and unproductive. Thus the factors that favour settlement are absent, and people avoid such areas as much as possible.

However, south-facing mountain slopes are warmer than north-facing slopes, because of the effect of **aspect**. Thus a higher density of settlement may be found in these sunnier areas, especially on valley slopes in upland areas where sheep farming is practised and where access is easier along valley routes.

Settlement is also regularly absent from flat, low-lying areas on the flood plains of rivers in their lower courses. Such low-lying areas are prone to flooding during periods of heavy rainfall. At such times, rivers are no longer confined to their channels and spread across their flood plains and cause widespread flooding, for example on the callows near Clonmacnoise on the River Shannon. Settlement avoids these areas, and where it does exist it is confined to dry points on elevated patches of ground above the flood plain.

People also avoid both steep, elevated areas and low-lying areas that are prone to flooding. Route construction and maintenance in such areas is expensive.

PATTERNS OF DRAINAGE

1 Dendritic Pattern

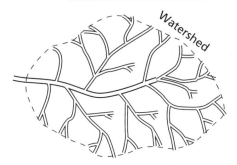

dendritic pattern

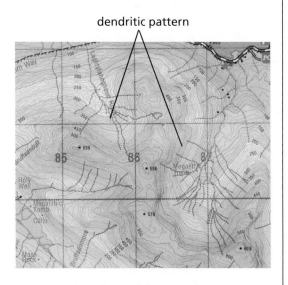

Déndron is the Greek word for 'tree'. Thus a dendritic pattern is tree-shaped (e.g. Shannon).

▲ Fig. 1.17 Dendritic pattern

▲ Fig. 1.18 Dendritic patterns

Déndron is the Greek word for 'tree'. Thus a dendritic pattern is tree-shaped. On a newly formed landscape, the first streams and rivers will flow according to the fall of the land. These rivers are called **consequent streams**. As they develop, tributaries flow towards these main valleys, joining the parent river obliquely, and in turn minor tributaries join them. If the rocks in the river's basin have equal resistance to erosion (e.g. all sandstone or all limestone) then each consequent stream will become the centre of a converging stream pattern, to which is given the name **dendritic drainage**. Every river appears to consist of a main trunk, fed from a variety of branches, each running into a valley proportional to its size.

2 Trellised Pattern

trellised pattern

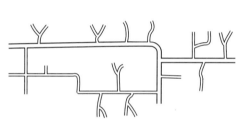

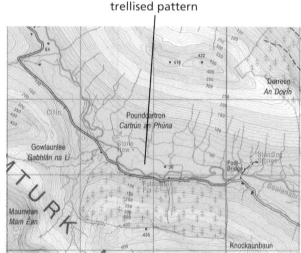

When tributaries flow into the main river at right angles, a trellised pattern is formed. This pattern occurs when valleys and ridges run parallel to each other (e.g. the Munster Blackwater).

▲ Fig. 1.19 Trellised pattern   ▲ Fig. 1.20 Trellised pattern

When tributaries flow into the main river at right angles, a trellised pattern is formed. If the land surface consists of rocks of varying degrees of resistance – in other words, if the land is composed of bands of hard (sandstone) and soft (limestone) rocks at right angles to the consequent stream – streams called **subsequent streams** will develop along the softer bands of rock. These subsequent streams will form broad valleys through the process of headward erosion, and they will be flanked on each side by parallel ridges. Tributaries will develop and flow from these ridges to join the subsequent streams at right angles. River capture frequently occurs in areas of trellised drainage, such as on the Blackwater River at Cappoquin in Munster.

Rectangular patterns are quite similar to trellised patterns, except that both the main streams and the tributaries follow courses with right-angled bends. Lines of weakness, such as faults and joints, may be responsible for such patterns.

3 Radial Pattern

radial pattern

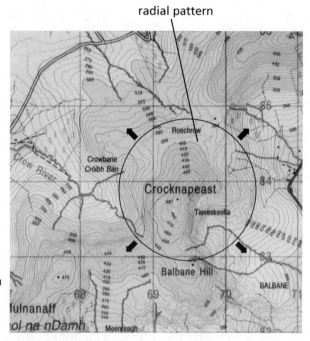

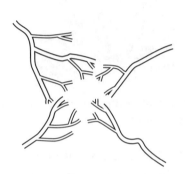

When several streams radiate (flow outwards) in all directions from a mountain or hill they form a radial pattern of drainage

▲ Fig. 1.21 Radial pattern

▲ Fig. 1.22 Rivers radiate from a central elevated area

Rivers that radiate outwards from a mountain form a radial pattern. This is best displayed in well-defined circular or oval upland areas. Some of these rivers may in fact display a different drainage pattern from the others, but together they may radiate outwards (north, south, east, or west) from a central elevated area. They all share a common watershed at their highest source streams.

KG.

4 Deranged Pattern

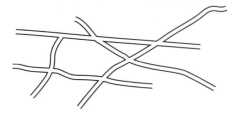

deranged pattern

This is a river pattern that generally develops in a lowland area. Rivers have a chaotic appearance.

▲ Fig. 1.23 Deranged pattern

▲ Fig. 1.24 Deranged pattern rivers have a chaotic appearance

Deranged drainage generally develops in a lowland area. Rivers have a chaotic appearance, with streams intersecting each other and flowing in no apparent direction. It generally develops as a result of widespread deposition of glacial material through which postglacial streams have had to find a route. An example of deranged drainage is to be found on the coastal plain west of Cahore Point in Co. Wexford.

PATTERNS IN THE DISTRIBUTION OF WOODLAND

DISTRIBUTION OF WOODLAND IN ELEVATED AREAS

Land in elevated areas may be purchased at a low price per hectare by Government bodies, such as Coillte. Much of it is commonage, and because of rural depopulation many farmers are willing to sell their land for investment elsewhere. As Ireland is the least-forested country in western Europe, it is Government policy to continue with a heavy planting commitment in the future.

■ Climate

Trees on mountains or high upland areas must withstand hard climatic conditions: extremely cold winters and short, cool summers. They must also withstand a continuously damp climate and often winter precipitation in the form of snow. Conifer trees such as Sitka spruce, Norway spruce, contorta pine and Scots pine are generally grown in coniferous forests because they can cope with these harsh climatic conditions. Their needle-shaped leaves reduce transpiration to a minimum, and their compact conical structure both helps their stability against the wind and prevents too heavy an accumulation of snow on the branches as in the colder northern lands of the Boreal Region. Conifer trees will grow quickly in exposed mountain areas. They produce a big proportion of soft wood in a relatively short time, while their foliage allows the maximum utilisation of sunlight throughout the growing season. South-facing mountain slopes capture the warm, high-angle rays of the sun. These slopes, which are sheltered from cold northerly winds, produce high growth rates in species such as Sitka spruce. It is a valuable alternative land use in areas that would otherwise be non-productive. It also provides a supplementary income for subsistence farmers in areas of heavy out-migration.

■ Soil Type

Conifer trees are undemanding in their needs. They will thrive in soils such as leached soil or bog, where other tree types, such as deciduous trees, will not grow.

High upland and mountain areas in Ireland receive between 1,500 and 2,000 mm of rainfall annually. This gives rise to **leaching**. Percolating water seeps down into the ground, and iron hydroxides and the humus from rotting vegetation near the surface are carried to the lower soil layer, thus leaching the topsoil or upper horizon. This top zone is thus changed in colour to a predominantly greyish tint; this type of soil is called a **podzol**. The leached iron and humus-rich material accumulates at a depth of a few centimetres, where, mixed with particles of clay and silt, it forms a hard cemented band or hard pan that prevents further drainage and leads to waterlogging. So there is a marked tendency for bogs to develop. Trees may be planted on steep mountain slopes. The tree roots help to bind soil particles together, thereby preventing erosion. The trees also prevent rapid surface water run-off. Thus areas that might otherwise be non-productive agriculturally are now put to a commercial use.

DISTRIBUTION OF WOODLAND IN LOWLAND AREAS

■ Demesne Woodland or Parkland

NOTICE!
Give map
reference

In the eighteenth and nineteenth centuries a system of large landed estates embraced the whole country. Their boundaries were often defined by high stone walls. These are represented by a well-defined line that encloses a wooded area on Ordnance Survey maps, such as at .... The main characteristics were great houses or castles with numerous outbuildings, set in parkland with ornamental trees, gardens, and lakes. On the inside and running parallel to the perimeter wall was a narrow strip of deciduous trees, such as beech, oak, and chestnut. Other parts of these estates may have been cordoned off by walls for the production of commercial timber.

■ Mixed Soils

Some lowland areas have soils that are not desired for immediate agricultural use. Such soils may be too wet or too dry for high agricultural yields. These may be gainfully put to use for long-term investment, and so conifer trees may be planted for the following reasons:

1. Coniferous trees produce a big proportion of wood in relation to the space occupied when compared with deciduous trees.
2. Conifer trees grow very quickly in lowland areas and are ready for felling in forty to sixty years.
3. Pines thrive on dry, sandy soils; spruce thrives on damper soils such as flood plains; while larch thrives on soils of fair quality.

ABSENCE OF WOODLAND

■ Elevated Areas

High upland and mountain land is often devoid of forest. This may occur for a number of reasons:

1. Some mountain areas are too high – greater than 600 m (2,000 feet) – for the growth of trees. In elevated areas such as these, insufficient heat and exposure to strong winds limit growth to grasses, mosses, and lichens.

2. Most high mountain areas have little or no soil cover. This absence of soil occurs because the agents of **denudation** (weathering and erosion) constantly remove **regolith** or weathered material, thus restricting the growth of soil.

■ Lowland Areas

3. Most lowland areas have no forest cover. Lowland is generally used for agricultural purposes. Farming activities such as tillage or dairying are intensive forms of land use and so produce high yields each year. Forestry, on the other hand, does not produce a return for at least forty years, and so is seen as a long-term investment. So it is restricted to marginal lands.

CASE STUDY

TIPS
Choose a theme for each developed statement. 1. In this example the chosen theme is *aspect*, and all information in the paragraph relates to this theme. 2. Other suggested themes for other examples may be climate, aspect, soil type, elevation, or demesne woodland.

■ Analysis of Question

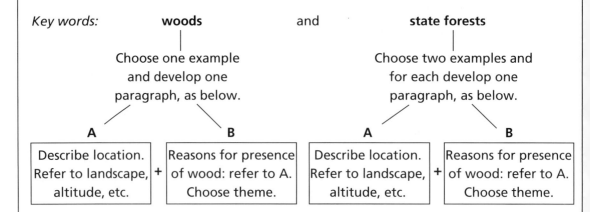

Key words: **woods** and **state forests**

| Choose one example and develop one paragraph, as below. | Choose two examples and for each develop one paragraph, as below. |

A	B	A	B
Describe location. Refer to landscape, altitude, etc.	+ Reasons for presence of wood: refer to A. Choose theme.	Describe location. Refer to landscape, altitude, etc.	+ Reasons for presence of wood: refer to A. Choose theme.

Sample answer of one developed point

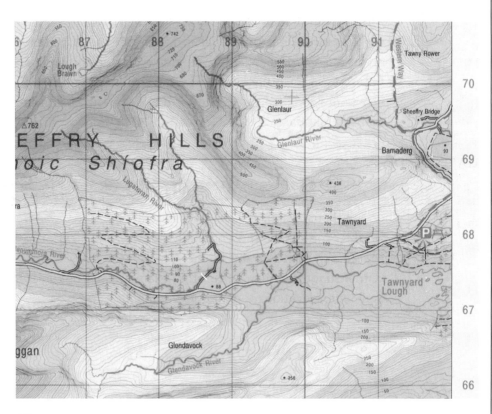

▲ Fig. 1.25 A state forest in the Glenummera Valley (Mweelrea Mountains extract map in map supplement book)

There is a large coniferous plantation in the valley of the Glenummera River at grid ref. L 88 68. It is on both sides of the valley but is mainly concentrated on the northern side. Both sides of this valley are steeply sloping and are open to the east. This suggests that the plantation takes advantage of the early morning sunshine that comes from the east. The greater portion of the plantation faces south on the steeply sloping side of the Sheefry Hills and is able to trap the sun's rays throughout the day. This ensures maximum growth of the trees in this elevated area. The plantation reaches an elevation of 370 m on these warmer, south-facing slopes, whereas it is limited to 250 m on the north-facing side. This indicates the limiting effects of aspect and slope on the plantation.

Annotations
Location + grid reference
Location + description
Explanation
Location + description
Explanation
Location + description
Explanation

Theme – aspect

TIP

As with most Ordnance Survey answers, refer regularly to the map, and describe the landscape and features. Write as much as you can.

2

UNDERSTANDING THE HISTORY OF THE IRISH LANDSCAPE

FIELD PATTERNS

Today the most common feature of the social landscape is the farm, giving us a **bocage** landscape (fields enclosed by clay or stone fences with hedging on top). In the eighteenth century, farms with their fields and fences were called **enclosures**. This name derived from the fact that all land before the eighteenth century was commonage, and the **rundale** and the open-field systems of farming were practised. The rundale system was practised in the parts of the country that had not been planted, for example in the western counties of Mayo, Galway, Donegal, and Kerry. Central to this system was the 'clachán' or unplanned cluster of farmsteads (fig. 2.1). The **infield** (a large field enclosed with a rail or wattle fence) was situated near the clachán and was divided into strips and tilled by the families. Oats, barley, wheat and rye were grown. Potatoes and turnips were introduced later. Surrounding the infield and beyond it lay the **outfield**, which was grazed in common by all the farmers. 'Booleying' or **transhumance** was practised on the upland slopes. Remnants of this farming system are still to be found in remote parts of the west today.

The **open-field system** was practised in the rest of the country. This consisted of a village, more formal in plan than the clachán, located near the manor. Surrounding the settlement were three large open fields. One of these was generally left fallow, while the others were divided into long, scattered and unfenced strips of land for each farmer. This ensured an equal distribution of land of varying quality. Each open field could be hundreds of acres in area. Landless peasants supplemented their meagre incomes by grazing one or two cows on the commons that surrounded the open fields. When land was enclosed, they were unable to continue this practice. In some western areas, enclosure fences are superimposed on the old tillage patterns that are indicative of the rundale system.

Farm dwellings in ruins

Ploughing ridges showing evidence of original infield

▲ Fig. 2.1 A clachán

THE ENCLOSURES

By the early eighteenth century the rundale and open-field systems had started to disappear. Commonage was enclosed with fences and hedges, and the land was redistributed among the strip holders. The enclosed farms were better managed; they used new farming methods such as crop rotation and seed drills, which led to much heavier crops and healthier, better-fed animals.

Each tenant built a house on his newly enclosed farm, and old villages or clacháns were pulled down. Thus a new land-holding system evolved, and a change came about in the settlement pattern of the Irish landscape. Each individual farmer now held a farm of his own and no longer held a farm in common with others. The elimination of many nucleated clusters or villages led to a dispersed rural settlement pattern similar to that of today's landscape. Each enclosure is divided into fields, which are separated by fences or ditches of stone or clay, or both, upon which hedges of whitethorn grow. Farms are separated from each other by **bounds ditches**, which are generally wider and thicker in their hedging than fences.

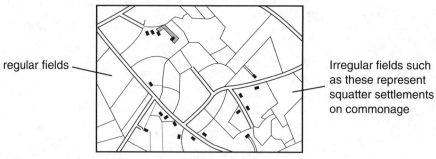

regular fields

Irregular fields such as these represent squatter settlements on commonage

▲ Fig. 2.2

In hilly areas or places where land was of varying quality, such as sloping land leading down to a river, improvers of the eighteenth and nineteenth centuries used a system of enclosure known as **striping**. In such cases the farmland was organised in single narrow strips or stripes arranged in parallel rows.

On lowland plains, where land was of uniform quality, a system known as **squaring** was arranged. This was a grid-iron pattern of farms interconnected by a complicated pattern of tracks or 'bohereens'.

THE HISTORICAL GROWTH OF TOWNS

SAMPLE ANSWERS

Q. Describe the history of the town from a study of its buildings.

TIP
For each building – (a) give an exact location on the photograph (b) describe size, architecture and materials of building if possible (c) describe its association with the growth of the town.

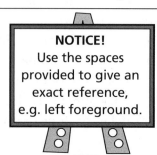

NOTICE!
Use the spaces provided to give an exact reference, e.g. left foreground.

▲ Fig. 2.3 Kells, Co. Meath
Round tower and graveyard indicate monastic origin

■ Round Tower: an Early Christian Settlement

There is a **tall circular** and **tapering stone** building in the ....
of the photograph. It has **openings** near its top. This suggests that it is a
round tower and that the openings were part of its belfry to warn the
local inhabitants of a possible attack by the Vikings. Round towers were
important buildings in Early Christian monastic settlements. Therefore
this part of the settlement must have its origin in Early Christian times,
possibly in the sixth, seventh or eighth century. At that time this
settlement would have had churches, graveyards, and smith's workshop.
It would have had a school, as most religious sites attracted students from
surrounding areas and from abroad. Thus it would have had religious,
social and educational functions.

There is a **circular street** around this oldest portion of the town.
It curves from the .... to the .... of the
photograph. This street may have replaced the original stone wall of the
monastic enclosure. It thus supports the idea of monastic origins for
this town.

Give exact photo references

▲ Fig. 2.4 Thomond Castle and St Mary's Cathedral, Limerick

Give exact photo references

■ Castle and/or Abbey: a Defensive Norman Settlement

There is a castle in the .... of the photograph. It is a **high stone** building with **thick walls** and has a **rectangular ground plan**. It is sited by the river that runs along the .... of the photograph. This represents the second stage of development of this town. The streets near the castle in the .... appear narrow and varying in width. This indicates a medieval type of street plan. Markets such as fish markets were held at such street junctions. This town would have been surrounded by high defensive walls during medieval times. Defensive walls became obsolete, and later they were demolished and new developments covered their foundations.

Castles were built in such defensive riverside sites by the Normans as they captured and secured river crossings in the twelfth and thirteenth centuries. They quickly moved across the country from the south-east and laid claim to the lands east and south of the River Shannon. They always chose important strategic sites for their settlements in fertile, low-lying areas. These sites therefore survived and thrived as commercial centres. The town in the photograph would have developed accordingly, and it would have been a **market town** for the local farming area. Norman farmers would have lived close to the castle for **security** and **protection** against attack from the Celtic Irish, while their produce could have been sold in the town on market day.

There is an abbey in the .... of the photograph and it is sited near the castle. It is a large stone building with a cross-shaped plan. At its centre there is a rectangular tower with pointed gothic-style windows similar to those in the castle. Irish abbeys are of Norman origin. European religious orders were invited to Ireland by Norman lords, who sometimes built these churches for the Augustinians, Cistercians, Franciscans, or Dominicans. These abbeys would have played an important role in the life of towns such as the one in the photograph. This abbey would have been multifunctional, providing education for the young, accommodation for travellers, and health care for the sick, as well as religious functions. This abbey was probably part of a much larger complex in Norman times. It would have had a cloister, kitchen, stores, and chapter-house. The river would have been a source of fresh water and fish for the monks and the people of the town. Thus abbeys would have attracted people to the town to live and so further encouraged the development of the town.

Give exact photo reference

▲ Fig. 2.5 Donegal town

PLANTATION TOWNS OF THE SIXTEENTH AND SEVENTEENTH CENTURIES

■ The Diamond

Give exact photo reference

There is a triangular 'square' in the .... of the photograph. Three main streets converge on this square, and two and three-storey commercial buildings line each side of the square. Such a plan suggests that it is a plantation town of Ulster built after 1609. The establishment of such towns in Ulster played an important part in encouraging settlers and creating economic development. The square or diamond would have served primarily as a market-place, which encouraged trade. Traders from other such towns would assemble and sell their goods, while local farmers sold their produce to urban folk on market day. The diamond also provided the town with an easily defended central area in the event of attack from the dispossessed Irish.

■ The Castle

Give exact photo reference

There is a castle in the .... of the photograph close to the diamond. It is sited on a river loop for defensive reasons. The plan and appearance of this castle differ greatly from Norman buildings. This structure has a large rectangular and spacious two-storey section with large **mullion windows** (windows with stone divisions). The remainder of the building seems to be three storeys high and has a square plan with small towers at its corners. This castle was probably owned and built by the 'undertaker' of the local plantation. In acquiring this estate he undertook to fulfil certain conditions, one of them being to build a castle of a particular size. He would also have interested himself in the plan of the adjoining town, as its appearance and prosperity would have played a crucial role in his own income and prestige. His castle and the entire town as it then was would have been surrounded by high stone walls for security against attack. Such walls were later demolished, as they were no longer needed during peaceful times.

■ Protestant Church

Give exact photo reference

There is a church in the .... of the photograph. It is gothic in its style of architecture, and has a tall pointed spire over its belfry at its front entrance. There are four small pointed projections on each corner of the belfry. Its side windows are pointed in the gothic style. This style of architecture suggests that it is a Protestant church built during plantation times. The fact that it is just off the diamond suggests that it is one of the town's original buildings. There is a small graveyard in the church grounds. In Ulster, Protestantism was introduced during plantation times. The church occupies a central location in the town, as Protestantism was the religion practised by the planters. This central location ensured that the church formed an integral part of the social and cultural life of the townspeople.

■ Catholic Church

Give exact photo reference

There is a large gothic-style church on the outskirts of the town in the .... of the photograph. It appears much larger than all the surrounding buildings, and appears to be a newer structure than the church in the town's centre. There is a car park adjoining the church. The peripheral location of the church suggests that it is a later addition to the town, which suggests that it is a Catholic church built after Catholic Emancipation in 1829. During the seventeenth and eighteenth centuries the Penal Laws forbade the native Irish from attending Mass. Churches and schools were closed during this time. Large neo-gothic churches such as that shown here display the freedom of the Catholic Church after emancipation, as well as displaying the wealth and numbers of the local community. Thus at the time of its construction the local community were prosperous and numerous, and it was a time of peace, as it would have been located far outside the site of the original town wall.

PLANTATION TOWNS OF THE EIGHTEENTH AND NINETEENTH CENTURIES

Give exact photo reference

The town in the photograph displays many features of a plantation town. The square in the .... of the photograph indicates that this part of the town was built in the eighteenth century. Fairs were held at least once a year in these open spaces, as towns acted as market centres for the rural farming community. They were designed by the local landlords to play a major role in the economic development of the town, as markets were held in the squares at regular intervals. There is a monument in the centre of the square to commemorate the local landlord.

▲ Fig. 2.6 Birr, Co. Offaly

Give exact photo reference

The streets are wide and regular in their width, and they appear to focus on the square, a common feature of planned towns. In the .... of the photograph there is a gothic-style church. Its tower has a number of tall spires, which is characteristic of Protestant churches of plantation times. A tree-lined street seems to lead away from the church to the .... of the photograph. High terraced buildings similar to Georgian houses seem to line this street. This is probably the mall, a wide and spacious street of the eighteenth century. On the .... of the photograph some buildings are also of Georgian design. Some houses are two-storey, others three-story, with classical features.

▲ Fig. 2.7 Carlow town

■ A Mill: Industrial Growth

Give exact photo reference

There is a long four or five-storey building in the .... of the photograph. It appears to be built of cut stone. It is a narrow structure with numerous evenly spaced windows on each floor level. This type of architecture indicates that it is a mill or grain store. Flowing alongside one wall of this building is a narrow stream, which represents the original mill-race that was used to work the mill wheel, the source of power in the factory. The presence of such a factory in a town indicates that during the eighteenth and nineteenth centuries this town was a prosperous industrial centre. Grain milling at this time was a labour-intensive industry, while brewing in some towns added to the number of jobs available. In such brewing and distilling centres grain was carried up to the top floors and spread out to mature. A combination of heat and dust increased the possibility of fire, and numerous windows were needed to reduce temperatures on these upper levels.

Such industries indicate that the town was a market centre for local farmers. They would bring their farm produce, such as grain, to the mills and distilleries for sale. This gave them a guaranteed income at harvest time.

■ Canal town

▲ Fig. 2.8 The canals

The waterway in the photograph (Fig 2.9) displays a canal section in the .... of the photograph. The docking area in the .... of the photograph has a stone quayside with large warehouse or granary-like buildings, now standing roofless. These structures were used to store bulky goods such as timber, coal and grain along the canalside. This dock would have been the centre of transport activity during the eighteenth and the beginning of the nineteenth century. Canals were used to transport bulky goods as well as people. Canal boats were at first pulled by horses at a speed of up to 10 miles an hour. This type of transport was favoured because it was more comfortable and reliable than horse-drawn coaches. Hotels were built near the quaysides to cater for the needs of the many passengers who used barge transport. The high three-storey plastered building in the .... of the photograph may be the old hotel, which now appears to be a ....

Give exact photo reference

Canal

▲ Fig. 2.9 Tullamore, Co Offaly

Such canal towns went into industrial decline with the construction of the railways. Many canal towns were by-passed, and as the railways were a more efficient form of transport their trade faltered.

■ Railways

The development of the railway greatly influenced urban development in Ireland during the late nineteenth and early twentieth centuries. The first railway was laid in 1834, and by 1912 there was a total of 5,500 km (3,500 miles) of track laid. This new form of transport became an overnight success, as it was cheaper, faster and more comfortable than either the canal barges or road coaches. The British government encouraged investment in the railways, and more than twenty companies came into existence.

Towns that were fortunate enough to be on railway lines grew, while less fortunate settlements, such as some canal towns, declined, for example Daingean in Co. Offaly, Killaloe in Co. Clare, and Graiguenamanagh in Co. Kilkenny.

The arrival of the railway in small towns added to the settlements' prosperity and increased their nodality for such events as fairs, which were held annually in market towns throughout the country. Railways

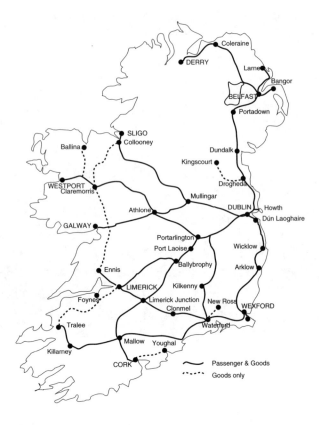

▲ Fig. 2.10 The main railway lines in operation today

were used to carry cattle from market centres in such areas as the Golden Vale to the fattening lands of Co. Meath, to the factories for processing, or to the ports for exporting, thus boosting exports. Nearly all the new lines that were built in the late 1800s were intended to improve access to ports. The railways brought thousands of tourists, of both the upper and middle classes, from urban centres such as Dublin and Limerick to the west and south. This in turn encouraged the development of seaside resorts such as Kilkee in Co. Clare and Youghal in Co. Cork.

The layout of such resorts was often determined by the shape of the coastline. Straight coastal beaches were backed by a linear pattern of tall terraced houses, often taking advantage of a high vantage point for a view out to sea, or by low Italianate villas along the sea front. Crescentic or bay-head beaches had dwellings that followed the shape of the bay, as at Kilkee in Co. Clare.

3

PHYSICAL GEOGRAPHY

■ The Earth

The **crust** consists of solid rock, mostly basalt and granite.

The **transition zone** lies directly inside the crust. It consists of hot molten rock and semi-solid matter.

The **mantle** consists of heavy rocks. Many of these are in a molten or liquid state because of the very high temperatures (4,000°C). Here rock is so hot that it has melted and flows like a river.

The **core** is made up of iron and nickel. It is the hottest part of the earth. Temperatures are greater than 4,000°C.

■ The Plates of the Earth's Crust

- The earth's crust is made up of **plates**. These fit together somewhat like a jigsaw. These huge plates float on a heavy semi-molten rock and are moved around by convection currents beneath them.
- As the plates move around slowly, so do the continents and oceans that sit on top of them. This movement of the continents is known as **continental drift**.
- In places, these convection currents
  (*a*) drag the plates apart – these are **plates in separation** – or
  (*b*) push the plates together – these are **plates in collision**.
- High mountain ridges occur on the ocean floor in places where plates separate. These are known as mid-ocean ridges. Volcanic islands, such as Iceland, occur on these mid-ocean ridges.
- **Fold mountains** are found in places where plates collide – e.g. the Armorican fold mountains of southern Ireland and the Andes in South America.

■ Earthquakes

- Earthquakes are sudden tremors or vibrations in the earth's crust.
- Colliding plates build up pressure beneath the earth's crust. The sudden release of this energy causes a violent shaking of the earth's surface.

- The **focus** is the place beneath the earth's surface where an earthquake occurs.
- The **epicentre** is the spot on the surface directly above the focus.
- **Shock waves** move out from the epicentre and focus. They reduce in strength with distance form the epicentre. (The shock waves may be compared to the ripples in a pool when a stone is thrown into the water.)
- Greater damage is done to built-up areas close to the epicentre than to places further away.
- The lines along which the plates meet are called **fault lines**. The San Andreas Fault in California is such an example. San Francisco and Los Angeles are close to this fault line and so experience earthquakes regularly.
- The largest earthquake and volcano zone lies along the Pacific Ocean. It is called the Pacific Ring of Fire.

■ Definitions

Tectonic:	belonging to the structure of the earth's crust and to general changes in it such as folding, faulting, etc.
Ocean trench:	a narrow scar thousands of metres deep along a destructive plate boundary.
Subducted:	At a destructive plate boundary where two plates come together, the heavier ocean plate sinks and is destroyed beneath the lighter continental plate.
Asthenosphere:	a zone within the upper mantle between the depths of 100 and 700 km in the earth's crust.
Lithosphere:	the rigid outer layer of the earth, including the crust and upper mantle.
Metamorphism:	the changes in mineral composition and texture of a rock subjected to high temperature and pressure within the earth.
Composite cone:	a volcano composed of both lava flows and volcanic ash and cinder.
Tsunami:	the Japanese word for a giant wave caused by an earthquake under the ocean floor.

PLATE TECTONICS

The theory of plate tectonics suggests that the earth's crust is divided into huge slabs of creeping rock that move slowly across the surface of the globe. The slabs or plates are driven by enormous convection currents within the earth's core and mantle. Alfred Wegener, a German meteorologist, proposed this idea in 1912 in a book called *The Origin of Continents and Oceans*, and today it is accepted as one of the most important theories of earth science. Simply, he proposed that all the continents of the modern world had drifted apart from an original 'supercontinent', which he called Pangaea (meaning 'all land'). Others before him, intrigued by the 'jigsaw puzzle' shape of the continents, had suggested a similar hypothesis, but Wegener was the first to support it with evidence, systematically collected and analysed.

Wegener based his proposals on

(a) the distribution of identical fossils on continents separated by thousands of miles of ocean

(b) the matching shapes of the African and American coastlines

(c) the presence of marine sediments on high mountains.

Wegener also argued that no evidence existed for most of the temporary land bridges that scientists of the time proposed as an explanation for the migration of species from one continent to another.

However, Wegener was unable to offer an explanation for the mechanics of what came to be called continental drift, and that flaw was fatal to his theories. His critics maintained that he was a meteorologist, not a geologist, and that he was out of his depth. It was not until the 1950s that interest in continental drift began to revive as a result of research into rock magnetism and sea-floor spreading.

THEORIES ASSOCIATED WITH PLATE TECTONICS

■ Continental Drift

The theory of continental drift suggests that the continents have moved great distances on the earth's surface and are still moving today. According to the theory, the continents once formed part of a single land mass, called Pangaea. The world's single ocean, called Panthalassa, surrounded Pangaea. About 200 million years ago, according to the theory, Pangaea began to break apart. It split into two land masses, called Gondwanaland and Laurasia. Gondwanaland then broke apart, forming

Africa, Antarctica, Australia, South America, and the Indian subcontinent. Laurasia split into Eurasia and North America. The formation of the present continents and their drifting into their present positions took place gradually over millions of years.

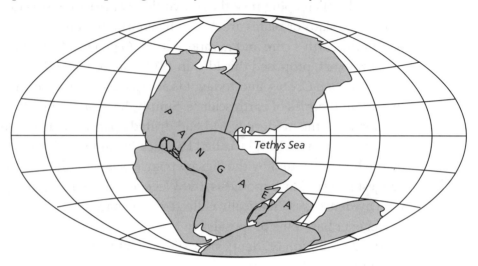

▲ Fig. 3.1 Reconstruction of Pangaea as it is thought to have appeared 200 million years ago

During the present century scientists gathered information to support this theory.

1. Geological studies of ancient mountain systems show a connection between the continents. These studies suggest that the Appalachian Mountains of the eastern United States extend through Newfoundland. The Appalachians may have been connected to the Caledonian mountain system, which runs through the north of Ireland, Scandinavia, and Scotland.

2. Other evidence for such a connection comes from palaeontologists (scientists who study fossils). They have found fossils of similar land mammals in the rocks of Asia, Europe and North America that are 100 million years old. It seems unlikely that similar animals could develop on widely separated continents.

3. In the mid-1960s scientists using radiometric methods for dating rocks found specimens of the same age and type in Africa and South America.

4. During the 1950s the study of magnetism in ancient rock helped support the idea of continental drift. When igneous rock is hot and liquid, magnetic particles in it (such as minerals of iron oxide) are free

to point towards the magnetic poles, like tiny compass needles. But after the rock cools and hardens, the particles stay pointed in the direction of the pole when the rock cooled. This **fossil magnetism** thus provides a record by which the position of the magnetic pole at various times can be established.

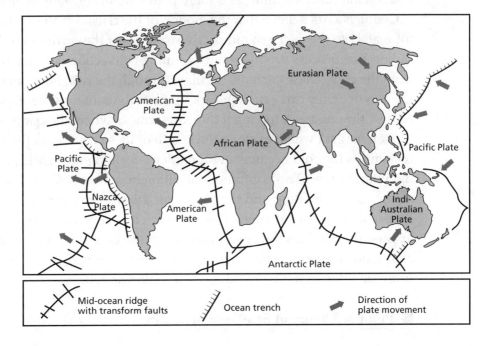

▲ Fig. 3.2 Plate boundaries, indicated by mid-ocean ridges, oceanic trenches, and transform faults

The British geophysicist S. K. Runcord established the earth's magnetic poles at the time the rocks were formed. He found that the positions of the poles determined from European rocks differed from those determined from North American rocks; the difference matched the width of the Atlantic Ocean. Runcord's studies indicated that the two continents were connected before the ocean was formed between them.

CONSTRUCTIVE PLATE BOUNDARIES

By the middle 1950s oceanographers had mapped a worldwide system of deep ocean trenches, island arcs (curved chains of islands), and mid-oceanic ridges or mountains. Seismologists (scientists who study earthquakes) noted that many deep earthquakes occur beneath ocean trenches. They also observed that volcanic activity is concentrated along the ocean ridges that correspond to plate boundaries.

■ Sea-Floor Spreading

The idea of sea-floor spreading explains how the continents moved. Sea-floor spreading involves the idea that the earth's surface is not rigid at all. It is divided by a series of fractures into twelve large **crustal plates** that float on the earth's mantle, and these plates are in constant motion.

Geophysicists believe that the motion of the crustal plates is due ultimately to the decay of radioactive isotopes at the earth's core. This radioactive process produces heat, forming convection currents that rise from the core. These currents circulate through the soft, hot material of the mantle. They carry molten rock up from the asthenosphere, pushing it against the crust and forcing it into large cracks where the plates separate. Molten magma wells up along the length of these cracks. As the molten rock meets the cold ocean water it hardens, forming new rock and high mountain ridges. This continuous addition of new rock along the ridges pushes the ocean floor and the continents away from the ridges, forcing the sea floor to spread apart. This is known as a spreading zone, and apparently provides the power that drives the plates. In other words, the convection currents in the rock carry the newly formed crustal plate away from the ridge as if it were riding on a conveyor belt.

■ Proof of Theory of Sea-Floor Spreading

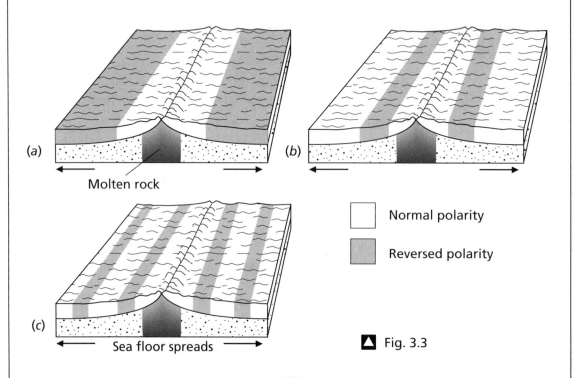

(a) Molten rock

(b)

☐ Normal polarity

▨ Reversed polarity

(c) Sea floor spreads

▲ Fig. 3.3

In 1963 the British geophysicists F. J. Vine and D. H. Matthews used palaeomagnetic measurements near the oceanic ridges to prove the sea-floor spreading theory. They based their experiments on two facts:

1. Magnetic particles in the sea-floor rocks recorded the direction of the earth's magnetic field when the rock hardened.
2. The direction of the field reversed itself from time to time as the ocean floor was formed.

If the sea floor spreads, the pattern of normal and reversed magnetism should match on both sides of the ridge. Vine and Matthews's experiments found these matching patterns. Following their work, many scientists accept the basic idea that the continents have moved in the past as part of large rigid plates. However, there is no proof yet that convections exist to cause this movement.

The **Mid-Atlantic Ridge** is a range of submerged mountains that runs north-south down the centre of the Atlantic Ocean. It was formed because of sea-floor spreading. The Mid-Atlantic Ridge in some places is over 800 km (500 miles) wide. Generally the top of the ridge lies 2,500–3,000 m (9,000–10,000 feet) below the ocean surface; but in some places it juts out of the water and forms such islands as Iceland and Ascension. The Mid-Oceanic Ridge and these islands consist of new crust formed along a constructive plate boundary.

DESTRUCTIVE PLATE BOUNDARIES

Fig. 3.4 ▶

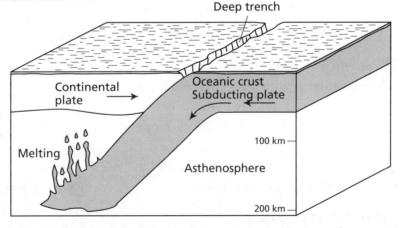

There is good evidence that the earth is not expanding, so there must be a global conveyor belt system linking zones of creation to zones of destruction. Thus a second simultaneous requirement for continental drift is a zone of subduction, where a moving plate is pulled down into the mantle and destroyed. This occurs along the zone of collision with another plate, such as the meeting of the Pacific and Eurasian plates.

VOLCANOES

■ Types of Volcanoes

Explosive types

1 Ash (Cinder) Cone

During a violent eruption, lava is blown high into the sky. Rocks, ash, cinders and volcanic bombs fall down around the vent and begin to build up into a steep-sided volcanic mountain (e.g. Paracutin in Mexico).

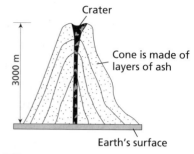

▲ Fig. 3.5 Ash and cinder cone

2 Composite Volcano

During a violent eruption a layer of ash is deposited, and later acid lava flows out to cover the ash. Successive eruptions lead to the building up of layers of ash and lava. The sides of the cone may be steeper towards the top, and conelets develop around the sides. Vesuvius in Italy is of this type.

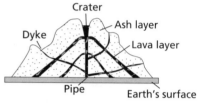

▲ Fig. 3.6 Composite volcano

3 Dome Volcano

When thick acidic lava, containing large quantities of gases, bursts through the crater, it flows only a short distance and cools quickly. As a result the cone has a blown-out appearance, like the *puys* of the Massif Central.

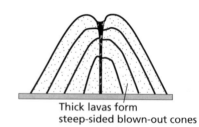

▲ Fig. 3.7 Dome volcano

Non-explosive types

4 Shield Volcano

When basic lava, which is extremely fluid, pours out, it flows quickly over a great distance. It forms a cone with gentle slopes, on average 5°, as in Hawaii, where the volcano Mauna Loa is further increased in size by smaller fissures on its sides.

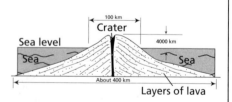

▲ Fig. 3.8 Shield volcano

VOLCANIC ISLAND ARCS

Volcanic island arcs are found
(*a*) at the convergence of oceanic plates such as in the Pacific Ocean (oceanic-oceanic convergence), e.g. Aleutian Islands, Mariana Islands
(*b*) at the convergence of two continental plates such as the African and Eurasian Plates (continental-continental convergence).

■ Oceanic-Oceanic Convergence

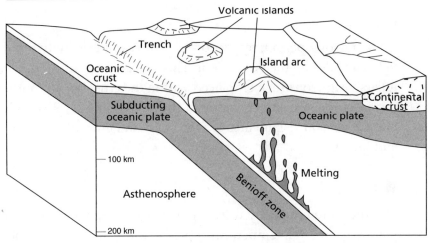

▲ Fig. 3.9 Formation of a volcanic island arc

Deep ocean trenches occur in places where slabs of oceanic crust are subducted into the upper mantle. As an oceanic plate sinks, it carries sediments and ocean crust containing abundant water downwards. Since water reduces the melting point of rock, it aids the melting process, which occurs at a depth of approx. 200 km (125 miles). Magma forms and migrates upwards, as it is less dense than the surrounding rocks. The presence of water contributes to the high gas content and explosive nature of the magma. Volcanoes form on the ocean floor, and dry land eventually emerges from the ocean depths.

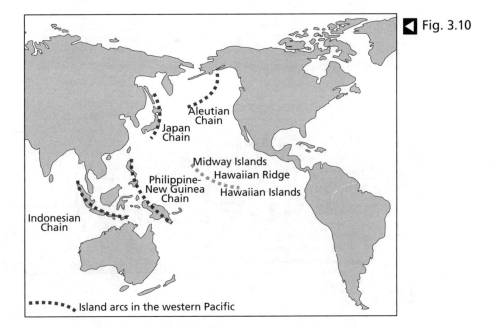

◄ Fig. 3.10

49

In the early stages of development, this newly formed land consists of a chain of small volcanic islands called an island arc (e.g. the Aleutian Islands).

Over a long period, many episodes of volcanic activity build large volcanic piles on the ocean floor. This volcanic activity, together with intrusive igneous rock emplaced within the crust below, gradually increases the size and elevation of the developing arc. Examples of such mature volcanic island arcs are the Alaskan Peninsula, the Philippines, and Japan.

■ Hot Spots

Hot spots are unusually warm spots found deep within the earth's mantle. Here high temperatures produce a rising plume of molten rock, which frequently initiates volcanic activity that may emit magma onto the earth's surface. Most evidence indicates that hot spots remain relatively stationary. Of the 50 to 120 hot spots believed to exist, about 20 are near divergent plate boundaries, whereas the others are not associated with plate boundaries. A hot spot beneath Iceland is thought to be responsible for the unusually large accumulation of lava found in that portion of the Mid-Atlantic Ridge. Another hot spot is believed to exist beneath Yellowstone National Park in the United States and is responsible for geysers such as Old Faithful.

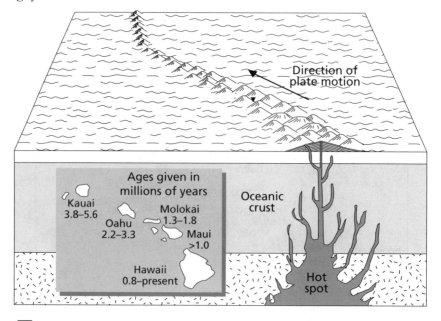

▲ Fig. 3.11

Ocean mapping in the Pacific Ocean revealed a chain of volcanic structures extending from the Hawaiian Islands to Midway Island and then continuing northwards towards the Aleutian Trench. Researchers believe that as the Pacific Plate moved over the hot spot, successive volcanic structures were formed. The age of each volcano indicates the time when it was over the relatively stationary hot spot.

To support this theory, older volcanic islands should show greater signs of erosion than newer islands. According to this theory, Kauai, the most northerly and the oldest of the Hawaiian Islands, should show the greatest signs of denudation. Kauai indeed displays such evidence, as its many extinct volcanoes have been eroded into jagged peaks and deep canyons. By contrast, the south slopes of the island of Hawaii consist of fresh lava flows, and two of Hawaii's volcanoes, Mauna Loa and Kilauea, remain active.

■ Continental-Continental Convergence

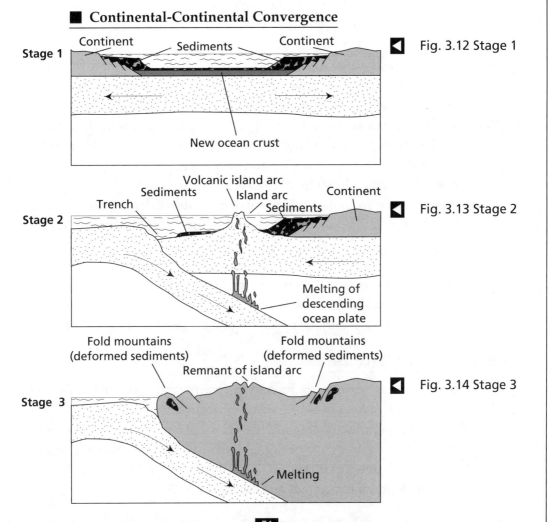

Fig. 3.12 Stage 1

Fig. 3.13 Stage 2

Fig. 3.14 Stage 3

■ Folded Mountains

All major mountain belts, including the Alps, Urals, Himalayas, Appalachians, and Caledonian Mountains of Scotland and north-eastern Ireland, are **complex fold mountains**.

Although major mountains differ from one another in particular details, all possess the same basic structures. Mountain chains generally consist of roughly parallel ridges of folded and faulted sedimentary and volcanic rocks, portions of which have been strongly metamorphosed and intruded by younger igneous bodies. In most cases the sedimentary rocks were formed from igneous accumulations of deep-water marine sediments that occasionally exceeded 15 km (10 miles) in thickness, as well as from thinner shallow-water deposits. Thus most of these deformed sedimentary rocks are older than the mountain-building event. This indicates that a long, stable period of deposition was followed by an episode of deformation (changes in shape).

A simple chronology of the events that gave rise to fold mountains is as follows:

Stage 1. After the break-up of a continental landmass, a thick wedge of sediments is deposited along the newly formed continental margins, thereby increasing the size of the newly formed continent.

Stage 2. For reasons not yet understood, the ocean basin begins to close and the continents begin to converge. Plate convergence results in the subduction of the intervening oceanic slab and initiates an extended period of igneous activity. This activity results in the formation of a volcanic arc. Debris eroded from the volcanic arc and material scraped from the descending plate add to the wedges of sediment along the continental margins.

Stage 3. Eventually the continental blocks collide. This event, which often involves igneous activity, severely deforms and metamorphoses the entrapped sediments. Continental convergence shortens and thickens these deformed materials, producing an elevated fold mountain belt.

CORAL REEFS AND ATOLLS

Coral reefs are mainly confined to the warm waters of the Pacific and Indian Oceans. Reef-building corals grow best in waters with an average annual temperature of about 24°C. They can survive neither sudden temperature changes nor prolonged exposure to temperatures below 18°C. In addition, coral requires clear, sunlit water. For this reason the limiting depth of active reef growth is about 45 m (150 feet).

There are three main theories on the formation of coral reefs and atolls.

1. Murray's theory states that coral reefs and atolls formed on submarine hills or plateaus within 55 m (180 feet) of the surface.
2. Daly's theory suggests that a rise in sea level was responsible for their formation, and that coral growth kept pace with the rising waters.

Fig. 3.15 ▶

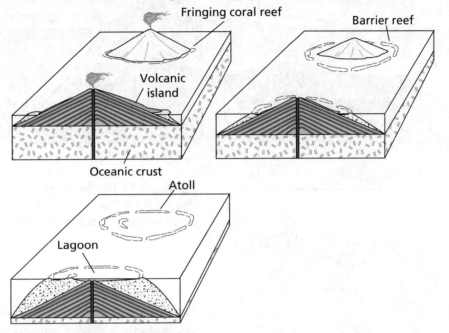

Fringing coral reef

Barrier reef

Volcanic island

Oceanic crust

Atoll

Lagoon

3. Darwin's theory stated that because coral requires shallow, sunlit waters no deeper than 45 m (150 feet) to live, coral reefs form on the flanks of sinking volcanic islands. As an island slowly sinks, the corals continue to build the reef complex upwards. Thus atolls are thought to owe their existence to the gradual sinking of the oceanic crust. American scientists made extensive studies of two atolls (Eniwetok and Bikini) that were going to be sites for testing atomic bombs. Drilling operations at these atolls revealed that volcanic rock did indeed underlie the thick coral reef structure. This finding was a striking confirmation of Darwin's explanation.

EARTHQUAKES

An earthquake is a vibration of the earth produced by the rapid release of energy or tension within the earth's crust. The energy produced radiates in all directions from its source, the **focus**. The surface point directly above the focus is called the **epicentre**. An earthquake generates seismic waves that radiate throughout the earth. This energy decreases rapidly with increasing distance from the focus.

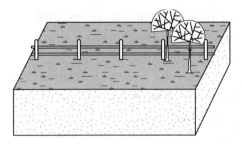

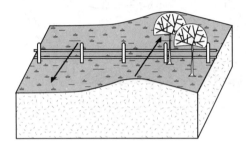

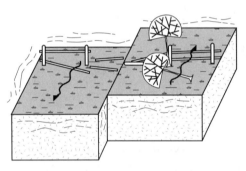

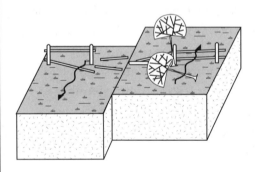

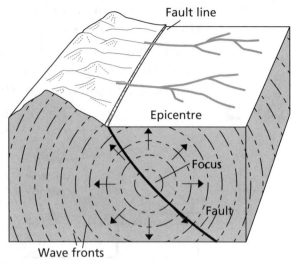

Fault line

Epicentre

Focus

Fault

Wave fronts

▲ Fig. 3.17 The focus of all earthquakes is deep within the earth. The surface point directly above it is the epicentre.

▲ Fig. 3.16 Deformation of rocks As rock is deformed it bends, storing elastic energy. Once the rock is strained beyond its breaking point it ruptures, releasing the stored energy in the form of earthquake waves.

Earthquake movements are frequently associated with large fractures in the earth's crust called **faults**. Tectonic forces (e.g. moving plates) ever so slowly deform the crustal rocks on both sides of the fault. Under such conditions, rocks are bending and storing elastic energy, much like a wooden stick if it were bent. Eventually the frictional resistance holding the rocks together is overcome, and slippage occurs. This slippage allows the deformed rock to 'snap back'. The vibrations we know as an earthquake occur as the rock elastically returns to its original shape. The adjustments that follow a major earthquake often generate smaller earthquakes, called **aftershocks**.

Distribution of Earthquakes

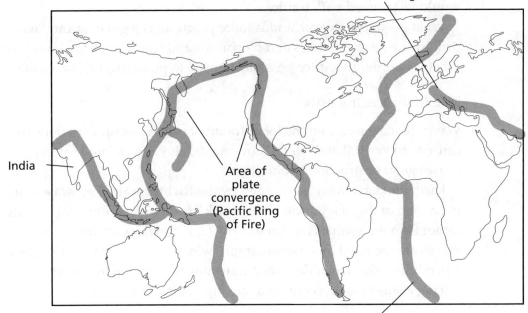

▲ Fig. 3.18

The global distribution of earthquakes appears to be directly associated with the theory of plate tectonics. Earthquakes occur in areas of plate convergence and plate divergence.

Three categories of earthquakes – shallow, intermediate, and deep – occur at various depths as an oceanic plate is subducted beneath a continental plate, such as along the deep ocean trenches off eastern Asia (e.g. Marianas Trench) and along the western edge of South America. Shallow earthquakes occur near **transform faults** (where plates slide past one another), such as near San Francisco, and along areas of separation, such as the mid-oceanic ridges.

■ Predicting Earthquakes

Seismologists constantly monitor earth movements in order to predict more accurately and understand more fully the forces that give rise to earthquakes. By the regular recording of data they are now able to predict the probability of major earthquakes occurring in certain areas within a reasonable time limit. However, the exact time cannot be predicted. Therefore in many large conurbations, such as Los Angeles, an earthquake alert may not be practical. Mass exodus from such urban areas would not be possible in a short time, as roads and motorways would be jammed with traffic.

What is done, however, and is more practical, is regular earthquake drill by the rescue services and by parents and teachers within homes and schools in order to reduce possible damage to property and loss of life.

■ Earthquake Intensity

Waves passing out from the focus (point of origin) set up vibrations that cause both vertical and lateral movements, and this violent shaking causes great destruction to buildings.

Earthquake intensity is recorded by the **Richter scale**. This scale is an indication of the magnitude of the shock, based on instrumental records rather than on results. A magnitude of 7.0 is a major earthquake. Shock waves are recorded on a **seismograph**, which is based on the principle of a pendulum that when disturbed transmits this motion to a needle tracing a continuous record on a moving drum.

■ Effects of Earthquakes

1. They can cause vertical and lateral displacement of parts of the crust.
2. They can cause the raising or lowering of parts of the sea floor.
3. They can cause the raising or lowering of coastal regions, as in Alaska in 1899, when some coastal rocks were lifted 15 m (50 feet).
4. They can cause landslides, as in the loess country of north China.
5. If shocks are experienced in densely populated and closely built-up areas, the results can be disastrous. Some of the worst earthquakes include that of San Francisco in 1906 and Tokyo-Yokohama in 1923, which killed 100,000 people. In October 1989, San Francisco suffered another earthquake, which recorded 6.9 on the Richter scale and killed sixty-two people. In January 1994, Los Angeles suffered a severe earthquake centred on the San Fernando valley. Roads and buildings collapsed, and twenty-two people were killed.

In most areas of the industrialised world that are liable to earthquakes, modern buildings are specially constructed so that they transmit the shock and vibrate; steel and pressed concrete are used, and the buildings may be erected on a thick raft of concrete sunk beneath the surface.

Developed country

Developing
country

6. In many areas of the developing world, buildings are subject to severe damage by earthquakes. On 31 October 1993 an earthquake that reached 6.4 on the Richter scale devastated some fifty villages in western India. The poorly constructed houses made of mud, stone and thatch crumbled, killing at least sixteen thousand people.

7. Some gaping cracks or subsidences are formed, railways and water pipes are cut, and bridges collapse, causing massive structural damage and loss of life. Fires result from leaking gas pipes, while disease may occur in some areas from a combination of burst sewerage mains and high temperatures.

8. Where an earthquake affects the ocean floor, great waves, known as seismic waves or tsunamis, may spread outwards across the ocean at speeds of 500–800 km/h (300–500 miles an hour) and sometimes cause great damage to coastal areas such as those of Bangladesh. Upon entering shallower coastal waters, these destructive waves are slowed, and the water begins to pile up to heights that occasionally exceed 30 m (100 feet).

REVISION

To revise the formation of physical landforms it is often best to concentrate on just four features: some landforms of erosion and others of deposition.

When writing a description of each landform, it is important to include the following:

(a) name of landform (F)
(b) example (E) of landform in Ireland
(c) explanation (E) of formation, including processes involved
(d) diagram (D) of landform fully labelled.

Tip...Feed

The following chapter examines four landforms of ice, rivers, sea, wind and limestone landscapes in an organised examination format.

NOTICE
For each landform:
Always explain fully the processes involved in the formation of the landform

THE WORK OF WIND

REVISION AID

The wind is the main force of erosion in desert and semi-desert regions.
Land slip also changes the character of a desert. Wind carrying sand
abrades rocks and rock fragments to form more sand.

Sand formations such as the **barkhan** and the **seif dune** are common to
most desert areas. Both are formed by the wind and get their shapes from
wind direction.

Wind-blown sand abrades or wears down ranges of rock into a number
of unusual shapes. These include mushroom rocks, buttes, canyons,
mesas, and pinnacle rocks.

Depressions in the desert may be caused by sand being scooped out by
the wind or by a fault that occurs beneath the surface.

A river flowing through a desert area can cut a deep canyon in the soft
layers of its bed.

Springs and artesian wells supply remote desert areas with water.

LANDFORM NO. 1: *LANDFORM OF EROSION*

Processes involved: abrasion, sand-blasting effect, undercutting

■ Rock Pedestals

Wind abrasion (wind plus sand) attacks rock masses and sculpts them
into unusual shapes. As wind blows across a desert region it picks up
grains of sand. The stronger the wind speed, the greater the size and the
number of sand particles it can carry. The sand-blasting effect of wind
carrying a load of hard quartz grains is of great potency. This sand-blast
effect can leave rock surfaces smooth and polished.

Desert weathering produces rock waste small enough to be moved by
the wind. Fine particles of rock waste called 'desert dust' are easily picked
up by the wind and may be carried great distances from the place of
origin. Coarser and heavier particles called sand, however, are bounced
over the surface for short distances. These larger particles cause greater
erosion at the base of rock outcrops than the more elevated smaller dust
particles. So undercutting occurs, leaving rock pedestals.

Example: Mushroom blocks called gour (singular gara) are formed in the
Sahara.

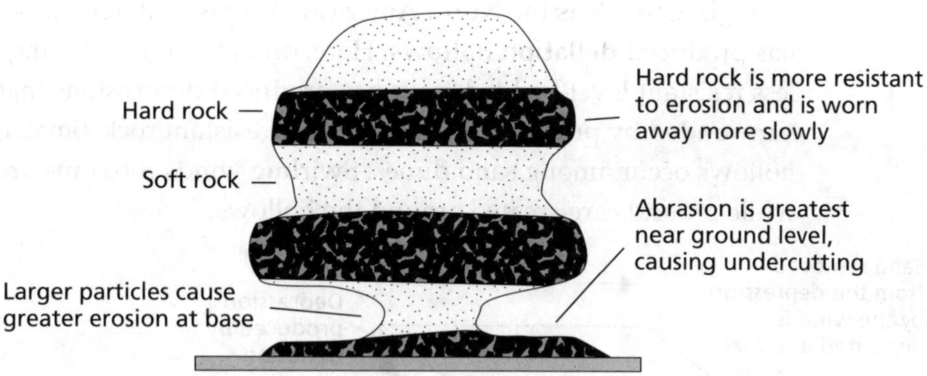

Hard rock —

Soft rock —

Hard rock is more resistant to erosion and is worn away more slowly

Abrasion is greatest near ground level, causing undercutting

Larger particles cause greater erosion at base

▲ Fig. 3.19 Rock pedestal: smooth rocky mass formed of alternate layers of hard and soft rock

LANDFORM NO. 2: *LANDFORM OF EROSION*

■ Deflation Hollow

Processes involved: abrasion, eddying

This involves the lowering of the land surface through the blowing away of any unconsolidated material. Faulting may initiate a depression. In this way a resistant surface rock layer (cap) is broken, so the wind can attack the underlying softer rock. A small blow-out or hollow forms and is gradually enlarged and deepened by **eddy** action (swirling action of wind with sand particles).

Example: The Qattarah Depression in Egypt.

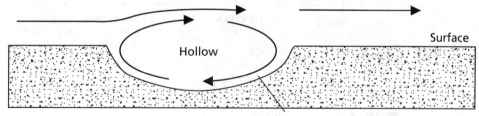

Surface

Hollow

Swirling movement of wind and sand

▲ Fig. 3.20 Eddying

The Qattarah depression, in a limestone plateau west of the River Nile in Egypt, whose floor reaches 400 m (1,300 feet) below sea level, may have been formed in this way.

Similar but shallower depressions are found in the Kalahari Desert in south-western Africa, in western Australian deserts, and in Mongolia. Many depressions contain oases or salt lakes on their floors, indicating that the water-table, the limiting factor in the wind's deflating effect, has been reached.

In places such as the North American deserts, differential weathering has produced **deflation hollows**. Here, differential weathering of areas of less resistant level-bedded rocks has produced depressions that are surrounded by pronounced rims of more resistant rock. Small deflation hollows occur among sand dunes. Swirling winds rob some areas of sand, while mounds are created around the hollows.

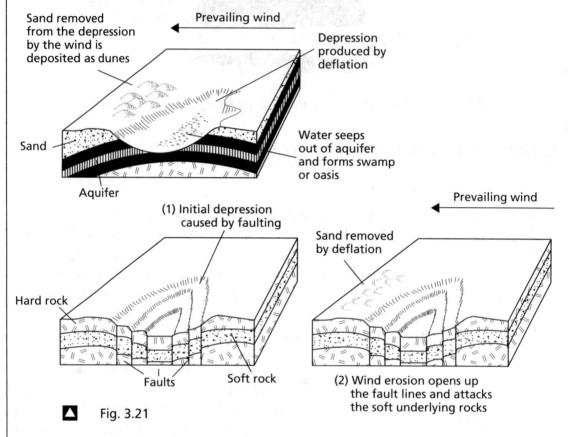

Fig. 3.21

LANDFORM NO 3: *LANDFORM OF EROSION*

■ Yardangs

Processes involved: differential erosion, abrasion

Differential weathering takes place where there are rocks of varying degrees of hardness. Soft rock is worn away at a faster rate than hard rock. This effect creates fluting, honeycombing, grooving, and etching.

When rocks of differing resistance occur in bands roughly parallel to the direction of the prevailing wind, a ridge-and-furrow landscape may be produced. The bands of hard rock are more resistant to erosion and stand up as rocky ribs up to 50 m (160 feet) in height. Abrasion produces blunt, rounded fronts facing the wind, with sharp keel-like crests. The ridges are separated by shallow grooves or furrows. In places such as the central Asian deserts, wind abrasion and deflation operate together and cut into areas of bare rock. The furrows or grooves gradually merge, until the most resistant masses remain.

Example: Atacama Desert, South America.

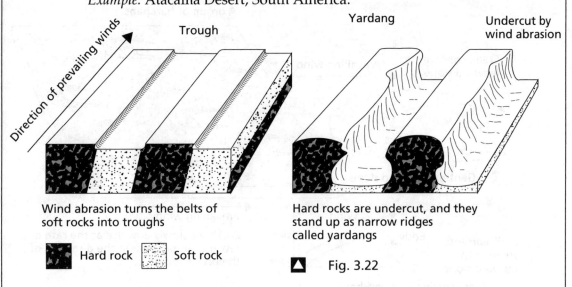

Wind abrasion turns the belts of soft rocks into troughs

Hard rocks are undercut, and they stand up as narrow ridges called yardangs

▲ Fig. 3.22

LANDFORM NO 4: *LANDFORM OF DEPOSITION*

■ Barkhan Dunes

Processes involved: deposition

Barkhan dunes, otherwise known as crescentic dunes, derived their name from the deserts of Turkestan. They have a crescentic shape and lie across the direction of the wind, with their 'horns' trailed out in the direction towards which it is blowing.

Patches of pebbles or sudden wind fluctuation may cause the accumulation of a low heap of sand, around which the barkhan dune forms. They occur on fairly level open surfaces. The direction of movement of barkhan dunes is dependent upon the wind. In Turkestan, for example, the wind changes seasonally, blowing alternately southwards and northwards, and the dunes change likewise, their horns swinging right round. Barkhans are sometimes found as isolated hills. Generally, however, they occur in swarms, sometimes as a regular series, more often as a chaotic, ever-changing pattern of partially joined ridges at right angles to the prevailing wind.

As sand accumulates to form a barkhan, movement is slowest at the centre of the dune, since more energy is needed to move sand up the gentle windward slope to the crest. At the edges, where the dune is lower,

the movement is faster. Thus 'horns' develop, and a crescent shape forms. Barkhans vary in height from 1 to 30 m (1–100 feet).
Examples: Libya and Egypt.

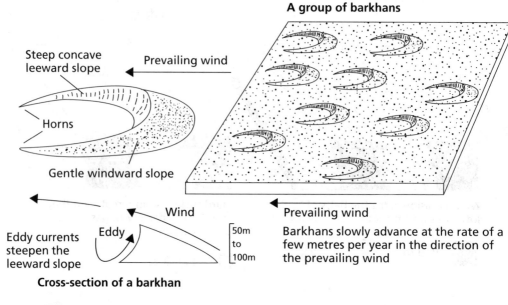

Fig. 3.23. Barkhans

THE WORK OF RIVERS

REVISION AID

A **basin** is the area drained by a river. The pattern of drainage in a basin may be (a) **dendritic**, when tributaries form a pattern like the branches of a tree, (b) **trellised**, when tributaries run parallel to each other towards the main course, or (c) **radial**, when streams have a watershed following the pattern of the spokes of a wheel.

Waterfalls occur where a layer of hard rock lies across a river bed. Softer rocks downstream are worn down, and the waterfall retreats.

Ox-bow lakes are meanders that have been cut off by the river as it lays down silt.

Deltas are built up at the mouth of a river that lays down heavy deposits of silt and mud where the river meets the sea.

Flood plains are level stretches of land on either side of a river in its mature and old stages.

Alluvium is fine material of silt and clay deposited by a river on its flood plain during times of flooding.

Hydraulic action is the breaking up of rock caused by the force of moving water.

Corrasion is the use by a river of its load to erode the banks and bed of the river.

Cavitation occurs when bubbles of air collapse and form tiny shock waves against the outer bank of a river.

Deposition material is dropped on the bed or flood plain of a river when the slope, the speed or the volume of a river is reduced.

■ Definitions

Source: the place where a river begins.
Tributary: a river that joins a larger one.
Confluence: the place where rivers join.
Mouth: the place where a river enters a sea or lake.
Estuary: that part of a river's course that is tidal.
Basin: the entire area drained by a river and its tributaries.
Watershed: the high ground that separates one river basin from another.

LANDFORM NO. 5: *WATERFALLS*

Landform of erosion; youthful state
Examples: Asleagh Falls on the Erriff River; Torc Waterfall in Killarney; Niagara Falls on the Niagara River. Local example: …

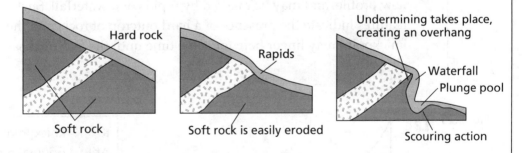

▲ Fig. 3.24

■ Formation

1. When waterfalls occur in the upper course of a river, their presence usually results from a bar of hard rock lying across the valley of the river. This interrupts the river's attempts towards a graded profile. If this slab of rock is dipping gently downstream, it results in a series of rapids with much broken water. If, however, the bar of rock is

Processes involved in formation:
hydraulic action, corrasion, eddying, solution, rejuvenation

horizontal or slightly inclined, a vertical fall in the river results. The scouring action of the falling water and the river's load at the base of the fall cut into the underlying soft rock, creating a **plunge pool**. Two processes are involved in creating the plunge pool: **hydraulic action** and **corrasion**. Hydraulic action is caused by the force of the falling water. By rushing into cracks, the water can help to break up solid rock. Corrasion is the use by the river of its load to erode the side and bed of the river. At the base of a waterfall, turbulent water and **eddying** by the river and its load erode the bed to form a plunge pool. Undermining causes an overhanging ledge of hard rock, pieces of which break off and collect at the base of the waterfall (the process of solution may also cause undermining if rocks such as limestone are present). As the fall recedes upstream, a steep-sided channel is created downstream of the falls. This feature is called a **gorge**.

2. If a waterfall appears in the middle course of a river, it may be the result of **rejuvenation** (to rejuvenate means to make young). This may be caused by a fall in sea level, a local uplift of land, or the presence of glacial debris. This causes a steeper slope and a greater river velocity and so renews downcutting or vertical erosion. When a fall in base level occurs, the river begins to cut upstream from its mouth. This produces a new curve or profile of erosion that intersects with the old curve at the **knickpoint**. Thus the knickpoint is distinguished by a marked break of slope at the junction of the old river profile and the new profile, and may be marked by rapids or a waterfall. Such features indicate the presence of a hard outcrop of rock, and the knickpoint may linger here for some time until the feature disappears altogether.

Fig. 3.25 ▶

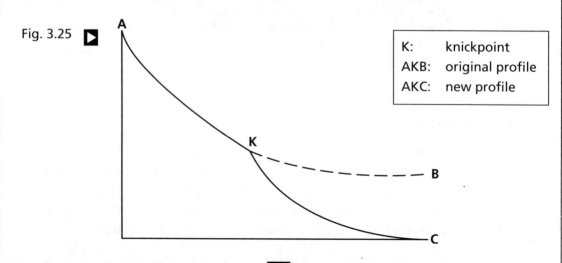

K:	knickpoint
AKB:	original profile
AKC:	new profile

LANDFORM NO. 6: *OX-BOW LAKE*

Feature of erosion and/or deposition; mature or old stage
Example: River Shannon; River Amazon. Local example: …

A neck of land separates two concave banks where erosion is active	Neck is ultimately cut through; this may be accelerated by river flooding	Deposition seals the cut-off, which becomes an ox-bow lake

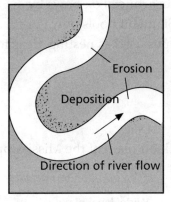
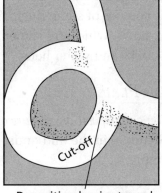
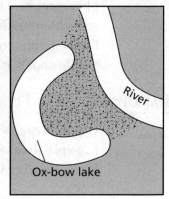

Erosion
Deposition
Direction of river flow

Cut-off

Deposition begins to seal up the ends of the cut-off

River
Ox-bow lake

A looping meander occurs where a narrow neck of land separates two concave banks that are being undercut	Erosion has broken through the neck of land; this generally happens when the river is in flood	Deposition takes place along the two ends of the cut-off, and it is eventually sealed off to form an ox-bow lake

▲ Fig. 3.26

■ Formation

Processes involved in formation: hydraulic action, corrasion, cavitation, deposition

Ox-bow lakes are relics of former meanders and are often called cut-offs. They may occasionally occur in a mature valley, but they are common on the lower courses or old valley floors of rivers. As meanders move downstream, erosion of the outside bank leads to the formation of a loop in the river's course, enclosing a peninsula of land with a narrow neck. Three main processes of river erosion act together to create the ox-bow lake. **Hydraulic action** is caused by the force of the moving water. By rushing into cracks and by direct contact with the river banks it can help to break up solid rock and undermine the banks. **Corrasion** is the use by the river of its load to erode, in this case, the river bank. Along the side of the outer bank turbulent water and **eddying** (swirling movement) by the river and its load create a river cliff. Erosion also occurs because of **cavitation**, when bubbles of air collapse and form shock waves against the outer bank. Loose clays, sands and gravels are quickly worn away by this type of process.

Finally, during a period of flood the river cuts through this neck and continues on a straight and easier route, leaving the river loop to one side. Deposition occurs at both ends of this loop to form an ox-bow lake.

After a long time these ox-bow lakes are filled with silt from flood water and finally dry up. At this stage they are called **meander scars** or **mort lakes** and are clearly visible on some old valley floors from aerial photographs. Drainage schemes may create artificial ox-bows by straightening the courses of some rivers. Stagnant pools of water fill the floors of these ox-bows, which are sometimes used as nesting areas for wildlife such as ducks and water hens.

LANDFORM NO. 7: *FLOOD PLAIN*

Landform of erosion and deposition; mature or old stage
Example: River Shannon in the midlands; flood plain of the Mississippi River. Local example: ...

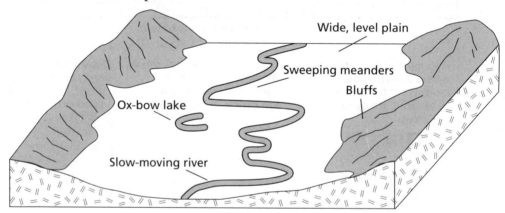

Fig. 3.27

■ Formation

Processes involved in **formation:** undercutting, divagation, deposition

When meanders migrate downstream, they swing to and fro across a valley. As a result the river swings from side to side. As the water flows around a bend, it erodes most strongly on the outside, forming a river cliff. **Undercutting** of the bank takes place. Little erosion takes place on the inside of a bend, but deposition often takes place, causing a gravel beach or slip-off slope. The valley has been straightened at this stage, with interlocking spurs removed by the lateral erosion of the meanders (**divagation**), and a level stretch of land is created on both sides of the river. This is called a **flood plain**.

During its youthful and mature stages, a river flows quickly and is able to transport a large amount of material, called its **load**, by the processes of solution, suspension, and saltation. However, in the late mature and old stages the speed of a river is reduced, because of the more gentle slope of the valley floor. At this stage the river is able to carry only the smallest particles of silt and clay, collectively called **alluvium**.

A flood plain is a wide and flat valley floor that is often subjected to flooding during times of heavy rain. When this occurs, the river spreads across the flat flood plain and deposits a thin layer of alluvium. Alluvium is fine material consisting of silt and clay particles and is rich in mineral matter, transported by a river and **deposited** at places along the flood plain. This deposit enriches the soil and leads to the creation of fertile farmland. The crops suited to such a soil are often determined by the local climate. For instance, in the flood plain of the River Po in Italy and in the Rhine Rift Valley in Germany, the climate is hot in summer, and tillage is practised on a large scale. In Ireland, however, crops of hay and silage are harvested along the flood plain of the River Shannon, as the weather is unpredictable and generally cool and wet.

LANDFORM NO. 8 *DELTA*

Landform of deposition; old stage
Example: Roughty River in Co. Kerry; River Nile in Egypt.
Local example: …

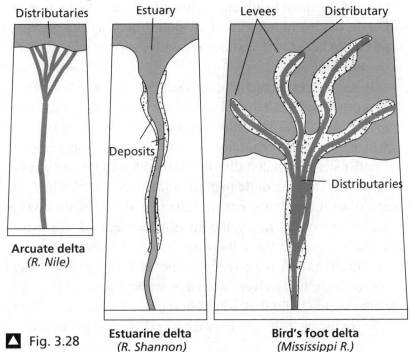

Distributaries   Estuary   Levees   Distributary

Deposits

Distributaries

Arcuate delta
(R. Nile)

▲ Fig. 3.28

Estuarine delta
(R. Shannon)

Bird's foot delta
(Mississippi R.)

■ **Main Types of Marine Deltas**

1. **Arcuate.** This type of delta is triangular in shape, like the Greek letter *delta* (Δ). The top of the triangle points upstream. Arcuate deltas are composed of coarse sand and gravels and where sea currents are relatively strong, which limits delta formation.
   Examples: River Nile in Egypt; River Po in Italy.
2. **Estuarine.** These form at the mouths of submerged river estuaries. The estuarine deposits form long, narrow fillings along both sides of the estuary.
   Examples: River Shannon; River Seine in France.
3. **Bird's foot.** These deltas form when rivers carry large quantities of fine material to the coast. Impermeable deposits such as these cause the river to divide into only a few large distributaries. **Levees** develop along these distributaries, and so long, projecting fingers extend out into the sea to form a delta similar in plan to that of a bird's foot.
   Example: Mississippi River.

The materials deposited in a delta are classified into three categories.
1. Fine particles are carried out to sea and are deposited in advance of the main delta. These are the **bottom-set beds**.
2. Coarser materials form inclined layers over the bottom-set beds and gradually build out, each one in front of and above the previous ones, causing the delta to advance seawards. These are the **fore-set beds**.
3. On the landward margins of the delta, fine particles of clays, silts and muds are laid down, continuous with the river's flood plain. These are the **top-set beds**.

When a river carries a heavy load into an area of calm water, such as an enclosed or sheltered sea area or a lake, it deposits material at its mouth. This material builds up in layers called **beds** to form islands, which grow and eventually cause the estuary to split up into many smaller streams, called **distributaries**. Should this occur in a lake it is called a **lacustrine delta** (e.g. Glendalough, Co. Wicklow). If it occurs at a coast it is called a **marine delta** (e.g. the Roughty River in Kenmare Bay, Co. Kerry; the River Nile in Egypt). The material that builds up to form the delta is composed of alternate layers of coarse and fine deposits, which reflect times of high and low water levels, respectively, in the river. Mountain streams flowing into glaciated valleys often build deltas in ribbon lakes. This causes a filling in of the lake, reducing its length over time or dividing ribbon lakes into

Process involved: deposition

smaller ones. These may occur at any stage of a river's course.

This has occurred at the western end of the Upper Lake in Glendalough, where large amounts of sediment have been deposited by a mountain torrent. An alluvial flat now occupies a large area at the upper end of this glacial lake. The Upper and Lower Lakes at Glendalough once formed a single lake. The north-flowing Pollanass river deposited material in the lake, forming a delta. This delta grew across the lake, thus dividing the lake into the Upper Lake and the Lower Lake.

ADVANTAGES OF RIVERS TO PEOPLE

- Rivers are dammed for the generation of hydro-electric power. Such dams are found on the River Shannon at Ardnacrusha, on the River Liffey at Cathleen Falls, and on the River Lee at Inniscarra. However, most hydro-electric dams are found in mountain areas, either high up on the benches or across the valley floors. Norway produces vast amounts of hydro-electricity, while the Alps in Italy provide power from the fast-flowing mountain streams such as the River Ticino. Hydro-electric power is produced when there is a large volume of water, a constant supply, and a high **head** (fall) present.
- River reservoirs are used for urban water supplies throughout the world. Blessington Lake on the River Liffey and Lough Derg on the River Shannon are two such reservoirs. In the United States, water from the Colorado River is diverted to supply the city of Los Angeles. Los Angeles is built in a semi-desert area and does not have sufficient water locally for its inhabitants.
- River reservoirs are also used as a source of water for irrigation. In California the Sacramento River has been dammed in a number of places to supply the central valley with water for its crops of cereals and vegetables. Canals carry this water to the valley, where it is channelled into irrigation sprayers that turn the central valley into the largest vegetable-producing area in the world.
- Since the Stone Age, rivers have been used by people as a source of transport. In Ireland dug-out canoes were discovered in the midlands, which indicates the importance of water transport in early times. Today rivers form some of the most used and most important transport routes in the world. For example, the rivers of Europe are connected by a system of canals. At the heart of this system is the River Rhine, which is often referred to as the lifeline of Europe. It is

connected to the Seine, the Rhône, the Danube, the Ems, the Weser, and the Elbe, as well as the Oder. Constant barge traffic has led to the development of port settlements along each of these routes, bringing raw materials to industries as well as transporting finished products. Europoort at the estuary of the Rhine is the largest port in the world.

■ Rivers are used by people for recreation. Water sports, such as fishing, sailing, and swimming, are much loved by people throughout the world.

■ Rivers form an important part of the water cycle. They return rainfall to the sea. In this way land is constantly drained and kept sufficiently dry for daily life to continue. When rivers are unable to do this, either because of heavy, continuous rainfall or the collapse of underground channels, vast areas are flooded, as often happens in parts of the midlands and west of Ireland.

Rivers also provide people with a constant water supply, which is necessary for our everyday existence.

THE WORK OF ICE

REVISION AID

Permanent ice and snow remain in areas where the temperature does not rise above freezing point for long enough during the day to melt the ice. During the Ice Age a change in climate caused the polar ice-cap to extend as far south as Ireland, which was fully covered by an ice-cap over 2,000 m (6,500 feet) deep.

Ice plucks, ploughs, carries and deposits material. The plucking action gives us **arêtes**, **corries**, and jagged mountain slopes. The ploughing action cuts U-shaped valleys and leaves hanging valleys, truncated spurs, and scrapes or **striae** on rock faces.

The material carried is laid down as lateral, medial or terminal moraines. **Drumlins** are formed when the glacier pauses; **erratics** are left in unexpected places; and **eskers** are laid down by melt-water streams under the glacier.

Other features include **crag and tail**, **kames** and **kettle holes**, **outwash plains** and **pro-glacial lakes**. Coastal landforms include **drowned drumlins** and **fjords**.

Plucking occurs when the base and sides of a glacier pluck out chunks of rock in its journey down the glaciated valley.

Abrasion is the scouring, polishing and scraping of the rock as a glacier or ice sheet passes over the surface.

Freeze-thaw is what happens when by day melt-water seeps into cracks in rock and at night this water freezes and expands, breaking up the rock.

■ Definitions

Glacier: a river of ice.

Glaciated valley: a steep-sided and flat-floored valley (U-shaped) formed by the action of a glacier.

Crevasse: a long, narrow and deep crack in the surface of a glacier.

Fjord: a glaciated valley that has been drowned by sea water.

Erratic: a large boulder that was carried a long distance from its place of origin.

Outwash plain: a large, gently sloping area of sand and gravel that was dropped by streams that flowed from the front of an ice-sheet.

Overflow channel: a V-shaped valley cut by water that flowed from an ice-dammed lake.

Pyramidal peak: a peak formed when there were three or more cirques back to back and pointed by frost action (e.g. Carrauntoohill, Co. Kerry).

Arête: a knife-edged ridge formed where two cirques formed side by side.

LANDFORM NO. 9: *CIRQUE*

Highland erosional landform

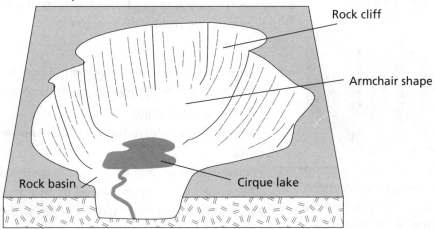

▲ Fig. 3.29 A cirque

A cirque is an amphitheatre-shaped hollow in a mountain area. Examples: Coomshingaun in the east Comeraghs; the Devil's Punch Bowl in Mangerton; Macgillycuddy's Reeks in Co. Kerry. Local example: …

■ Formation

The upper end of a glaciated valley generally consists of an amphitheatre-shaped rock basin, known variously as a **cirque**, **corrie**, or **coom**. These cirques have steep, rocky walls on all sides except that facing down the valley. Cirque lakes regularly occupy overdeepened hollows at the base of these rock walls. They are generally the source of ice for valley glaciers.

Cirques are formed when pre-glacial hollows are progressively enlarged on north or north-east slopes. A patch of snow produces alternate thawing and freezing of the rocks around its edges, causing them to 'rot' or disintegrate. The weathered debris is transported by melt-water, forming a **nivation hollow**. This process is called **snow-patch erosion**. As snowfall accumulates, large masses of ice form a **firn** or cirque glacier.

At this stage the ice moves downslope and pulls away from the headwall of the cirque, to which some ice remains attached. This gaping crack or crevasse is called the **bergschrund**. The backwall of the cirque maintains its steepness from melt-water, which seeps into cracks and, after alternate thawing and freezing, shatters the rock face. This action produces debris that falls down the bergschrund and freezes into the base of the ice field and acts as an abrasive. Ice movement pivots about a central point in the cirque. By **plucking** and **abrasion**, this action increases the depth of the hollow, which often contains a lake when the ice finally disappears.

Processes involved: abrasion, plucking, freeze-thaw

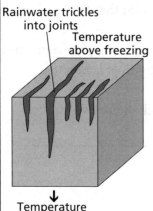

Rainwater trickles into joints

Temperature above freezing

↓

Temperature below 0°C

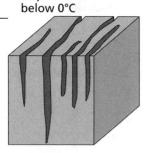

▲ Fig. 3.30. Water expands when it freezes. Ice crystals grow and exert pressure on the joints. Splitting of the rock results.

■ Features

1. Amphitheatre or bowl-shaped hollows found mainly on north-facing mountain slopes where ice remained for a longer time.
2. Steep rock cliffs form the backwall and sides of the cirque.
3. A cirque lake or **tarn** may occupy an overdeepened hollow or may be impounded by moraine debris.
4. Mountain lakes whose names begin with 'cum' or 'coom' or end in 'tarn' are cirque lakes.

LANDFORM NO. 10: *U-SHAPED GLACIATED VALLEY*

Highland erosional landform

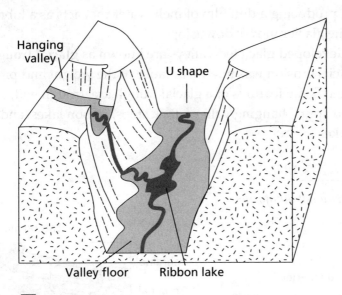

▲ Fig. 3.31

Example: Gap of Dunloe in Co. Kerry. Local example: ...

■ Formation

Processes involved: abrasion, plucking

When glaciers moved downslope through pre-glacial river valleys, they changed their V-shaped profile into wide, steep-sided U-shaped valleys. As the ice proceeded down the valley it used material that it **plucked** out from the valley floor to increase its erosive power. This material accumulated on top of the glacier, within the glacier, and beneath the glacier. Thus, gathered debris was used to increase vertical and lateral erosion in the valley. These processes of plucking and **abrasion** changed the pre-glacial V-shaped valley into a U-shaped glaciated valley. Most of our mountain valleys were glaciated (e.g. Cumeenduff Glen in Co. Kerry and Glenariff in Co. Antrim).

A glacier is a solid mass of ice that moves down a valley. Because of its solid nature it may have difficulty in negotiating a route through a winding valley that may also vary in width from place to place. However, it overcomes this difficulty in a number of ways:

1. Pressure is exerted on a glacier as it passes through a narrow neck in a valley. **Compression** produces heat, and some ice melts, allowing the glacier to squeeze through, only to freeze again when the pressure is released. Elsewhere obstacles in the glacier's path have a similar effect

on the ice, and local melting on the upstream side allows the glacier to move over or around these obstacles as it moves downhill.

2. **Friction** between the base of the glacier and the valley floor causes melting, producing a thin film of melt-water that acts as a lubricant, and so the glacier moves downslope.

Well-developed glaciated valleys are known as **glacial troughs**. Here glacial erosion was intense because of the weight and pressure of the glacier. Some features of a glacial trough are: trough end, truncated spurs, hanging valleys, rock steps, ribbon lakes, and pater-noster lakes.

LANDFORM NO. 11: *MORAINE*

Upland and lowland depositional landforms

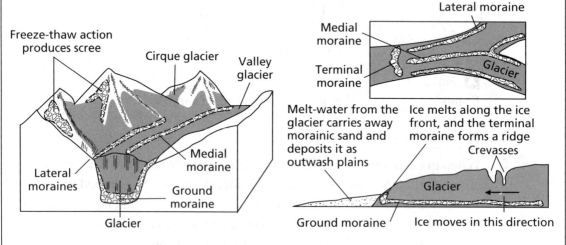

▲ Fig. 3.32

Example: Cumeenduff Glen in Co. Kerry. Local example: …

All rock material transported by a glacier, including boulder clay, is called **moraine**. Rock fragments range in size from large boulders to particles of dust.

■ Lateral Moraine

Long, sloping ridges of material left along valley sides after a glacier has melted are called **lateral moraine**. Freeze-thaw action is active on the **benches** (ridges) above glaciers, and angular rocks of all sizes fall onto the glacier edges below. This material accumulates to form lateral moraine. Vegetation may cover this material in time and may now be recognisable only by its lesser angle of slope than the valley walls or as a rocky sloping surface along valley sides.

Process involved: deposition

■ Medial Moraine

A medial moraine is formed from the material of two lateral moraines after a tributary glacier meets the main valley. These lateral moraines join and their material is carried down the valley by the main glacier. It is laid down as an uneven ridge of material along the centre of the main valley. There may be many such medial moraines in a valley, the number varying according to the number of tributary glaciers.

■ Terminal and Recessional Moraines

When glaciers stopped for a long time during an interglacial or warm spell, they deposited an unsorted and crescent-shaped ridge of material across valleys and plains. These deposits have an uneven surface and are composed of moraine. In some instances they have caused moraine-dammed lakes to form by impeding drainage. In relation to upland areas, terminal moraines are found across the lower part of the mouth of a valley, while recessional moraines are found at higher levels up the valley. In relation to lowland areas, over the Central Plain, chiefly in Co. Westmeath, moraines have dammed water into lakes. These were formed by an ice sheet that covered Ireland during the Ice Age.

LANDFORM NO. 12: ESKER

Lowland depositional landforms

Fig. 3.33 ▶

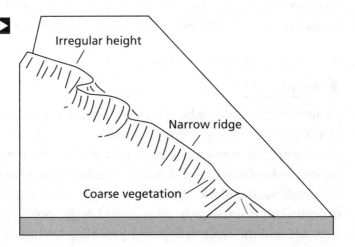

Irregular height

Narrow ridge

Coarse vegetation

1. As ice melts, melt-water channels form under the ice.

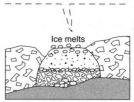

2. Sand, gravel and boulders are deposited, depending on the speed of melt-water flow.

3. Melt-water channel fills with deposits as the ice melts.

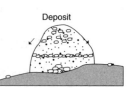

4. After the ice has melted, esker slopes stabilise, leaving a ridge of sand, gravel and boulders.

▲ Fig. 3.34

Example: Eiscir Riada, near Clonmacnoise, Co. Westmeath; north and south of the River Brosna in Cos. Offaly and Westmeath.

Local example: …

■ Formation

Process involved: deposition

An esker or **os** is a long, low and winding ridge of sand and gravel that is oriented in the general direction of ice movement. Sections through eskers have revealed alternate strata of coarse and fine deposits, representing times of rapid and slow ice melting, respectively. They represent the beds of former streams flowing in and under ice sheets. Changes in discharge routes sometimes led to a section of tunnel being abandoned by the main stream flow. It would then silt up with sand and gravel; when the ice ultimately disappeared, the tunnel-fill would emerge as an esker, a ridge running across the country for several kilometres and bearing no relation to the local topography.

The surrounding landscape has a boulder clay covering, giving rise to rich farmland, which often stands in stark contrast to the sandy soils of an esker, which may display a poor-quality grass surface or coarse grasses and scrub. The esker was formed as the ice retreated rapidly.

THE VALUE OF GLACIATION TO THE IRISH ECONOMY

■ Boulder Clay

Farming thrives where boulder clay deposits are found on well-drained, sloping or undulating ground. Such ground will provide a deep and fertile soil, rich in minerals, especially if it had been eroded from a limestone landscape. Well-known expanses of rich farmland – such as the Golden Vale, the Blackwater valley in Cos. Cork and Waterford, the drumlin belt from Sligo to Strangford Lough, north Kildare and Meath in Leinster, and the river valleys of Armagh – owe much of their fertility to the minerals that were deposited in their boulder clays.

■ Lake Beds

Old glacial lake beds are generally fertile. Rich alluviums that once collected on the floors of these lakes now produce tillage crops or are used as rich pasture for dairy or beef herds. The Glen of Aherlow in Co. Tipperary was at one time such a lake, which drained southwards through a glacial spillway towards Galbally.

■ Eskers

These winding and stratified ridges of sand and gravel are found scattered over the Central Plain and the river valleys of Ireland. Their gravels and sands form the raw materials for the construction industry in the manufacture of concrete blocks, pavements, and ready-mix concrete. Quarrying along some eskers is quite noticeable in places, such as at Donohill, Co. Tipperary, and in Co. Westmeath near Clonmacnoise. Eskers were used in ancient times as roads that were free from flooding, especially in the Central Plain, while their sands and gravels are in constant demand for road building today.

■ Scenery

Glaciated mountains attract tourists in large numbers to such areas as Killarney in Co. Kerry, the Glendalough area in Co. Wicklow, and the Connemara area in Co. Galway. The ruggedness of these areas, caused by the erosive action of glaciers, has stamped a wild beauty on each region. Hotels, guesthouses and numerous service industries earn substantial incomes as a result of ice action!

Some glaciated areas have been designated national parks, such as Glenveagh National Park in Co. Donegal. Other such areas are Glendalough in Co. Wicklow and Killarney's lake district in Co. Kerry.

■ Energy and Water Supply

Glaciated lakes are used as reservoirs for urban areas (e.g. Blessington Lake for Dublin), while other lakes are used as reservoirs for the generation of hydro-electric power, such as Lough Derg, Blessington Lake (Poulaphuca), and Lake Nahanagan (Turlough Hill).

THE WORK OF THE SEA

REVISION AID

The waves of the sea cut, carry and deposit material. The cutting action gives the coastline many of its features, including cliffs, wave-cut platforms, bays, promontories, and beach material.

Beaches are formed between high and low water lines. The upper beach has heavy material such as angular rocks, and lower down are smaller rocks and pebbles, then sand, and finally mud.

Cliffs are formed when a steep coastline is undercut by waves. Hard rocks hold out longer than softer types. In this way bays and promontories are formed. Weaknesses allow the sea to cut caves, blow-holes, tunnels, arches and sea-stacks on a cliff coastline.

Longshore drift builds up **spits**, **bars**, and **lagoons**. Salt marshes form in sheltered estuaries. This sea-built land may be reclaimed for agriculture, as in the case of the Dutch polders. A sandy beach and an on-shore wind can cause sand dunes to build and spread inland. Grasses help to halt the invasion of land by these dunes.

Corrasion occurs when boulders, pebbles and sand are pounded by the waves against the coastline.

Hydraulic action is the direct impact of strong waves on a coast.

Compression is the breaking of rock by compressing air in cracks and caves.

■ Definitions

Wave:	Wind causes water particles on the surface of the sea to move in a circular motion and form a wave shape. This disturbance is transmitted to neighbouring particles, and so the wave shape moves forward (not the actual water).
Swash:	water that rushes up a beach following the breaking of a wave.
Backwash:	the return of the water down the beach.
Longshore drift:	the movement of material along the shore.
Load:	mud, sand and shingle carried along the shore by the sea.

LANDFORM NO. 13: *LANDFORM OF EROSION*
SEA-STACK

Example: Kilkee coast in Co. Clare. Local example: …

Fig. 3.35

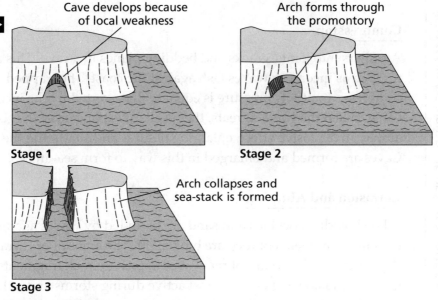

Cave develops because of local weakness

Arch forms through the promontory

Stage 1

Stage 2

Arch collapses and sea-stack is formed

Stage 3

■ Formation

Stage 1: Cave

Caves form in areas of active erosion where there is some local weakness. A jointed or faulted zone with a regular outline might be seen at a cave entrance. The sea erodes more effectively at such places. The joints are gradually opened up to form cavities, which in turn are enlarged to form caves.

Stage 2: Sea-arch

When a cave increases in length through a narrow headland or meets another cave from the opposite side, a sea-arch is formed. If a portion of a cave roof collapses, a bridge-like arch may also form. Example: the Bridges of Ross in Co. Clare.

Stage 3: Sea-stack

Sea-stacks form when arches collapse, leaving small islands of rock isolated from the coastline, normally very close to a cliff. A sea-stack is formed because of the processes of hydraulic action, compression, and abrasion.

Processes involved: hydraulic action, compression and abrasion

Hydraulic Action

The direct impact of strong waves on a coast has a shattering effect as it pounds the rocks. Strong waves breaking against the base of a cliff force rocks apart, creating a cave.

Compression

Air filters into joints, cracks and bedding planes in a cave. This air is trapped as incoming waves lash against the coast. The trapped air is compressed until its pressure is equal to that exerted by the incoming wave. When the wave retreats, the resultant expansion of the compressed air has an explosive effect, enlarging fissures and shattering the rock face. Caves are formed and enlarged in this way to form sea-arches.

Corrasion and Abrasion

When boulders, pebbles and sand are pounded by waves against the coastline, fragments of rock are broken off. The amount of corrasion is dependent on the ability of the waves to pick up rock fragments from the shore. Corrasion is therefore most active during storms and at high tide, when incoming waves throw water and suspended rock material against the coastline, eroding the sea arch until it collapses, leaving a sea-stack isolated from the coastline.

LANDFORM NO. 14: *CLIFF*

Landform of Erosion
Example: Cliffs of Moher, Co. Clare. Other example: …

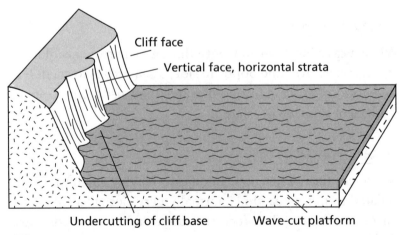

Cliff face

Vertical face, horizontal strata

Undercutting of cliff base   Wave-cut platform

▲ Fig. 3.36

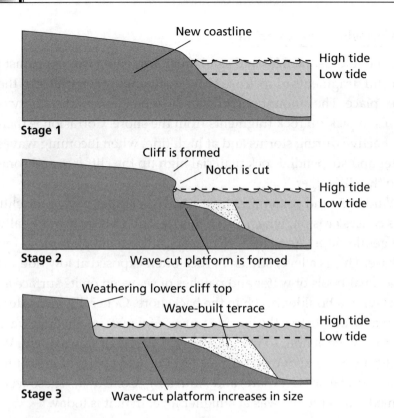

Fig. 3.37

Stage 1

New coastline

High tide
Low tide

Stage 2

Cliff is formed
Notch is cut

High tide
Low tide

Wave-cut platform is formed

Stage 3

Weathering lowers cliff top
Wave-built terrace

High tide
Low tide

Wave-cut platform increases in size

Processes involved: hydraulic action, compression and abrasion

■ Formation

As destructive waves lash against a shoreline, a wedge of material is eroded to form a notch. As the notch is enlarged, a steep cliff is formed. Undercutting of this cliff face occurs as the waves continue to strike at the base of the cliff. In time the overhang collapses and the cliff retreats. The following processes of erosion are involved in cliff formation.

■ Hydraulic Action

The direct impact of strong waves on a coast has a shattering effect as it pounds the rocks. Strong waves breaking against the base of a cliff force rocks apart, making them more susceptible to erosion. Cliffs of boulder clay are particularly affected, as loosened soil and rocks are washed away.

■ Compression

Air filters into joints, cracks and bedding planes in cliff faces. This air is trapped as incoming waves lash against the coast. The trapped air is compressed until its pressure is equal to that exerted by the incoming wave. When the wave retreats, the resultant expansion of the compressed air has an explosive effect, enlarging fissures and shattering the rock face.

■ Corrasion and Abrasion

When boulders, pebbles and sand are pounded by waves against the foot of a cliff, fragments of rock are broken off, and undercutting of the cliff takes place. The amount of corrasion is dependent on the ability of the waves to pick up rock fragments from the shore. Corrasion is therefore most active during storms and at high tide, when incoming waves throw water and suspended rock material high up the cliff face and sometimes onto the cliff edge.

Wind, rain and sometimes frost attack the upper part of the cliff face. This causes erosion, which also helps the cliff to retreat and finally reduce to a gentle slope. As a cliff face retreats, a wave-cut platform is formed at its base. This is a level stretch of rock often exposed at low tide, with occasional pools of water and patches of seaweed on its surface and displaying a boulder beach in the backshore. Generally the wider a wave-cut platform, the less the erosive power of waves, as shallow water reduces wave action, so the rate of coastal erosion slows down. Wave-cut platforms occur above present sea level in some parts of the country, such as at Black Head, Co. Clare, and Annalong, Co. Down. These were formed when the sea was at a higher level than it is today.

LANDFORM NO. 15: *BEACH*

Landform of deposition
> *Example:* Dollymount Strand, Dublin. Other example: …

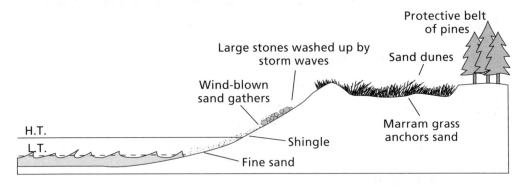

▲ Fig. 3.38 Composition of a beach

The term **beach** is applied to the accumulation of material between low tide level and the highest point reached by storm waves. This material usually consists of stones, pebbles, shingle, and sand, all of which were deposited by constructive wave action.

On an upland coast a beach may be just a loose mass of boulders and shingle under the cliffs, while a bay between headlands generally has a crescentic beach at its head, called a **bayhead** or **pocket beach**. Example: Sauce Creek near Brandon Head. The most typical beach is one with a gently concave profile, the landward side backed by dunes succeeded by a stretch of shingle and sand and sometimes rock covered by seaweed, indicating the underlying wave-cut platform.

An ideal beach profile has two main parts:

(a) the **backshore**, which is composed of rounded rocks and stones and broken shells, pieces of driftwood, and litter thrown up by storm waves. This part of the beach has a steep gradient and is reached by the sea during the highest tides or during storms;

(b) the **foreshore**, which is composed of sand and small shell particles, has a gentle gradient, and is covered by the sea regularly each day.

■ Runnels and Ridges

Broad, gently sloping ridges of sand and shallow, gently sloping depressions may be found on the seaward edge of the foreshore and parallel to the coastline. At low tide the runnels or depressions may contain long pools of water that was trapped by the ridges as the tide was receding.

The ridges are formed by constructive waves. As the waves break, sand accumulates on the landward side and forms ridges parallel to the breaking wave. The long, shallow depressions that form in between the ridges are called runnels.

■ Longshore Drift

Longshore drift is the movement of material (sand and shingle) along a shore. When waves break obliquely onto a beach, pebbles and sand are moved up the beach at the same angle as the waves by the swash. The backwash drags the material down the beach at right angles to the coast, only to meet another incoming wave, and the process is repeated. In this way materials are moved along in a zigzag pattern.

When a wave approaches a beach at an angle, the swash runs up the beach at the same angle, carrying material. The backwash flows straight down the slope at right angles to the coastline. The next wave carries the material at an angle up the beach again; so it moves along the shore in a zigzag manner.

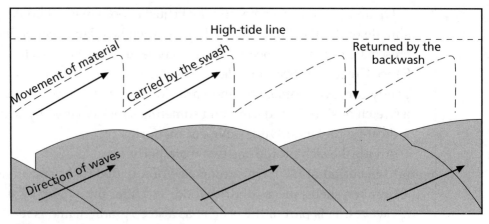

▲ Fig. 3.39. Longshore drift

LANDFORM NO. **16:** *LAGOON*

Landform of deposition

  Example: Roonagh Lough, Co. Mayo. Other example: …

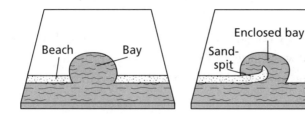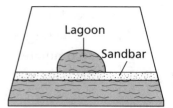

▲ Fig. 3.40 Method no. 1

■ Sandspit

Process involved: deposition

A spit is formed when material is piled up in line-like form but with one end attached to the land and the other projecting into the open sea, generally across the mouth of a river. Spits generally develop at places where longshore drift is interrupted and where the coastline undergoes a sharp change of direction, such as at river mouths, estuaries, and bays, or between an island and the shore.

  In long, funnel-shaped inlets of the sea, such as rias, spits are sometimes built out at right angles to the shore some distance up the bay, where the force of the incoming waves is markedly weakened. In such cases, **deposits** are carried seawards and they gradually build up to form a projecting ridge of beach material. This growth continues for as long as the amount of beach material being deposited is greater than the amount that is removed.

A sandbar may form as a result of the growth of a sandspit across a bay. When a bay is cut off from the sea, a **lagoon** is formed. Sometimes where tidal or river scouring takes place, a bar may be prevented from completely sealing off the bay, as is the case along the coast near Wicklow. This type of sandbar is called a **baymouth bar**.

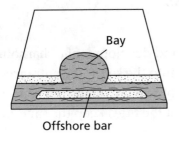

Bay

Offshore bar

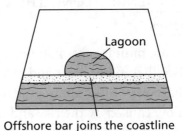

Lagoon

Offshore bar joins the coastline to form a baymouth bar

▲ Fig. 3.41 Method no. 2

■ Offshore Bar

An offshore bar is a ridge of sand lying parallel to a shore and some distance out to sea. On gently sloping coasts, **breakers** (large ocean waves) break, dig up the sea bed, and throw the loose material forward to form a ridge of sand. Once the ridge is formed, the bar increases in height by constructive wave action. Longshore drift may lengthen the bar at both ends. Offshore, these ridges are pushed along in front of the waves until finally they may lie across a bay to form a baymouth sandbar. Lady's Island Lake and Tacumshin Lake in Co. Wexford were originally bays of the sea before being cut off by such a sandbar.

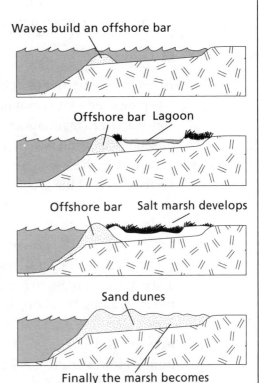

Waves build an offshore bar

Offshore bar Lagoon

Offshore bar Salt marsh develops

Sand dunes

Finally the marsh becomes an area of sand dunes

▲ Fig. 3.42

Processes involved: deposition, longshore drift

■ Stages of a Lagoon

A lagoon is formed when waves build a bar above water and across a bay or parallel to the coastline. Waves wash sand into the lagoon, and rivers and winds carry sediment into it. The lagoon becomes a marsh. Finally, the work of waves, rivers and winds turns the marsh into an area of sand dunes.

HUMAN INTERFERENCE ALONG THE COAST

■ Jetties

Jetties are built for the maintenance and development of harbours. They are usually built in pairs and extend into the sea at the entrances to rivers and harbours. By confining the flow of water to a narrow zone, the ebb and flow caused by the rise and fall of the tides keep the sand in motion and prevent deposition in the channel.

However, the jetty may act as a dam against which the longshore current and beach drift deposit sand. At the same time, destructive wave action removes sand on the other side, causing erosion and finally removal of the beach if it existed.

■ Groyne

A groyne is a barrier built at right angles to a beach for the purpose of trapping sand that is moving parallel to the shore. Groynes are constructed to maintain or widen beaches that are losing sand because of erosion. The result is an irregular but wider beach.

However, these groynes are so effective in places that the longshore current beyond the groynes is sand-deficient. Longshore current may therefore remove sand from here to compensate for its load deficiency and so give rise to erosion. Increased groyne development will counteract this erosion, and so groyne development continues.

Groynes may be built from timber stakes that are set into the ground in a line at right angles to the coastline. These lines of stakes are built at set intervals along the shore. Others may be built from large boulders forming a ridge in a similar manner. Timber groynes were built at Rosslare Strand, Co. Wexford, to limit erosion of the beach and sand dunes. However, erosion has continued, and recently stone groynes were added to help with defensive work.

■ Breakwaters

A breakwater is a coastal barrier that may be constructed parallel to the shoreline. The purpose of such a structure is to protect boats from the force of large breaking waves by creating a quiet-water zone near the shore. However, when this occurs the reduced wave activity along the shore behind the barrier may allow sand to accumulate. If a marina exists it may fill up with sand, while the downstream beach erodes and retreats.

■ Coastal Protection Methods

Concrete honeycomb: Blocks ranging from 0.25 to 1.25 m (1–4 feet) across, usually with a hexagonal profile, are laid interlocking on a slope of 30–60°. The wave energy is dissipated as water rushes into the circular core of each block. The block size and slope angle depend on the direction and strength of the waves.

Example: coastline at Nice in southern France

Mock rocks: These range from small natural rocks bonded together with bitumastic material to form larger rocks to reinforced concrete moulded into four-legged 0.5–1.25 m (2–4 feet) high shapes like oversize jacks (as in the children's game).

Hydrodynamic curve walls: The wave attack on a curved face is turned back on itself, dissipating the energy as turbulence. The walls can be combined with large pipes beneath the shingle, and water surges in and out of them, decreasing scour, which can erode the wall toe. Large boulders (5–7 tonnes) can also be put at the foot of the wall to protect the toe. Example: Lehinch, Co. Clare.

Example: Lehinch in Co. Clare

▲ Fig. 3.43

LIMESTONE LANDSCAPES

REVISION AID

Pervious rocks allow water to pass through them; **impervious (impermeable) rocks** do not. **Porous rocks** absorb water, somewhat like a sponge. The water in a well comes from a layer of rocks that has been waterlogged by rainwater.

Features formed by underground water are usually found in limestone areas, because rainwater can dissolve limestone more rapidly than other rocks.

A **karst** (limestone) landscape may be cut into a pattern of **grikes** and **clints** to form a limestone pavement. **Swallow-holes** are cut through the karst by rainwater. Below the surface, underground caverns are formed, where **stalagmites** and **stalactites** grow. **Potholes** are also a feature of the karst.

■ Definitions

Cavern:	a large underground chamber in a limestone region dissolved by rainwater.
Stalactite:	a slender column of calcite that hangs from a cavern ceiling.
Stalagmite:	a thick column of calcite that forms on a cavern floor directly underneath a stalactite.
Pillar:	a column of calcite in a limestone cavern formed when a stalactite and a stalagmite join together.
Curtain:	a continuous sheet of calcite formed when rainwater drips from a fissure in a cavern roof.
Passages:	long tunnels formed by underground streams.

Fig. 3.44 Features of a limestone region ▶

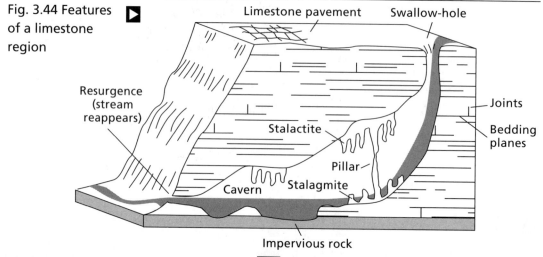

Limestone pavement Swallow-hole

Resurgence (stream reappears)

Joints

Stalactite

Bedding planes

Pillar

Cavern Stalagmite

Impervious rock

LANDFORM NO. 17: *DRIPSTONE*

Underground landform of deposition

Example: Mitchelstown Caves. Other example: …

Evaporation takes place as water seeps from limestone joints in cavern roofs. When this happens, some carbon dioxide is released from the solution and the water is unable to hold all the calcium carbonate. Calcium carbonate deposits are left on the ceiling or wall of the chamber or on the floor as the water falls because of gravity. All these calcium carbonate deposits are called **dripstone**.

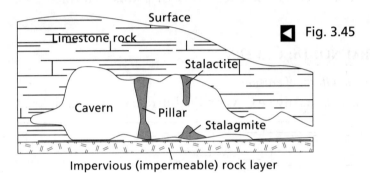

Fig. 3.45

■ **Dripstone Deposit Types**

1 Stalactites

Continuous seepage of water through cavern ceilings produces constant dripping and evaporation at specific places. As drips of water fall from the ceiling of the cavern, they leave behind a deposit of calcium carbonate. Deposition of the calcium carbonate occurs fastest at the circumference of the drop. A hard ring of calcite develops and grows down to form a tube that eventually fills up to form a solid stalactite. Calcite is a mineral formed from calcium carbonate. In its purest form it is white; however, as seeping water will have impurities in solution or suspension, they will discolour the calcite, causing brownish or other discolorations. These discolorations are especially noticeable on stalagmites.

2 Stalagmites

If seeping water does not entirely evaporate on the cavern ceiling, it falls to the floor or to sloping sides along the width of the cavern. Wider and shorter stumps or domes of calcite deposits build up to form stalagmites.

Process involved: evaporation

Their shape results from dropping water 'splashing' onto the floor, spreading out and thus forming a larger base than that of the stalactite.

3 Columns

As stalactites grow downwards they meet stalagmites growing upwards, thus forming columns or pillars.

4 Curtains

As water seeps out of a continuous narrow fissure on cavern or cave roofs, a curtain-like feature of dripstone is formed. This is called a curtain.

LANDFORM NO. 18: *CAVERN*

Underground landform of erosion

Example: Ailwee Cave in the Burren. Other example: …

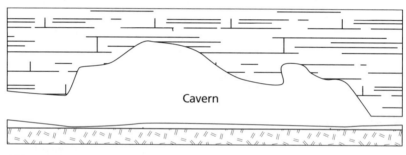

Cavern

▲ Fig. 3.46

Processes involved: hydraulic action, carbonation, solution

Underground streams in limestone landscapes form a maze of channels that run in some places for many kilometres underground. Their waters chiefly come from streams pouring through swallow-holes on the surface. Groundwater also seeps into these passages from the surrounding bedrock. In some interglacial and immediately postglacial periods these underground streams carried much more water than at present. Huge caverns were created by the hydraulic force of melt-water and are now left dry because of a lowering of the **water-table** (zone of saturation rock beneath the surface).

Streams flowing underground act upon fissures, enlarging them. Finally huge underground passages are formed. These are called **caverns** and may often be as large as a cathedral and indeed may even resemble one from within – so individual caverns may have such titles as 'the Cathedral' or 'the Dome'.

In limestone regions the water-table fluctuates regularly, and because the surface run-off is so rapid, the underground channels and caverns often quickly fill to capacity. A sudden downpour may cause such a rapid rise that **speleologists** (cave explorers) may be trapped or may have to make a speedy retreat to the surface.

■ Formation

Limestone has a number of characteristics that aid the denudation processes:
1. It is porous – small spaces between the rock particles can hold water.
2. It is pervious – it is well-jointed, which allows water to pass freely through its many lines of weakness.

■ Carbonation

Rainwater falling through the atmosphere combines with small amounts of carbon dioxide to form a weak carbonic acid. As it reaches and percolates through the ground, it changes carbonate compounds to soluble bicarbonate compounds. This process is particularly effective on chalk and limestone, where **carbonation** converts calcium carbonate to calcium bicarbonate, which is soluble in water and may be removed in solution: $CaCO_3$ (limestone) + H_2CO_3 (carbonic acid) = $Ca(HCO_3)_2$ (calcium bicarbonate). Karst landscapes such as the Burren are greatly affected by this process.

LANDFORM NO. 19: *DRY VALLEYS*

Surface landforms of erosion

Example: near Lisdoonvarna, Co. Clare. Other example: …

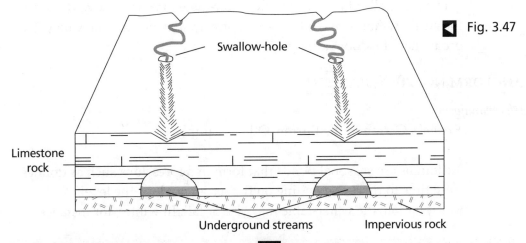

◀ Fig. 3.47

Swallow-hole

Limestone rock

Underground streams   Impervious rock

Processes involved: abrasion, solution

■ Dry valleys

These are extinct or partially used river valleys that are without running water for all or most of the year. Such valleys were formed in the following ways:

1. Some were carved by glacial melt-water when the ground was frozen and so impermeable. These were left dry as the ice disappeared.
2. Some are caused where large rivers **cut vertically down faster** than other neighbouring streams, thereby causing a fall in the water-table. This leaves the smaller streams without a water supply, and so their valleys are dry.
3. When a surface stream enters a swallow-hole, the valley below is left dry. Later, other swallow-holes are formed upstream, and in this way the surface stream shortens and the dry valley increases in length.

Swallow-holes are sometimes known as 'sink-holes', 'sluggas', or 'dolines'.

Swallow-holes are openings in the beds of rivers that flow over limestone rock. These holes, which were formed by **abrasion** and **solution**, allow the river water to disappear underground to solution channels, which wind their way under the surface. Swallow-holes generally form the shape of an inverted cone. They may be several metres in diameter as well as over a hundred metres in depth. In the Burren in Co. Clare, however, they are not very deep. Examples of such features in the Burren are Poll na gColm, Poll Binn, Poll an Phúca, and Poll Eilbhe.

A river that disappear through a swallow-hole may reappear further downslope as a spring. The point at which an underground river emerges from the earth is a **resurgence**. Such waters are not true springs, and their waters have not been filtered by bedrock. The Aille River in the Burren and Gort River in Co. Galway are examples of such a feature.

During spells of heavy rain the water-table may rise above the level of the swallow-holes, and a temporary stream may occupy the valley. This occurs near Lisdoonvarna in Co. Clare.

LANDFORM NO. 20: *TURLOUGH*

Surface landform

> *Example:* Carran in the Burren. Other example: …

Turloughs are seasonal ponds that form in depressions such as dolines from time to time. Depending on the season and/or the level of precipitation, the water-table may rise or fall. In winter, for instance,

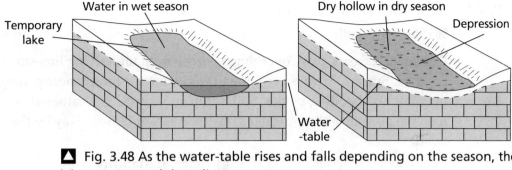

Fig. 3.48 As the water-table rises and falls depending on the season, the lake appears and then disappears

heavy rains will cause these hollows to fill with water, while in summer, because of a shortage of water, they will dry up. Soil gathers in such hollows and produces a rich grass that is grazed in summer if the water-table is sufficiently low.

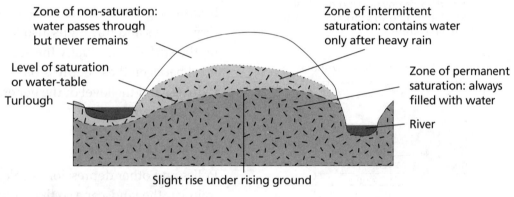

Fig. 3.49

■ **Formation**

Water entering the surface rocks will eventually move downwards until it reaches a layer of impermeable rock. At this stage it can no longer travel downwards and so it saturates the overlying rock layers, filling all pores and crevices. The portion of this where water is permanently stored is called an **aquifer**. The upper level of this water supply is called the **water-table**. Its level runs generally parallel to the ground surface, rising slightly under high ground and dipping down under low ground. The water-table may be permanently exposed in hollows, creating permanent water pools in fields. However, some pools, called **turloughs**, may be of a seasonal nature. In winter, for instance, slight hollows may fill with water, while in summer they dry up and disappear. These occur in parts of Cos. Clare and Galway.

Process involved: rising and falling of water-table

THE CYCLE OF EROSION IN A KARST REGION

■ Stage of Youth

Denudation wears away overlying bedrock until underlying limestone is exposed. Surface streams continue to erode into the limestone, opening up joints and bedding planes. Soil is thin and scarce, as weathered material is easily either washed away by rivers or blown away by the wind.

(a)　Normal surface drainage

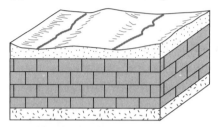

Youth: Streams flowing normally but beginning to work down into the limestone

(b)

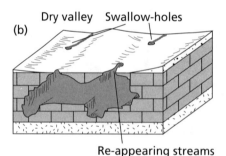

Dry valley　Swallow-holes

Re-appearing streams

(c)　Roof has collapsed　Dolines form

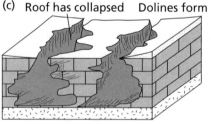

Maturity: Surface drainage non-existent

(d)　Hums　Impermeable rock

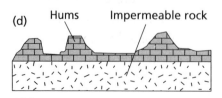

Old age

■ Stage of Maturity

At this stage all surface drainage has disappeared through swallow-holes into underground systems, and huge tunnels and caverns are formed below the surface. Tunnel and cavern roofs collapse, while joints in underlying limestone grow wider to form dolines. Dry valleys and turloughs also form on the surface. Gradually the surface level between these depressions reduces, and the level of the general area is lowered.

■ Stage of Old Age

Poljes and other depressions coalesce to lower the landscape so that only small hills called **hums** remain. Underground cavern systems disappear, and surface drainage resumes once again. The Burren is in a stage of maturity and displays all the features mentioned.

◀ Fig. 3.50 The cycle of erosion in karst areas

4

NATURAL VEGETATION, CLIMATE, AND PEOPLE

SUMMARY OF CASE STUDIES

Equatorial climate
Tropical-continental climate
Boreal climate

⎤ Effect of climate on vegetation
⎦ Effect of people on vegetation

Deforestation in the tropics

⎤ Causes of deforestation
⎦ Effects of deforestation

CASE STUDIES IN AFRICA

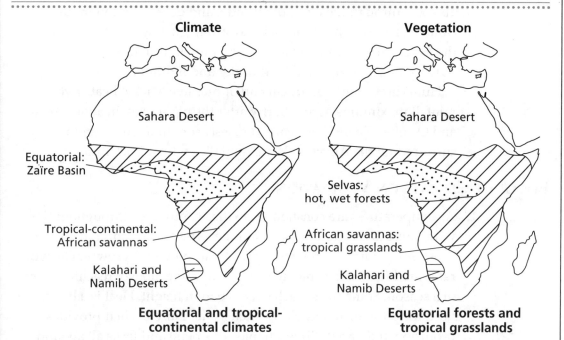

Climate

Sahara Desert

Equatorial:
Zaïre Basin

Tropical-continental:
African savannas

Kalahari and
Namib Deserts

**Equatorial and tropical-
continental climates**

Vegetation

Sahara Desert

Selvas:
hot, wet forests

African savannas:
tropical grasslands

Kalahari and
Namib Deserts

**Equatorial forests and
tropical grasslands**

▲ Fig. 4.1

CASE STUDY NO. 1: *THE ZAÏRE BASIN*

Examples of countries: Cameroon, Zaïre
Climate: Equatorial
Location: 0°–8° north and south of the Equator

1. **Temperature:** This region is on the Equator. Therefore the sun's rays strike the surface vertically. The midday sun is always near the vertical and it is overhead twice a year, at the equinoxes (March and September). Average daily temperatures are **26°C** throughout the year. These are well below the average daily temperatures of some other types of climate occurring outside equatorial latitudes. Extensive cloud cover and heavy rainfall prevent temperatures from rising much above 26°C. Temperatures are high and uniform near sea level, departing little from 26°C, and the annual range rarely exceeds 3°C. The diurnal (daily) temperature range is between 6°C and 8°C, which is greater than the annual range.

2. **Rainfall:** Low pressure dominates the Zaïre Basin throughout the year. Annual rainfall is about **2,000 mm**. Rainfall is heavy and is usually **convectional**. In the Amazon rain-forest the air is still. The hot, damp air creates rising thermal currents within a distance of about 10° north and south of the Equator. In the afternoon this rising air cools through the effect of altitude, and dark cumulonimbus clouds form. Air speed increases to strong gusting winds, which sway the forest canopy with great violence. Rain falls in torrential downpours, accompanied by thunder and lightning.

   Humidity is high, producing an oppressive 'sticky' heat. Two rainfall maximums occur shortly after the equinoxes, in about April and October. There is no marked dry season. In upland regions surrounding the Amazon Basin, rainfall can total 2,500 mm.

EFFECT OF CLIMATE ON VEGETATION

1. As temperatures are constant, growth is continuous throughout the year. There is only one season: summer. Trees shed individual leaves constantly, which are immediately replaced by new growth. **Growth rates are high**, with some tree species (e.g. the albitso) reaching 10 m in a season. Some trees reach over 100 m in height. Heat is a basic need for growth, and in places such as the Zaïre Basin it provides profusion and variety. Trees, **lianas** (creepers) and ferns all abound. Ecologists estimate that in equatorial areas some 25 million individual plants may populate a square kilometre of forest. Such forests are called **selvas**.

2. The combination of high temperatures and heavy rainfall throughout the year produces a dense vegetation cover, which shows a distinct arrangement in layers:

(a) the upper layer, consisting of tall trees whose broad evergreen leaves form a continuous canopy; the surface of the canopy is not level, as the crowns of the biggest trees, called **emergents**, project (e.g. kapok);

(b) the middle layer, an intermediate layer consisting of smaller trees, tree ferns, lianas, and numerous **epiphytes** (plants growing on others though not deriving their substance from them) (e.g. orchids and ferns);

(c) the **undergrowth** or lower layer, consisting of ferns and large herbaceous plants growing between the trunks of the trees.

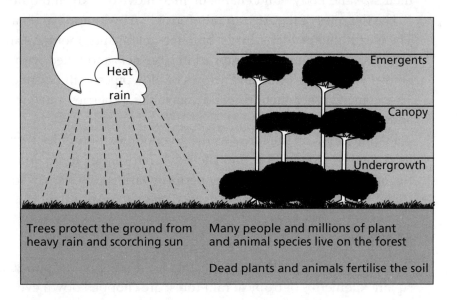

▲ Fig. 4.2

The tallest trees are supported by **plank buttress** roots. These roots, as well as those of other tree types, spread across the forest floor. They tap nutrients from the blanket of rapidly decaying vegetable matter, such as leaves, that litters the forest floor. The intense humidity within the forest creates an atmosphere where plants decay rapidly.

Soils in equatorial areas are **leached** (washed down to lower layers). The heavy rains dissolve most minerals in the A horizon and deposit them in the B horizon. Therefore forest soils contain little organic matter. Iron and aluminium hydroxides, however, are not dissolved and remain in the A horizon to form a **laterite** soil. The infertile soils, together with the absence of direct sunlight, limit the growth of plants on the forest floor.

HOW HUMAN ACTIVITIES INTERACT WITH THE EQUATORIAL RAIN FOREST

1 Positive

The Pygmies in Zaïre wear little clothing, because of the hot, moist climate of the equatorial regions. They are between 122 and 142 cm (48–60 in.) tall. They have reddish-brown skin and tightly curled brown hair (Negroid racial group), and have short legs and long arms. Some scientists believe that the physical characteristics of Pygmies developed over thousands of years, enabling them to adapt to their surroundings. The colour of the Pygmies' skin serves as a camouflage in the forest, and their size and body build enable them to move quickly and quietly.

The Pygmies of the African rain-forest live by hunting and gathering. The men hunt antelopes, birds, buffaloes, elephants, monkeys, and other animals. Most animals are trapped in large nets and killed with spears. Some Pygmies use bows and arrows or blowpipes with poisoned arrows. The women gather such fruit and vegetables as berries, mushrooms, nuts, and roots.

Pygmies look on the forest as the giver of life. It provides them with food, clothing, protection, and shelter. In return they try to do nothing that might harm the forest. They perform various ceremonies to maintain friendly relationships with the natural and supernatural world.

2 Negative

Equatorial forests are disappearing at an alarming rate. Up to 200,000 square kilometres of tropical rain-forest are chopped down every year to satisfy the life-style of the rich countries. According to the Food and Agriculture Organisation (FAO) of the United Nations, since 1945 nearly half of all rain-forests have been wiped out. At present rates almost one-fifth of the remaining tropical forests will be completely destroyed or seriously degraded by the year 2000.

Commercial logging is the activity most responsible for tropical forest destruction. In Japan, for example, almost all restaurants and canteens are now serving food with wooden chopsticks. Until recently chopsticks were washed after meals and used for years; but the development of disposable chopsticks, which are simply thrown away after a single use, has changed all that. They use up 200,000 cubic metres of tropical wood a year, although this accounts for only 0.2 per cent of Japan's total wood usage. The Japanese construction industry also uses hardwood as scaffolding, much of which is disposed of after a single use.

CASE STUDY NO. 2: *THE AFRICAN SAVANNAS (TROPICAL GRASSLANDS)*

Example of countries: Kenya, Sudan
Climate: tropical-continental
Location: 8°–18° north and south of the Equator

▲ Fig. 4.3 The African savanna with wildlife

1 Temperature

Between the equatorial belt of rainfall and the hot deserts lies a transitional zone called the tropical savanna lands. The savanna lands lie within the tropics, approx. 8°–18° north of the Equator, so temperatures are high (**25°C**) throughout the year. Maximum temperatures are reached before the arrival of the rains as a result of the dry air and cloudless skies. Average April temperatures reach **33°C**. The diurnal (daily) range of temperature is very noticeable, since the clear skies that promote daytime heating also cause night-time radiation (loss of heat).

2 Rainfall

This natural region has two distinct seasons:
(*a*) the dry season, from October to March
(*b*) the wet season, from April to September.

During the dry season the savanna lands are influenced by a belt of high pressure (**anticyclone**). At this time, cool descending air gets warmer as it approaches the earth and so retains its moisture. During the wet season the region experiences a period of convectional rain. A dominating low-pressure cell draws moisture-laden winds from the Atlantic Ocean and the Zaïre Basin. Rising **thermal** (warm) currents cause torrential downpours, rivers overflow their banks, and large tracts of the savannas are covered by flood waters.

Rainfall amounts vary within the basin. Elevated regions receive higher rainfall than lower areas. As distance from the Equator increases, both the rainfall total and the length of the rainy season decrease. Thus while southern areas receive 1,000 mm, northern areas have less than 250 mm of rainfall.

■ Effect of Climate on Vegetation

1. Tropical grassland or savanna may be classified as a transition zone between the equatorial lands and hot desert. So as one moves away from the Equator and towards the hot desert, one passes through tropical forest, tropical grassland, scrub, and desert. The savanna land partakes, to a varying degree, of the character of all four. As rainfall decreases from the Equator, so also does the density of vegetation. There is a mixture of trees and grasses near the edges of the selvas. As one moves away from the Equator, the number of trees reduces, giving way to open savanna grassland.

2. Savannas display a discontinuous cover of tufted grass, growing rapidly during the wet season to a height of 2 m as a stiff green plant. At this time, rivers are no longer confined to their channels and flood large areas. Grasses grow in these flooded places. During the dry season, rivers gradually return to their channels, while the grasses change to a yellow straw with silvery spikes. The tallest variety is elephant grass, often as much as 5 m high. As the desert approaches, the grass becomes shorter and more tufted, with bare sand between the scattered thorny bushes.

3. Many drought-resistant plants grow in the savannas. Palms, baobab and acacia are adapted to the drought of the dry season. They grow in hollows where ground-water approaches the surface. The leaves of the baobab appear in May. They are waxy and thin and form an umbrella shape to shade the roots from the heat of the sun. The baobab sheds its leaves in the dry season. The acacia has waxy leaves to prevent transpiration. All these plants have either large root systems on the surface for finding water or long, deep roots that reach down to the water-table.

HOW PEOPLE INTERACT WITH THE TROPICAL SAVANNA GRASSLANDS

■ Negative

Desertification: Within the savanna lands of North Africa, farming has worked its way northwards (Sahel region). Between the 1950s and the 1970s the southern fringe of the Sahara had a relatively large amount of rainfall, and this series of good years led to an invasion of farmers and the attendant land clearance in what had been a pastoral area. In Niger, for example, farmers pushed northwards, planting fields of millet and ground-nuts in the area traditionally occupied by nomadic herdsmen.

Agricultural demands let to the clearance of natural vegetation. Over the past thirty years the woods that covered the Sahel have been reduced by felling. The disappearance of tree cover has had serious consequences on the whole of the environment. Run-off accelerates, ground-water is no longer replaced, water-tables drop, and erosion attacks the soil, robbing it of its fertility. It has been estimated that in the Sudan a minimum of 548 million acacia shrubs a year were uprooted just for cooking. In this way, unexpected dry spells created a desert environment, and starvation followed.

CASE STUDY NO. 3: *THE SAHARA*

Examples of countries: Mali, Algeria, Chad
Climate: hot desert
Location: 18°–35° north of the Equator

1 Temperature

Hot deserts are characterised by the absence of a cold season, with no mean monthly temperatures below 8°C. In Africa there are two main areas of hot desert climate: (*a*) the Sahara and (*b*) the Kalahari.

The Sahara is classified as a continental hot desert (located mostly inland). This means that temperatures are far more extreme than along coastal areas. Temperatures above **55°C** are recorded. The world record shade temperature is reputed to be 65°C, recorded some 40 km south of Tripoli. The average July temperature is 35°C, while the average January temperature is 20°C.

The diurnal range is very pronounced. The clear skies that allow great insulation during the day cause rapid radiation by night. As a consequence there may be a fall of 20°C in the couple of hours succeeding sunset. Diurnal ranges of 35° or 43°C are commonly recorded.

2 Rainfall

High pressure dominates the Sahara region. For much of the year the Sahara is influenced by the trade winds (0–30° N), which blow from the continent of Europe. These are dry winds that retain their moisture as they approach the Equator. There is practically no rainfall in this region. Rain-bearing winds from the Gulf of Guinea on the Equator lose their moisture over the tropical rain-forest areas and are dry when they reach the Sahara. Winds that blow from the Atlantic lose their moisture over the Atlas Mountains in Morocco, and so this northern portion is in the rain shadow.

■ Effect of Climate on Vegetation

The Sahara is arid. Therefore much of the region has only a rock and sand cover, and vegetation is absent. Where vegetation does exist it consists of scrub and semi-desert plants. These plants are **xerophytes** (plants adapted to living in drought conditions). Waxy skin and spiky leaves prevent loss of moisture, while a large top-root system gathers precipitation from a wide area and from deep underground.

The bare rock or **hamada** areas and the gravel or **reg** areas of the Sahara have scattered clumps of leafless thorny **perennials** (plants lasting throughout the year). Elsewhere dwarf salt-bushes, prickly plants, cactus and thorn bushes of the scrublands are found, but much more stunted and sparsely. Most vegetation exists in an apparent dormant state for long periods and instantly reacts to a sudden downpour. This physical reaction causes seed pods to open and to scatter their seeds. These will germinate, grow and cover the area with colourful blooms within a week to repeat the cycle.

HOW PEOPLE INTERACT WITH HOT DESERTS

■ Positive

The Nomads

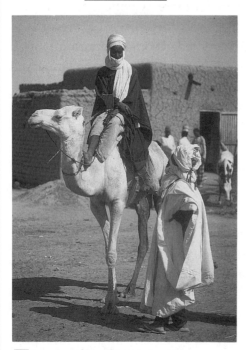

Various groups inhabit hot desert areas. Some are nomads, while others are **sedentary** (settled people).

The nomads such as the Tuareg of the Sahara are Berbers. They roam the desert with herds of camels, goats, and sheep. They wander from oasis to oasis. Their shelter consists of light skin tents, which protect them from the heat of the day and the cold of the night. Their clothing, often of white woven material, serves the same purpose. Wanderers such as the Tuareg depend to a great extent on their camels, their date-palms, and above all on the precious water, which they carry in leather containers beneath their camels' bellies.

▲ Fig. 4.4 Tuareg nomads with camels

The Settled People (Farmers)

The settled inhabitants of the oases are engaged in the growing of cereals, the rearing of sheep and goats, and the cultivation of date-palms. Some oases need the dwellers to persist with the removal of sand, as dunes threaten to overcome their area. The oasis-dwellers build houses with thick stone or mud walls to keep them cool. Flat roofs are used, as there is no necessity to guard against rain.

In Egypt the people live in the Nile Valley. For centuries they cultivated the alluvial soils of the flood plain using irrigation (screw pump and water-wheel) as a means of watering their crops. Egyptian farmers ploughed and seeded their fertile fields as soon as the flood waters of the Nile went down. In the hot climate, farmers could grow two or three crops a year.

Tourists

In recent decades tourists are attracted to the Mediterranean fringe on the desert coastlands of North Africa. Morocco, Algeria and Tunisia have developed holiday resorts to cater for this growing demand. The people of the industrialised countries of western Europe seek dry, sunny areas for their holidays.

▲ Fig. 4.5 Simple irrigation methods in the Nile Valley

DEFORESTATION IN THE TROPICS

The world's tropical forests are being cleared at the rate of 14 hectares per minute or 7.3 million hectares a year. As a result, fragile tropical soils are being turned into wastelands, many tribal peoples are being decimated, and thousands of unique plant and animal species are being destroyed.

CAUSES OF DEFORESTATION

1 Demand for Wood

▲ Fig. 4.6 Deforestation in a tropical forest

In 1983, 20,000 million pairs of disposable wooden chopsticks were used in Japan – 170 sets for every person – using up to 200,000 cubic metres of timber a year. Most of this wood comes from south-east Asia, and accounts for 2 per cent of Japan's timber imports. Western Europe, the second-largest importer of tropical wood, received 12 million cubic metres of tropical round wood in 1984. France, Britain, Germany, Italy and the Netherlands are the main users. The wood is used in construction and is also valued for expensive office and household furniture, and for fittings such as doors, floors, and window frames. For the manufacture of mahogany toilet seats alone, 4 million hectares of rain-forest are destroyed each year.

2 Ranching

Since 1960 more than a quarter of all Central American forests have been destroyed for conversion to pastureland. The grass-fed cattle are mainly exported as beef, almost all of it to the United States. There it is bought by fast-food chains, which process it to meet the American and multinational appetite for hamburgers. Hundreds of American and other foreign companies in Central America are involved in cattle-related activities, with interests ranging from financing and ranching to processing and marketing.

▲ Fig. 4.7 Cattle ranching in the Amazon Basin

However, the main purpose of cattle ranching in the Amazon is as a device for claiming land and for speculation rather than for the production of beef. Landless labourers and drought-stricken farmers from the *sertão* (north-eastern Brazil) flock to the Amazon Basin to win land from the forest. Settlers grow rice, corn, coffee and manioc for a few years, until the meagre soil is exhausted, then move deeper into the forest to clear new land. This cycle of burning and clearing continues until the pioneers give up, suffering from disillusionment and malaria. The abandoned fields end up in the hands of ranchers and speculators who have access to capital. Thanks to tax relief and subsidies, these groups can often profit from the land even when their operations lose money.

3 Demand for Cash Crops

The Sahel region of Africa – a dry land 63 times the size of Ireland, straddling parts of six of the world's poorest countries – was at one time a prosperous empire where trading, herding and farming tribes interacted well and kept their environment in balance. They exchanged meat and milk for cereals and vegetables. In the dry season, herds grazed the left-over cereal plants and manured the land in doing so. Rotational grazing (grazing cereal stubble) and farming patterns placed no strain on the soil.

Colonisation (by France, Spain, and Portugal), private land rights and cash-cropping have damaged the delicate ecological balance in the Sahel. Over the past twenty years much of the best land has been turned over to cash-cropping.

Cash-cropping was imposed through taxes. Ground-nuts, cotton, coffee and tobacco replaced cereals. These cash crops were used to provide exports for money needed to repay ever-growing national debts. These crops drain minerals from the soil and hasten erosion. The land devoted to cash crops could not be grazed. Traditional farmers were pushed out of the lands into the semi-arid wastelands. Here livestock overgrazed these marginal lands. Land that used to be green pasture during short wet spells turned into desert after four years without rain. Parched trees provided the only source of income for those whose livestock had died. This accelerated the spread of the deserts, as the woods had previously prevented erosion and retained moisture in the land.

In 1968, when the rains failed, there were no natural reserves left in the environment. The region was plunged into a long and painful famine, from which it has never recovered. Between 1968 and 1973 crops shrivelled, over 3 million cattle perished, and over 150,000 people died.

EFFECTS OF DEFORESTATION

■ Local Effects

Example 1: *Industrial Development*

The Tucuruí hydro-electric dam project in north-eastern Brazil is a government-sponsored scheme intended to provide cheap electricity for the multinational companies in the area. These companies are owned and run by Japanese, American and British industrialists on the north-east coast. Of all the Amazon development programmes, the Tucuruí project has caused most controversy. The Tucuruí dam is the second-largest hydro-electric scheme in Brazil and the fourth-largest in the world. The first stage cost the Brazilian government over £5,000 million; the cost to the local environment and its people, however, has been higher.

Over 2,500 square kilometres of rain-forest was flooded, and many thousands of trees were destroyed, while rising water levels trapped and drowned thousands of animals. Chemicals such as Agent Orange (dioxin), which is highly toxic, were used to clear the area of undergrowth. Hundreds of people were forced to leave their homes and were given land that belonged to Native Americans ('Indians'), who were willing to defend it at all costs.

Some 20,000 people were forced to leave their homes on the coasts in order to clear a site for a factory that was associated with the project. The evicted people had to build shanty-houses on land that was liable to flooding. Because of this they suffer from tuberculosis, leprosy, pneumonia, and diarrhoea.

Example 2: *Desertification in North Africa*

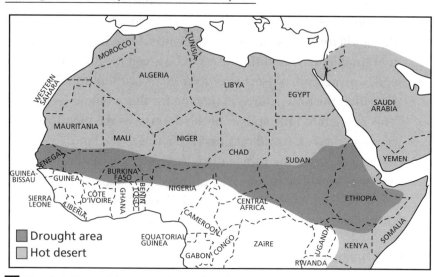

▲ Fig. 4.8 Drought areas of North Africa

Until recent times, 70 per cent of the Sudan was covered with tropical forest vegetation or savanna woodland. Many of these trees were cut down as the demand for cash crops increased to feed national debts.

Because of this the area devoted to agriculture increased and encroached into marginal regions that were unsuited to such activities. When the rains failed, the soils were left exposed to the winds, which caused erosion of the soil. In colonial times, administrative centres grew up across the Sahel. This urban development continued into recent times, creating a huge demand for wood for fuel and construction.

This deforestation in association with global warming (the 'greenhouse effect') has increased the water supply problem in marginal areas and has led to desertification. Climate change is brought about by the interaction between the forest and the atmosphere. Of the rainfall, 25 per cent drains into the rivers, 25 per cent evaporates off the leaves, and 50 per cent returns to the atmosphere through transpiration and makes clouds. When trees are absent, so are clouds. With no clouds, the land becomes dried up by the equatorial sun. When rain does fall, the full force of the rain reaches the ground, and **sheet erosion** occurs. Nutrients and topsoil are washed into rivers and estuaries, creating problems of silting.

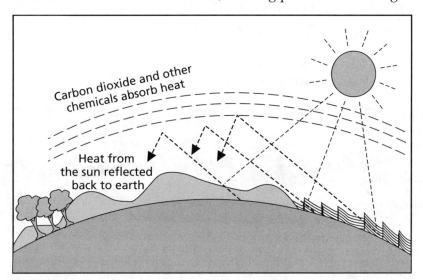

Carbon dioxide and other chemicals absorb heat

Heat from the sun reflected back to earth

▲ Fig. 4.9 The greenhouse effect

■ Global Warming: the Greenhouse Effect

Scientists are concerned that the destruction of the Amazon Basin could lead to climatic chaos. Because of the huge volume of clouds it generates, the Amazon system plays a key role in the way the sun's heat is distributed around the globe. Any disturbance of this process could produce far-reaching and unpredictable effects. Moreover, the Amazon region stores at least 75,000 million tons of carbon in its trees, which when burned emit carbon dioxide into the atmosphere. Since the air is already dangerously overburdened by carbon dioxide from the cars and factories of industrialised countries, the burning of the Amazon forests could magnify the greenhouse effect – the trapping of heat by atmospheric carbon dioxide. Scientists believe that increased carbon dioxide levels will cause the atmosphere to warm up and will bring on devastating climatic changes, such as the melting of polar ice-caps.

The consequences of such changes can only be guessed at at present. Melting polar ice and increasing water temperatures would raise the sea level, flooding low areas; increased evaporation might lead to increased rainfall and to reduced sunshine in wet temperate zones and cause droughts in central continental areas.

According to the Worldwatch Institute, one of the hundreds of environmental pressure groups advising the Earth Summit in Rio de Janeiro, the world has lost 200 million hectares (500 million acres) of trees since 1972, an area roughly one-third the size of the United States.

CASE STUDY *IN THE NORTHERN LATITUDES*
CONIFEROUS FOREST REGION (TAIGA)

Climate: Cold continental (inland location)
Location: Coniferous Forest Region (taiga)

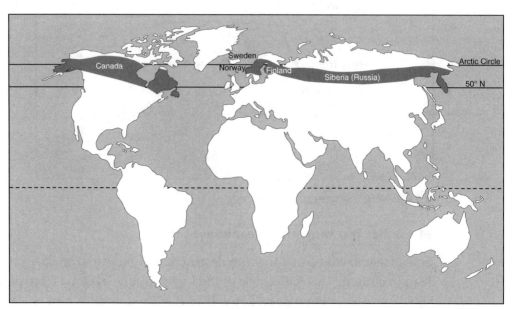

▲ Fig. 4.10 World distribution of coniferous forest lands. They stretch across the landmasses of the northern hemisphere between 50° N and the Arctic Circle.

■ Distribution

The coniferous forest proper is found in high latitudes or on high mountain slopes. The Siberian name of **taiga** is given to this belt. Their greatest development is in the northern hemisphere, where the landmasses are at their broadest, and they extend right across North America and Eurasia. In western Europe they extend as far south as 60° N. Here the influence of the North Atlantic

▲ Fig. 4.11 Coniferous forest and sawmill in northern latitudes

Drift increases temperatures and thus limits the southward migration. In eastern Asia they extend to approx. 50° N because of the influence of the cold Kamchatka current (Oya Siwo), while in eastern Canada they extend as far south as 45° N because of the influence of the cold Labrador Current.

■ Temperature

This type of climate extends across North America from Alaska to the gulf of the St Lawrence River, and across Eurasia from the Scandinavian uplands to the Pacific. Bordering both oceans the climates are of the cold temperate type, with rainfall throughout the year. Temperatures rapidly become more extreme as the continental interiors are approached. In central Canada, Winnipeg has a January mean of –20°C, and Dawson City (at 14° of latitude further north) has a January mean of –31°C. In Asia the size of the landmass makes the winter cold even more intense. Winter nights are long with hardly any daylight, and summer days are long with hardly any night. Summer temperatures are warm at 19°C.

Extreme cold sets a limit to forest distribution at high latitudes and altitudes, where tree growth is stunted.

■ Precipitation

Precipitation is sparse because of the distance of these continental interiors from the sea. Some areas are in the rain shadow of mountain ranges, such as the Rockies and the Scandinavian Highlands. The total annual precipitation is approx. 250 mm, some of which falls as rain in summer and as snow in winter. Humidity is always low, because of low temperatures.

■ How the Trees Adapt to Their Environment

Soil Type

The soil type of the coniferous forest regions is called **podzol** (Russian for 'ashy grey soil'). Soils under coniferous trees show a well-developed soil profile. During winter, chemical and biological actions that produce quality soil are at a standstill, as the ground is covered by a blanket of snow. When the snow melts, water drains downwards, and iron hydroxides and the humus from rotting vegetation near the surface are carried in solution to the lower soil layer. This causes leaching of the topsoil or A horizon. This action bleaches the upper horizon to a greyish colour. The ferro-humus material gathers at a depth of a few centimetres, where, mixed with particles of clay and silt, it forms a deep brown (rust-coloured) layer. Regularly, this becomes a hard cemented layer called the **hard pan**, which is impermeable. This leads to waterlogging, and there is a tendency for bogs to develop. Podzol soils are not, therefore, rich in mineral matter. Plants that grow on such soils, like the conifer trees, have frugal needs and can thrive on these peaty or low-nutrient soils.

Conifer Plants

In order to survive in high latitudes, the conifer tree has adapted itself to its environment in the following ways.

1. Conifers must withstand long winters and short summers. Conifers have needle-shaped leaves. These allow for the minimum amount of moisture loss, as their pores are protected from the winds and they are also covered with a waxy skin. Because of the short summers at this latitude, the trees retain their leaves in order to maximise their growing season. Once the early spring sunshine heats the ground, growth can begin immediately.

2. Conifers grow quickly, and their compact conical shape both helps their stability against the wind and prevents too heavy an

accumulation of snow on the branches. They have shallow roots that quickly trap nutrients from the surface, and they occur in great uniform stands, which reduces competition from other plants.

■ How People Interfere with Coniferous Forests

Positive

Coniferous trees are used as a source of employment and raw material. As conifers are a renewable resource, planned development characterised by sustained yield can be achieved. In Sweden, for example, the forest stock is greater than at any other time in the twentieth century. In addition, annual growth rates of timber exceed cutting and add further to the country's stocks. Forest reserves are guaranteed, because disease controls, the application of fertiliser and better drainage of land all help to raise the productivity of the forest. In addition, continuous replanting in some areas and natural regeneration in other areas ensure a constant supply of timber in the future.

Forestry activities are labour-intensive and provide a valuable source of full-time and part-time employment in marginal areas such as Norrland. Logging, transporting and wood-processing are the main areas of employment. Sweden has some four hundred sawmills and accounts for 3 per cent of world timber output and 8 per cent of world exports. Some sixty-four integrated pulp and paper mills produce 10 per cent of world output, while 70 per cent of the pulp is processed into paper within Sweden, creating additional value and employment for the national economy.

Negative

In the industrialised countries of Europe, such as Germany and Britain, heavy **combustion** (burning) of fossil fuels such as oil and coal results in the emission of sulphur dioxide and nitrogen oxides into the atmosphere. Transformation of these gases into sulphuric acid and nitric acid leads to further acidification of the water vapour. This artificial acidification of the cloud water results in an increase in the acidity of the precipitation, giving rise to regular rainfall episodes with an acidity of less than pH 4.0 downwind of the source areas.

Acids also fall to the ground as dry particle deposition. Acids in cloud water and fog droplets are deposited directly by contact with forest vegetation. The prevailing south-west anti-trades that blow across Europe carry this pollution to forested areas such as Scandinavia and the Black

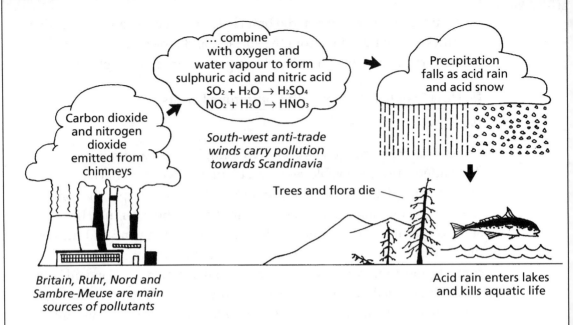

... combine with oxygen and water vapour to form sulphuric acid and nitric acid
$$SO_2 + H_2O \rightarrow H_2SO_4$$
$$NO_2 + H_2O \rightarrow HNO_3$$

South-west anti-trade winds carry pollution towards Scandinavia

Carbon dioxide and nitrogen dioxide emitted from chimneys

Precipitation falls as acid rain and acid snow

Trees and flora die

Britain, Ruhr, Nord and Sambre-Meuse are main sources of pollutants

Acid rain enters lakes and kills aquatic life

▲ Fig. 4.12

Forest in Germany. Scandinavia, with its heavily weathered sandy soils and acid soils overlying granite rocks, is particularly affected by this **acid rain**.

As acid rain penetrates the soil it leaches away important nutrients (e.g. calcium and potassium) and releases manganese and aluminium, which poison the tree roots, so restricting their ability to absorb moisture. The tops of the conifers turn yellow-green, growth stops, the lower branches shed needles, and the bark may split, letting in the cold winds in winter and the bark beetle in summer.

In the Black Forest area in Germany over 70 per cent of trees have been killed or are damaged. In Scandinavia an estimated 15 per cent decline in forest productivity has occurred because of acid rain.

5

POPULATION GROWTH, URBANISATION, AND MIGRATION (DEMOGRAPHY)

In studying social, economic and regional sections of the Leaving Certificate geography course, it may be helpful to learn key areas of study that can be used for a variety of answers. For example, the heading 'Congestion' can be used to answer part of the following questions:

1. Problems of increasing populations
2. Consequences of rapid urbanisation
3. Problems of developing economies

In a similar way, the study of western Europe can be made much easier. For example, southern Italy can be regarded as a region within Italy and at the same time a peripheral region within the EU and also an industrial problem region because of lack of resources.

One purpose of this book is to help students organise answers in a way that is advantageous in an examination. For many topics covered in these sections, only a few sample answers are given, but there may be other equally valid points that you may wish to develop. In such instances you should organise alternative information in a similar way to prepare for the examination.

■ Definitions

Demography:	the study of population.
Natural increase:	when the birth rate is greater than the death rate.
Overpopulation:	when the resources of an area are unable to support its population.
Conurbation:	the joining of two or more neighbouring urban areas (e.g. the Randstad in the Netherlands).
Megalopolis:	the joining of two or more conurbations (e.g. Los Angeles, or the eastern seaboard of the United States from Boston to Washington).
Shanties:	makeshift dwellings erected around the outskirts of cities in developing countries.
Push factors:	circumstances that force people to leave their homes (e.g. famine, war, flooding).
Pull factors:	circumstances that attract people to an area (e.g. jobs, climate, political freedom).

Ozone layer: a layer of ozone, a form of oxygen that creates a protective shield against the harmful ultraviolet rays of the sun.

Greenhouse effect: increasing amounts of gases in the outer atmosphere such as carbon dioxide and methane that are trapping too much heat and causing a gradual rise in global temperature.

POPULATION GROWTH

Around 5000 BC the population of the world was approximately 10 million. By the time of Christ it totalled about 100 million, and by 1600 it had grown to around 400 million. Population growth was slow and may have **oscillated** (moved slightly up and down) until the beginning of modern times.

THE POPULATION CYCLE

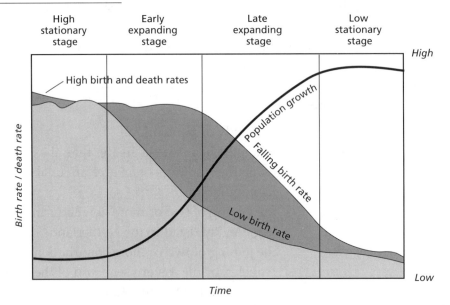

Fig. 5.1 The population cycle

■ Reasons for Slow Population Growth in the Past

1. Natural disasters such as earthquakes, flood, and fire (Pompeii destroyed in AD 79).
2. Famines in earlier times periodically reduced the population.

3. Diseases were common, such as the Black Death (bubonic plague), which wiped out a quarter of Europe's population in the fourteenth century.
4. Wars and persecution also contributed to loss of life throughout the centuries (Napoleonic wars, First and Second World Wars).

■ Recent Population Growth Trends

1. Improvements in health, such as the introduction of vaccination and the raising of standards of hygiene, have reduced the effects of disease and plagues.
2. The provision of a constant food supply and developments in science and technology have led to an oversupply of food in some parts of the world.
3. Urbanisation and improved living standards have aided population growth by increasing people's life expectancy.

    In 1972 the world's population was approx. 3,400 million and was increasing at a rate of 50 million a year. In 1988 the earth's population had increased to 5,000 million and was increasing at a rate of 90 million a year. Even though the rate of population growth has begun to decline, most demographers believe that population size will still pass 8,000 million during the next fifty years.

■ Problems Arising from Increasing Population

1 Unequal Growth and Food Supply

Population is not growing at the same rate everywhere. For example, the total population of Europe is approx. 500 million, and the average annual rate of growth over the region is only 0.3 per cent. In much of western Europe rates of natural increase almost balance, while West Germany before its union with the east had a negative growth rate.

On the other hand, Kenya's growth rate is near 4 per cent, the highest in the world. Its population is expected to double in about seventeen years, to 46 million people. Though predominantly a farming society, Kenya has not got much arable land. It has also suffered from the recurrent droughts that have afflicted all of Africa along the southern edge of the Sahara – the Sahel – since the 1960s. Food production has fallen far behind population growth, and economic growth has lagged. Thus the term 'overpopulated' can be applied to this region of Africa, where the resources as they are developed at present are unable to support the local population.

2 Environmental Damage

There is a direct connection between population growth and environmental problems. The mechanisms that supply people with the needs to survive are **ecosystems** – plants, animals and micro-organisms interacting with each other and their physical environments. Ecosystems supply us with the atmosphere, the regulation of climate, the generation and maintenance of soils, and provision of food from the sea. The energy that flows through ecosystems and the oxygen, nitrogen and carbon and other materials they recycle are the essence of the life support system within which the world's 5,000 million people live.

Population growth has a serious impact on these ecosystems. The birth of a baby in the United States imposes more than a hundred times the stress on the world's resources and environment of that of a birth in an African or Asian country. Children in the industrialised world grow up to expect to own motor cars and air-conditioners and to eat grain-fed beef. Their life-style requires huge quantities of minerals and energy, and their activities seriously undermine the life-support capability of the planet Earth.

Tropical forests are known to be the main reservoirs of raw materials that can supply people with many benefits, such as medicines. However, both industrialised and developing countries attack this uninvestigated and abundant reservoir with great ferocity. In Brazil the development of transamazonian highways has led to the rapid movement of people from the overpopulated and drought-stricken north-east to the Amazon Basin and away from the overcrowded cities of the east coast (e.g. Recife). These settlers are in search of farmland or gold, while others, such as multinational companies, are in search of pastureland for making pet-food and convenience food for foreign markets, especially the United States. In Papua New Guinea, forests are destroyed to supply cardboard packaging for Japanese electronic products. Thus a rich person thousands of miles away may be the cause of forest destruction because of a demand for luxury goods.

3 Air Pollution

Population growth in the industrialised world is directly related to a rise in atmospheric levels of carbon dioxide and methane. These 'greenhouse gases' trap heat near the earth's surface and thus alter the climate. Major sources of increased carbon dioxide are the burning of fossil fuels, which is related to high living standards (car exhausts) and the destruction of tropical forests. Major sources of methane include the intensive cultivation of wetland and the large populations of cattle.

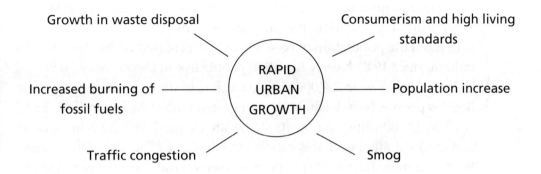

Growth in waste disposal

Consumerism and high living standards

Increased burning of fossil fuels — RAPID URBAN GROWTH — Population increase

Traffic congestion

Smog

▲ Fig. 5.2

The depletion of the ozone layer because of the use of chlorofluorocarbons (CFCs) is also related to high living standards and urban growth. **Smog** – a combination of smoke and fog – is a common problem in most urban areas of the temperate zone. It regularly occurs in densely built-up areas in winter under certain atmospheric conditions. When there is an **air inversion**, with cold, still air near ground level trapped by warmer air above and no wind to disperse it, chimney smoke builds to form smog. While smoke is visible, many chemicals, such as sulphur dioxide and nitrous oxides, are invisible but are harmful to human health. In November 1988, Dublin suffered from an acute smog. As a result, areas within the city were ordered to use smokeless fuels in the future.

4 Congestion

Cities of the developing world suffer from chronic congestion. There is a rapid growth of urban population in South America. No longer is any European city among the twelve largest in the world: by the year 2000 the eleven largest cities will be in developing countries, including São Paulo and Rio de Janeiro in Brazil. As a result of urban migration and a high birth rate, Brazil's cities are expanding at an alarming rate. In 1985, São Paulo had a population of 15.9 million. By the year 2000 this figure is expected to reach 26 million. Thus São Paulo's

▲ Fig. 5.3 Traffic congestion in New Delhi

population is growing by approximately half a million each year. Most of Brazil's urban population lives in shanty-towns.

In India the population of New Delhi has increased twentyfold, to 10.3 million, since 1947. Nearly 6 million people live in the slums of New Delhi, and each year 200,000 people migrate to the city in search of work. Besides people, New Delhi is also congested with vehicles. In 1947 the city had 11,000 vehicles; now its streets are clogged with 2.2 million cars and trucks, a number that is expected to double by the end of the century. Each year more than 1,700 people are killed on the streets of New Delhi.

New Delhi is one of the ten most populated cities in the world, along with Mexico, Seoul, and Beijing. New Delhi also suffers from acute water shortages, disruption of communications, and a general lack of basic services.

5 Urban Sprawl

In the second half of the twentieth century, increased concentration of population and economic activities within cities created increased demands for land. One response was to spread urban land uses into the adjacent countryside. **Suburbs** are mostly large-scale housing estates that are built to accommodate population increase. They are mainly composed of single-family houses of a detached or semi-detached type.

In parts of Germany and the Netherlands, apartment blocks are common. As the Randstad in the Netherlands became more and more crowded, villages, towns and cities expanded towards each other and threatened to overcome the 'greenheart'. In the United States, Los Angeles covers a vast area. Here many towns have joined together to form a **conurbation**, a sprawling city built on the edge of a desert in one of the most high-risk earthquake zones in the world. Yet it continues to grow outwards and into the surrounding mountains. In the north-eastern seaboard of the United States, cities such as Washington, Philadelphia, Atlantic City, New York, Jersey City and Boston as well as many neighbouring towns have expanded to form an urban environment that is sometimes called 'Megalopolis'.

▲ Fig. 5.4 Residential housing in a Los Angeles suburb

URBANISATION: THE GROWTH OF TOWNS AND CITIES

The following models have been devised to try to explain structures that are common to many cities. They are concerned mainly with showing how accessibility, land values and city growth affect the arrangement of zones.

MODELS OR THEORIES OF URBAN STRUCTURE

■ Concentric Zone Theory (Burgess)

Concentric zone model

1. Central business district
2. Wholesale and light manufacture
2A. Slums
3. Low-income residential
4. Medium-income residential
5. High-income residential
6. Heavy manufacture
7. Outlying business districts

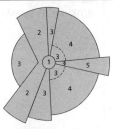

Sector model

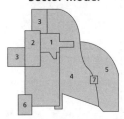

Multiple nuclear model

1. The central zone is often the oldest part of the town and is now the business centre, with its shops, offices, markets, and hotels. It is mostly non-residential.

2. The zone of transition surrounds the central zone. It is an area of decay, although in many towns clearance and rebuilding are taking place. Large old houses have been subdivided into apartments. Some businesses and light manufacturing are located in this zone.

3. The third zone consists of the homes of low-income people who have purchased their own houses. Much of this area was built up after the First World War.

4. The fourth zone consists of housing of middle and higher-income groups. These single-family houses are newer and larger and occupy larger sites. Some industrial estates also occupy areas within this zone.

5. The urban fringe is a commuting zone where dormitory towns and expensive residences are interspersed with open country.

◀ Fig. 5.5 Urban models

■ Sector Theory (Hoyt)

The sector theory is based on the idea that when different land uses arise near the central business district they grow outwards as sectors or wedges. These zones develop along arterial roads. Location near a railway or canal may result in a warehousing or industrial sector. Land near these activities tends to develop as low-income residential areas and may be confined to one side of a town. Middle-income residential areas may occupy wedges of land on the opposite side of the town to the industrial and low-income areas.

When a high-income residential area develops it expands radially, as the most desirable sites are along its outer edge.

■ Multiple-Nuclei Theory (Harris and Ullman)

This theory suggests that in addition to the concentric zone theory and the sector theory, development occurs around certain growth centres. Heavy manufacturing may develop around a port, retailing at a main route junction, and expensive housing on an attractive hillside site. In Ireland, growth centres might include hospitals, universities, shopping centres, and industrial estates. Once they have established themselves the land uses develop outwards, producing a cellular structure.

FACTORS IN THE GROWTH OF TOWNS AND CITIES

■ Historical Factors

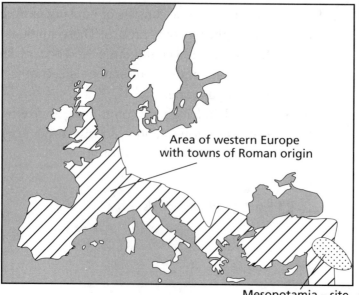

◀ Fig 5.6 The Roman empire in western Europe

Area of western Europe with towns of Roman origin

Mesopotamia – site of earliest towns

1 Food supply

The earliest towns appeared in the **Fertile Crescent** in the valleys of the Tigris and Euphrates in Mesopotamia (modern Iraq). Before this, people were hunter-gatherers. Then they realised that if wild seed could be collected and scattered on a suitable area of land, cereal would grow and flourish, providing a constant food supply in a particular region. Once this practice was established, food was in plentiful supply. This allowed some people to work for others in return for their food.

The first villages appeared in Mesopotamia approximately ten thousand years ago, while cities, such as Erech, were built some five thousand years ago. Babylon, built by the king Nebuchadrezzar, had massive defensive walls and imposing avenues, and accommodated eighty thousand inhabitants. Urban life, together with the knowledge of farming, diffused westwards to Europe and gave rise to the civilisations of Crete and Greece.

2 Roman Civilisation

The town was an instrument of Roman civilisation and defence. The Romans inherited urban culture from the Greeks and developed their own successful building techniques. They established towns north of the Alps, bringing urban life to traditional Celtic communities. Many European cities and towns owe their origins to the Romans. Roman architecture was copied wherever Rome ruled, and cities from England to Egypt were centred around structures similar to that of the Roman Forum. Those towns nearest to the margins of the empire were primarily for defence and administration. Most of the largest cities were in the eastern part of the empire, such as Athens, Constantinople, and Alexandria. Rome was the greatest of all.

3 Renaissance and Colonisation

With the collapse of the Roman empire in the fifth century there was a recession in urban life. However, from the eleventh century onwards a slow but steady urban growth occurred. Some Roman towns were redeveloped, villages became towns, and new settlements were established.

Two main areas of urban growth are recognised. One was in northern Italy, where cities such as Milan, Genoa, Florence and Venice flourished. Some of these cities also controlled large regions. Venice, for example, controlled most of the Plain of Lombardy, and its empire stretched eastwards to include the Aegean Islands, the Peloponnese, Crete, and part of Constantinople. The second area of urban growth was bordering the North Sea. Cities such as Bruges, Ghent, Amsterdam, Hamburg, Cologne and London emerged. Some of these, such as London and Amsterdam, were port cities, and trade with colonies boosted their development.

4 The Industrial Revolution

In 1750 the availability of coal and the development of factories led to the building of towns on or near coal-mines. At this time, agricultural developments released huge numbers of farm workers, who readily found employment in rapidly expanding factories. As workers needed to be near their place of employment, housing was provided in back-to-back terraces adjoining the factories. As a result, coal-mining villages became towns, and towns became cities. By 1900, Britain was the first urbanised country, followed by Germany, France, and the north-eastern United States.

5 Twentieth-Century Developments

The growth in manufacturing and the expansion in service employment have had a major influence on urbanisation. Employment has grown with economic development, rising living standards, and government administration. The perceived social advantages that cities have to offer, such as the excitement of city living, the easier life, shopping facilities, the varied educational opportunities, and medical services, draw people towards urban centres.

In the developing world, rural migrants flock to towns and cities. Depressed economic conditions in the overpopulated countryside encourage people to leave, in the belief that prospects are better in the city. This has given rise to the development of shanty-towns on the outskirts of cities. In the industrialised world, the expansion of cities in areas such as the Randstad in the Netherlands has led to the development of conurbations, where cities and towns have either joined or are near each other, while intervening areas have either become suburbanised or are very much subject to urban influences. On the north-eastern seaboard of the United States an urban environment has developed that has been called 'Megalopolis'.

CAUSES OF RAPID URBANISATION IN RECENT DECADES

1 Growth of Suburbs

Because of improvements in transport, people, especially those with young children, seek spacious housing and gardens on the less expensive land of the suburbs. Houses are generally single-family, detached or semi-detached. Many people desire modern housing with up-to-date facilities. They also wish to own their own house, which provides security and a sound financial investment.

As most of the owners of suburban houses are young couples, there is an associated high fertility rate. Young families therefore create a need for varied social services and amenities. At first there is a huge demand for schools, which diminishes with time as the population ages. The availability of landscaped, well-planned and reasonably priced houses on the outskirts of cities attracts buyers in large numbers. The stress of purchasing land and supervising construction is removed by the organised developer, who presents a package that is both desirable and affordable by young couples or second-time purchasers.

2 Rural-to-Urban Migration

In the non-industrialised countries, 'push' factors force people to leave their rural homes, while 'pull' factors encourage them to move to the cities, where they believe they will find a better way of life and a higher living standard for themselves and their families. In Brazil, for example, deforestation and desertification in the extremely poor north-east have helped to drive rural people to the cities of the east coast, such as São Paulo and Rio de Janeiro. Cities also offer the prospect of jobs, education, health facilities, and an alternative to their harsh rural existence.

In the industrialised world, cities also attract people at the expense of rural areas. Here industrial estates, modern housing and educational and other services continue to attract people, especially the young. The west of Ireland suffers from depopulation, many of its young people having migrated to Galway or Dublin or emigrated to cities in Britain or the United States.

Explosive population growth and constant migration from the countryside are creating cities that dwarf the great capitals of the past. By the turn of the century there will be twenty-one 'megacities', each with a population of 10 million or more. Of these, eighteen will be in developing countries, including some of the poorest countries in the world. Mexico City already has 20 million people and Calcutta 12 million. Some of Africa's cities are growing at the rate of 10 per cent a year.

SOCIO-ECONOMIC CONSEQUENCES OF RAPID URBANISATION

■ Developed World

Negative

1 Urban Sprawl

In the second half of the twentieth century, increased concentration of population and economic activities within cities created increased demands for land. One response was to spread urban land uses into the adjacent countryside. **Suburbs** are mostly large-scale housing estates that are built to accommodate population increase. They are mainly composed of single-family houses of a detached or semi-detached type.

▲ Fig. 5.7 Traffic jam on the M1 motorway in England

In parts of Germany and the Netherlands, apartment blocks are common. As the Randstad in the Netherlands became more and more crowded, villages, towns and cities expanded towards each other and threatened to overcome the 'greenheart'. In the United States, Los Angeles covers a vast area. Here many towns have joined together to form a **conurbation**, a sprawling city built on the edge of a desert in one of the most high-risk earthquake zones in the world. Yet it continues to grow outwards and into the surrounding mountains. In the north-eastern seaboard of the United States, cities such as Washington, Philadelphia, Atlantic City, New York, Jersey City and Boston as well as many neighbouring towns have expanded to form an urban environment that is sometimes called 'Megalopolis'.

2 Traffic Congestion

With improvements in transport came a rise in car ownership. By the mid-1980s there were 110 million private cars in western Europe. Concentration of office employment within the core gives rise to the pattern of a daily journey to work involving large numbers of commuters and of motor vehicles. Travel into the city from suburbs, satellite towns, commuter villages or individual homes in private cars creates traffic problems at peak travel times in the mornings and evenings. Traffic queues at these times in places like New York may be many kilometres in length and are regularly monitored from the air by helicopters.

Traffic congestion has given rise to a secondary and related problem of smog. Vehicle exhaust pollutes the air and is a major contributory factor in human respiratory diseases in many cities.

Positive

3 Increased Employment Opportunities

As cities expand, increased numbers of people are needed to supply the growing demand for services and products. The construction industry in particular is a labour-intensive industry that employs a wide cross-section of trades and professions, including carpenters, electricians, vehicle operators, engineers, and architects. New housing is constantly being added to the suburbs, while older inner-city buildings are either demolished and replaced or renovated. Industrial estates and port areas are generally associated with urban centres. Increased industrial activity and the rapid growth in water transport in recent decades continue to employ an expanding work force.

Temporary employment is usually available in many cities. New York, for instance, is the gateway to the United States and continues to offer initial employment opportunities to a young, mobile labour force such as students and school leavers in jobs for waiters and security guards and in low-paid manufacturing.

■ Developing World

1 Shanty-Town Development

Shanty-towns are slum areas on the outskirts of cities in the developing world. Houses in such areas are generally of a poor standard. Walls may be made from galvanised iron, plastic, or cardboard boxes, while the main frame of the dwelling is often of poles nailed together. Roofs are of similar materials, often stabilised with weights such as old tyres. In some parts of Calcutta, concrete pipes are used as shelters.

Some well-established shanty-towns, such as in parts of Rio de Janeiro, are of a higher standard, as income over a number of years is invested in the buildings. Newly established shanty-towns lack many facilities, such as sewerage, clinics, and proper water supplies. Some shanty-towns are built in tidal areas, others on rubbish dumps, such as 'Smoky Mountain' in the Philippines, or on land that is liable to flooding. Disease is rampant in areas such as these. Children are prone to infectious diseases such as malaria, typhoid fever, and tuberculosis. Fire is a constant danger. The

▲ Fig. 5.8 Favela, built on a rubbish dump in São Paulo, Brazil

density of housing is high, and the close association of shanty-towns and industrial areas has regularly led to large-scale loss of life such as in the Bhopal chemical plant tragedy in India.

2 Congestion

Cities of the developing world suffer from chronic congestion. There is a rapid growth of urban population in South America. No longer is any European city among the twelve largest in the world: by the year 2000 the eleven largest cities will be in developing countries, including São Paulo and Rio de Janeiro in Brazil. As a result of urban migration and a high birth rate, Brazil's cities are expanding at an alarming rate. In 1985, São Paulo had a population of 15.9 million. By the year 2000 this figure is expected to reach 26 million. Thus São Paulo's population is growing by approximately half a million each year. Most of Brazil's urban population lives in shanty-towns.

In India the population of New Delhi has increased twentyfold, to 10.3 million, since 1947. Nearly 6 million people live in the slums of New Delhi, and each year 200,000 people migrate to the city in search of work. Besides people, New Delhi is also congested with vehicles. In 1947 the city had 11,000 vehicles; now its streets are clogged with 2.2 million cars and trucks, a number that is expected to double by the end of the century. Each year more than 1,700 people are killed on the streets of New Delhi.

New Delhi is one of the ten most populated cities in the world, along with Mexico, Seoul, and Beijing. New Delhi also suffers from acute water shortages, disruption of communications, and a general lack of basic services.

PROBLEMS OF DEVELOPING COUNTRIES

1 National Debt

Developing countries owe one billion (a million million) dollars to the richer countries of the world. Many Latin American countries are now so deeply in debt that all their new loans are devoted entirely to paying the interest on the old ones. The result is more debt and yet more interest. Latin American countries account for over $400,000 million of this billion-dollar debt. Between 1982 and 1985 Latin America paid back over $106,000 million to foreign banks; at the same time they were getting poorer. Living standards fell 10 per cent in Mexico, 14 per cent in Peru, 17 per cent in Argentina, 25 per cent in Brazil, and 35 per cent in Venezuela. Until 1973 the Latin American debt was manageable. On 5 October 1973 the Organisation of Petroleum-Exporting Countries (OPEC) raised the price of crude oil from $3.65 to $17 a barrel. The Latin American countries had only one choice: to borrow more money to run their economies. Private banks in the richer countries lent money recklessly to any country that needed it, without monitoring the needs and the subsequent investments of these countries. Then in 1979 the price of oil was raised from $17 to $34 a barrel. Now developing countries were getting so heavily into debt that they could not even pay the interest. In May 1981 the interest rate on this borrowed money was 21 per cent. Brazil's repayments went up by $580 million a year.

Then the world economy started to go into recession. The price of thirty primary commodities, on which developing countries depend so heavily for exports, shrank by 34 per cent between 1974 and 1985. So the oil crisis, the interest rise and the fall in export prices brought about more borrowing to pay interest on the debt.

2 Cash Crops

As a result of colonialism, many African countries inherited agricultural economies geared heavily towards export cash crop production – a situation that remains to this day. Coffee in Tanzania, tea in Kenya, cotton in Sénégal and peanuts in Mali are some examples. In order to earn some foreign income, many governments increased production of these crops, and more and more land was given over to them. Much foreign aid (bilateral) and technical assistance was given to increase efficient production of these crops. When prices fluctuated or fell, governments responded by increasing production further. At the same time less attention was paid to food production for local consumption. For example, only 16 per cent of the millions of pounds of aid was given to this sector. Farmers throughout the region became dependent on cash crops for paying taxes and in some cases for buying food. Traditional farming practices were abandoned, and the soil came under heavy pressure to support increased production, often without the adequate use of fertiliser.

Many countries had become completely dependent on cash crops by 1980; for example, 75 per cent of Sénégal's export earnings came from peanuts, while 80 per cent of Chad's came from raw cotton. Thus today, developing countries produce cash crops on land that could be devoted to the production of food, in order to pay for debts and imports.

3 Shanty-Town Development

Shanty-towns are slum areas on the outskirts of cities in the developing world. Houses in such areas are generally of a poor standard. Walls may be made from galvanised iron, plastic, or cardboard boxes, while the main frame of the dwelling is often of poles nailed together. Roofs are of similar materials, often stabilised with weights such as old tyres. In some parts of Calcutta, concrete pipes are used as shelters.

Some well-established shanty-towns, such as in parts of Rio de Janeiro, are of a higher standard, as income over a number of years is invested in the buildings. Newly established shanty-towns lack many facilities, such as sewerage, clinics, and proper water supplies. Some shanty-towns are built in tidal areas, others on rubbish dumps, such as 'Smoky Mountain' in the Philippines, or on land that is liable to flooding. Disease is rampant in areas such as these. Children are prone to infectious diseases such as malaria, typhoid fever, and tuberculosis. Fire is a constant danger. The density of housing is high, and the close association of shanty-towns and industrial areas has regularly led to large-scale loss of life such as in the Bhopal chemical plant tragedy in India.

MIGRATION

An important aspect of demography is the movement of people from place to place. Movements are of three main kinds:
1. Unconscious drifts, such as the wanderings of early peoples
2. Enforced movements, such as the transporting of slaves
3. Voluntary emigration

Attractive Reasons ('Pull' Factors): Voluntary Migration

Among the varied reasons that attracted people to move and settle elsewhere were the following:
1. More congenial climatic conditions
2. Better economic opportunities
3. Higher standards of living
4. Freedom of thought and belief
5. Adventure, and the sheer attraction of 'foreign parts'

■ Repellent Reasons ('Push' Factors): Involuntary or Forced Migration

Some people left their homelands, voluntarily or involuntarily, for these reasons:

1. Harsh environmental conditions that make getting a living precarious (e.g. Highland Scotland, Norway).
2. Natural disasters, such as earthquakes, volcanic eruptions, floods, and famines.
3. Religious persecution (e.g. the Huguenots, who left France after the revocation of the Edict of Nantes in the reign of King Louis XIV, and the Puritans in seventeenth-century England).
4. Political persecution (e.g. Jewish refugees from Nazi Germany, and Baltic people from Russian communism).
5. Economic depression and lack of work, which compel people to seek work elsewhere.

VOLUNTARY MIGRATION

1 European Expansion

The European states that colonised the Americas in the sixteenth century, such as Portugal and Spain, were motivated by the promise of wealth and power. Some were *conquistadores*, such as Cortés and Columbus. They went in search of gold, land, and adventure. They colonised Latin America and brought the native peoples under their control.

The English colonised much of North America, and many British subjects emigrated to avail of the abundance of free land that was not available to them at home. Once America gained its independence from Britain, the new democracy attracted a flood of immigrants from impoverished places, such as the west of Ireland, the south of Italy, the Norwegian coastline, and Scotland. Freedom of religion, and career opportunities in a new, developing world away from the monarchies and oppression of Europe, were hard to resist. By 1914 an estimated 60 million people had left Europe for America.

2 European Opportunities

An industrial boom in the economic core of Europe in the twentieth century created a demand for labour within an expanding industrial and urban society. The countries that attracted the greatest number of immigrant workers were West Germany and France, each with some 2.5 million foreign workers. Within the countries of the EU only a quarter of the total immigrant labour force originated from other member-states. The great majority were attracted from the countries of the Mediterranean Basin, such as Turkey, Yugoslavia, Italy, Greece, Algeria, Morocco, and Spain. The non-industrialised economies of these countries and their growing populations meant that there was a surplus of labour in these areas. In Europe, labour was in short supply; a labour flow therefore occurred, which satisfied the demand for labour in the richer countries.

FORCED MIGRATION

1 The Great Famine

During the early part of the nineteenth century a large proportion of the Irish people lived habitually on the verge of destitution. The food of about one-third of the population was almost exclusively potatoes. A wet summer brought disaster in 1845, when potato blight wiped out the entire crop. Potato crops in 1846 and 1847 also failed. Most of the people in the western part of the country were affected by this crop failure. Because of British policy to export grain from the eastern half of Ireland, over a million people died during this famine. Others were forced to flee the country, and during the period 1845–47 more than a million emigrated, most of them to the United States.

This outward movement of people continued well into the twentieth century, as employment prospects were limited at home. In 1841 the population of Ireland was 8.2 million, and this had fallen to 4.4 million by 1911. During this period many tenants were evicted from their farms, as they were unable to pay their rents, and they were forced to make a livelihood elsewhere.

2 Marsh Arabs

Marsh Arabs live in the broad marshlands of southern Iraq, where the rivers Tigris and Euphrates flow together. Until recently this was an endless landscape of cane-breaks, shallow lagoons where time passed virtually unnoticed, unmarked by watches or calendars. This civilisation extends back six thousand years to the time when the first nomadic tribes settled in this wetland. The people of the marshes catch fish in the lagoons, bake bread in crude ovens, herd water-buffalo, and build arched huts of reeds. However, over the past few years the government of Iraq under Saddam Hussein has systematically tried to wipe out this ancient civilisation. Constant bombing of the area with chemical weapons has forced thousands to flee their homeland and to seek refuge elsewhere.

Parts of these wetlands have been drained by blocking the flow of rivers from the marshes and by the construction of canals. For those who remain, much of their area is poisoned with chemicals. Water is undrinkable, and the fish stocks in many areas have died. These people have asked for international aid to prevent a total destruction of their civilisation.

3 Tutsi Migrations in Rwanda

▲ Fig. 5.9 Tutsi refugees in Zaïre

Most of the people of Rwanda come from one of two tribes, the Hutu, who form the majority, and the Tutsi. Over the past thirty years both groups have struggled for political power, which up to 1962 was in the hands of Belgium, the colonial power. On 6 April 1994 the president of Rwanda, a member of the Hutu tribe, was killed when his plane was shot down over the capital, Kigali. His policy of power-sharing was unacceptable to some members of his tribe, who used his death as a way of wiping out the minority Tutsi tribe. This type of aggression is sometimes called **ethnic cleansing**.

Within minutes of the president's death, soldiers – who most resisted any sharing of power – took to the streets along with mobs of young men and began hunting down Tutsi civilians. Within days a killing frenzy had left up to 300,000 dead and forced 1.7 million others to flee to neighbouring countries, such as Tanzania and Burundi. In a single 24-hour period over 250,000 people fled across the border into Tanzania, creating an instant city and leaving relief agencies struggling to cope with food, medical and shelter supplies.

■ Consequences of Migration

Positive Effect

During the Great Famine, Ireland was overpopulated. This means that during famine times the country was unable to support its population. Emigration acted as a safety valve, so that the country could reach the situation where the food supply was in keeping with population demands. This was especially true in the west, where some areas of Cos. Galway and Mayo were classed as 'congested districts', i.e. were congested with people. The railway provided the means of transport in some instances to carry the emigrants to ports for passage to America.

Today this same safety valve of emigration has provided the Government with a means of solving part of its unemployment problem. During the late 1980s more than 40,000 people a year have left Ireland to seek employment elsewhere. Special visas allowed many to legally enter the United States in search of employment.

Negative Effect

As a result of the Great Famine, Ireland lost many of its young population. Of those who survived, many emigrated to the United States and Britain. This left the west of Ireland without its future work force. Many of those who remained were old and were unable to farm the land properly. Communities that were thriving before 1845 were decimated by 1850. In 1841 the population was 8.2 million; by 1861, death from starvation and emigration had reduced this to 5.8 million.

Irish was mostly spoken in the western regions. As a result of the famine and the subsequent emigration, these areas lost most of their native speakers. Since that time the numbers of Irish-speakers continued to decline, until recent times when a national revival helped to make Irish attractive once more. The reason for this decline was partly because Irish was associated with poverty, while English appeared to offer opportunity and prosperity.

4 The Buffer Theory

The energy crisis of 1973 and the economic depression that followed changed the job market in the core region. Demand for labour declined, and unemployment increased.

The 'buffer theory' was based on the principle that when such an economic depression occurred, immigrants would be **repatriated** (sent home). However, forceful repatriation did not seem socially or morally right to many people. This was partly because immigrant workers were concentrated in certain occupations and sectors of the economy of West Germany and France that were rejected by the domestic population.

Also, the buffer theory assumed **no family emigration**. However, long before 1973, immigrant workers were sending for their families to join them, and this gave a sense of permanence to the migration. Many of these immigrants had children born within the community, and this, together with the other factors, made it extremely difficult to reduce the numbers of foreign residents.

The presence of such immigrants can become a pretext for racial discrimination during an economic depression, while many immigrants tend to live in ghetto communities as their wages are low. Such concentrations present a poor image of the immigrants and may generate hostility from the host population (e.g. the burning of Turkish homes in Germany).

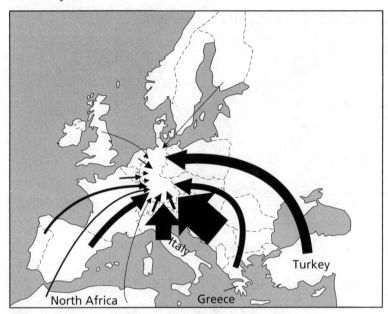

▲ Fig. 5.10 Emigration to West Germany, 1970

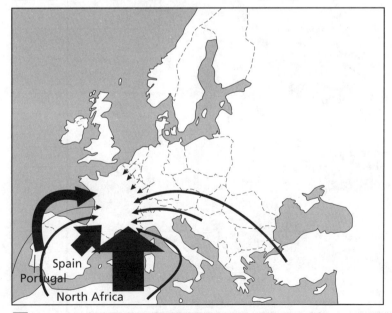

▲ Fig. 5.11 Emigration to France, 1970

6

ECONOMIC GEOGRAPHY

WORLD FISHERIES

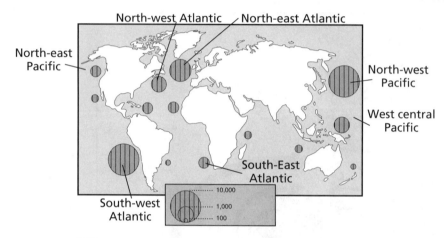

▲ Fig. 6.1 World distribution of fisheries

CASE STUDY: *THE NORTH-EAST ATLANTIC – ENTIRE AREA ICE-FREE*

▲ Fig. 6.2 Major fishing areas and ports of western Europe

FACTORS THAT HAVE INFLUENCED THE PRESENT DISTRIBUTION OF FISHERIES

1 The Continental Shelf – North-East Atlantic

This area includes the fishing grounds of the Barents Sea, Iceland, North Sea, and Bay of Biscay. These seas cover the continental shelf off Europe, which stretches approx. 500 km (300 miles) off the western coast of Ireland. Its waters rarely exceed 185 m (600 feet) in depth, and so sunlight can penetrate to the ocean floor.

Because of this and because many rivers drain into the north-east Atlantic, the area is rich in **plankton** – tiny floating animals and plants that many fish feed on and depend on for their food. They thrive where warm and cold bodies of water meet, e.g. the North Atlantic Drift and Arctic waters (the plankton also indirectly support other fish, which eat the plankton-eating fish). Plankton are created by **photosynthesis** (the process by which a plant makes food). This activity is generally confined to the upper 60 m of the sea, where sunlight, oxygen and carbon dioxide are available. Plankton are primary producers and convert simple mineral substances into the more complex biological molecules, using sunlight as the energy source. They not only serve as a food supply for higher marine organisms but also produce and release a number of complex substances. Dissolved organic carbon, for instance, is an important food source for many microscopic creatures.

2 Marginal Lands: Fishing an Alternative in Norway

Norway is the leading fishing country of Europe. Because of its high latitude, the harsh climate and rugged mountainous terrain make farming difficult. This, together with the absence of extensive mineral and forest resources, has caused Norway to turn to the sea.

Cod and herring fishing dominate Norway's fishing industry. Whaling in the Antarctic is also important. The numerous fjords provide excellent sheltered fishing areas and ports. The fjord coastline provides the main herring fishery, based on rich feeding and spawning grounds. In spring, huge shoals of cod migrate from the Arctic waters to their spawning grounds in the coastal waters around the Lofoten Islands. This fishery attracts large numbers of fishing boats from the south of Norway, as well as providing a rich harvest for northern fishermen. More than half of Norway's boats are registered in northern Norway and are engaged in cod fishing along the coast. Northern Norway's climate is most severe in this area, and the numbers of fishermen here reflect the attractive alternative that the sea offers. The main fishing ports are Hammerfest, Tromsø, and Vadsø. Co-operatives and quality control are playing an increasing role in providing a ready outlet for fish caught, some 90 per cent of which is exported.

3 Marginal Lands: Fishing an Alternative in the West of Ireland

Herring, mackerel

Haddock, monkfish

• Burtonport
• Killybegs

Rossaveal
•

Hake, monkfish

Dingle •

Castletown •
Bearhaven

Mackerel, herring

Celtic Sea

▲ Fig. 6.3 Main western fishing ports

Almost 75 per cent of the total value of fish caught in Ireland is landed along the west coast. This is an important source of income and employment for this depressed region. Much of the west of Ireland is mountainous, including large areas of Cos. Kerry, Galway, Mayo, and Donegal. Soils are leached and thin because of the heavy rainfall of 2,000 mm and the crystalline rocks of the area. Fishing provides an important economic alternative in an area that constantly suffers from rural depopulation. Burtonport, Killybegs, Rossaveal, Dingle and Castletown Bearhaven are some of the most important ports on the western coast. Much of the fish catch is processed at the ports, such as Killybegs, providing steady employment. Active government encouragement by An Bord Iascaigh Mhara (BIM) and increased market demand at home and abroad and port development on the west coast secure an important future for fishing off the western coast.

4 The North Atlantic Drift

The North Atlantic Drift is a continuation of the Gulf Stream, which flows from the Gulf of Mexico in a north-easterly direction across the Atlantic towards Ireland and Scandinavia. This drift is a body of warm water that encourages the presence of a wide variety of fish types, such as cod, herring, mackerel, turbot, haddock, and plaice. Other types, such as lobster, oyster, and mussels, are also found. These fish are in great demand throughout the world. The North Atlantic Drift is also directly responsible for the year-round fishing season. Because of its warm waters, the eastern North Atlantic is ice-free throughout the year, even within the Arctic Circle and as far north as Hammerfest in Norway. Waters in similar latitudes in other parts of the Atlantic, such as along the Labrador coast and the St Lawrence Estuary in eastern Canada, are frozen for up to three months of the year.

These ice-free waters off western Europe allow owner-skippers to constantly provide cash flow to meet heavy repayments on their fishing vessels. The number of larger vessels has increased in recent years, as has the use of expensive equipment to track and catch the fish (e.g. echo sounders). As fishing has become a specialist occupation and as levels of efficiency have increased, a large financial investment in trawlers is necessary. Therefore a steady cash flow is necessary, which can only be achieved in ice-free and sheltered fishing grounds. So the north-east Atlantic is a major fishing area.

5 Technology

Western Europe is one of the most densely populated areas in the world. As a result, a large market of 350 million people is available for fresh and processed fish. Western Europe is also one of the most technologically advanced regions, and this is reflected in its ability to land large catches of fish. Recently there is a noticeable increase in the number of larger and more modern fishing vessels. Advanced technology (e.g. sonar and radar to track the shoals of fish) and more efficient methods of fishing (e.g. power-hauling and seining) are used on these expensive boats. They have the added advantage of being able to stay away from port for several months and to work distant fishing grounds.

Killybegs is Ireland's main fishing port and home for most of its large, modern trawlers. In 1986 nine such vessels accounted for 50 per cent of Ireland's total annual catch. The EU encourages such specialisation, and finance is available to encourage the withdrawal of smaller, less efficient vessels and of part-time fishermen.

REASONS FOR THE COMMON FISHERIES POLICY (1983)

1. International agreements by Iceland, Canada, the Faroes and Russia to extend exclusive control over the resources within the waters and on the seabed up to 320 km from their shoreline in effect barred European fishing fleets from many rich fishing grounds. This led to the 'Cod War' between Britain and Iceland in 1974. It also led to the virtual collapse of the European distant-water fleet, which was forced to turn its attention to the territorial waters of the European states.

2. Before the signing of the Common Fisheries Policy, fishing in the waters of the North Sea and the north-east Atlantic was a free-for-all. Increased pressures on fish stocks, especially herring in the Celtic Sea south of Ireland, called for special measures to control and promote the development of fishing in all member-states of the EU.

THE COMMON FISHERIES POLICY

1 Conservation and Management of Stocks

1. Viable stocks must be maintained, and reduced stocks must be rebuilt. Before this policy, herring fishing was suspended by member-countries of the EC between 1978 and 1981 by voluntary agreement. The Common Fisheries Policy, however, set a total allowable catch for each year, which is divided among member-states to reflect traditional fishing activities. Each country is then allocated a national quota or percentage of the total allowable catch (TAC).
2. Conservation measures were decided, such as mesh sizes, access to certain fishing grounds at certain times of the year, regulations on the landings of fish, and an increase in the number of fishery protection vessels to check on the scale and type of fishing in member-states' waters.

2 Structural Changes

Payments are offered to encourage the withdrawal of boats from fishing. Incentives are also offered to those who wish to modernise equipment and who wish to explore the possibility of fishing for new species. **Grants** are available for improving marketing facilities and the modernisation of harbours in those areas that are heavily dependent on fishing (e.g. Killybegs and Howth).

3 Market

Guide prices are fixed at the beginning of each fishing season to ensure a minimum standard of income for fishermen. The development of co-operatives involving fishermen and processors should improve efficiency. Expansion of the consumer market depends on the industry achieving a high level of quality control.

4 Bilateral Agreements

Agreements have been reached between the EU and the Faroes, Norway, Sweden and Canada that allow their fleets some limited access to EU fishing grounds in exchange for similar access to their territorial waters.

THE PACIFIC OCEAN

■ The North-West Pacific

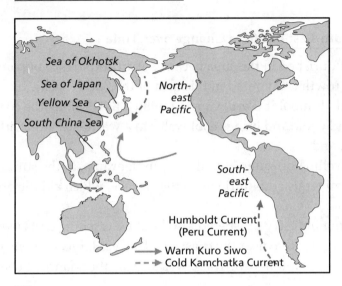

▲ Fig. 6.4 Sea areas in the Pacific Ocean

The fishing industry in this area is dominated by Japan, China, and Russia, the three leading fishing countries in the world. The Japanese industry in particular has expanded enormously in the present century. Japan has the highest per capita consumption of fish and the most valuable catch in the world. This is due to the scarcity of good agricultural land. Most of Japan is mountainous, with steep, rugged slopes. Land is also limited, as Japan is composed of islands on the edge of the continental shelf. Japan also has a high density of population, mainly living on coastal lowlands. This population can only be fed by exploiting the abundance of fish in the seas around Japan.

The large fisheries catch of this region is due to the presence of conditions similar to those in the north-east Atlantic. These conditions include

(*a*) the extensive continental shelf, which includes the shallow sea areas of the Sea of Okhotsk, the Sea of Japan, the Yellow Sea, and the South China Sea;

(*b*) the mixing of the cold Kamchatka current (Oya Siwo) and the warm Kuro Siwo.

Both currents have resulted in an abundance of plankton and fish.

In the colder northern waters, herring, flounder and pollack are the main varieties fished, while in the warmer southern waters flounder, mackerel, pilchard, tuna and sole are among the many varieties caught.

The coastlines of Japan, Russia and China are long and indented and provide many fine areas for inshore fishing as well as natural sheltered harbours.

■ The South-East Pacific: a Change over Time

Fish have flourished in this area because of an abundance of plankton. Plankton growth is favoured in this area of the South Pacific by
(a) the cold Humboldt (Peru) Current, which flows along the coasts of Peru and Chile and brings cool water to a warm-sea area within the tropics, and
(b) the upwelling of water from the ocean floor to near the surface; this brings minerals and nutrients to the surface, which aid the growth of plankton.

The fishing industry prospered also because catching costs were low. Fishing grounds were near the coast, stocks were large, and one species of fish – anchovy – dominated. There was also an abundance of cheap labour.

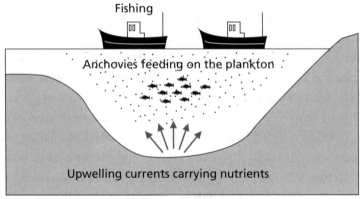

Fishing

Anchovies feeding on the plankton

Upwelling currents carrying nutrients

▲ Fig. 6.5 Fish cycle off the Peru coast

Investment from large American companies and loans from the International Monetary Fund (IMF) boosted the fishing industry, especially in Peru. Large fishing boats were constructed, although many were foreign-owned. Over thirty processing plants were constructed to process the huge catch, which represented nearly 20 per cent of the total world catch in 1970 (12.5 million tonnes). These developments made Peru the world's leading fish producer, and the industry contributed up to 33 per cent of Peru's foreign earnings.

Since the 1970s these fisheries have suffered a decline because of massive overfishing and a move in ocean waters. A warm current from the Equator called El Niño moved south along the Peruvian coast. El

Niño is low in oxygen and replaced the cold, nutrient-rich water, contributing to the decline in Peru's fishing. Today Peru's fishing industry is struggling to survive.

TOURISM IN THE EUROPEAN UNION

GENERAL REASONS FOR DRAMATIC GROWTH IN RECENT DECADES

▲ Fig. 6.6 European tourist destinations

1 Improvements in transport

Since the 1960s there has been a dramatic rise in the numbers of private cars in use. This has allowed great flexibility to people in choosing their holiday destination on the European continent. In 1985, 68 per cent of all holidays in the EC were undertaken by car. This has been aided by the improvements in roads throughout the EC. Motorways, mountain tunnels, such as the Mont Blanc tunnel, and 'piggy-back' transport in Switzerland and France have all helped to ease movement within and between countries. Car technology has also improved to produce faster, safer and more comfortable cars.

The introduction of ferries allows the easy transport of vehicles from islands to continental Europe and vice versa with the minimum of difficulty.

Developments in the aircraft industry have allowed for fast and cheaper package holidays. This, together with the creation of numerous airports at seaside resorts, such as along the Mediterranean coast (e.g. Nice in southern France and Palma on Majorca), has boosted international travel.

2 Industrialisation and Higher Incomes

Increased industrialisation and the higher wages that accompany this development led to a greater amount of disposable income among the work force. This guaranteed income together with paid annual leave encouraged people to travel on holiday. At first most holidays were confined within individual countries; later, especially since the 1960s, larger incomes have allowed for foreign destinations, especially along the Mediterranean coast. Increased productivity and demands within industry and the services create a need to 'get away' from the local culture to where people can relax in an outdoor setting away from the shop-floor or office environment.

3 Education and Living Standards

Higher living standards and increased educational standards have created a desire to travel and experience other cultures and environments. Television has played a great part in creating this desire, as images of sun-baked seashores attract travellers from the cool, damp and windy climates of western and northern Europe. Programmes specially produced for the tourist industry promote various resorts and present the advantages that these areas have for tourists.

4 Official Policy

EU policy has encouraged tourism as part of a programme to create a 'people's Europe'. The European Investment Bank and the European Regional Development Fund have spent millions of pounds in promoting the region's potential in the tourist trade. Governments have offered loans and grants to improve and increase tourist accommodation in hotels and guesthouses. Bord Fáilte was established to promote and develop tourism in Ireland. This has given rise to improved standards, which are regularly monitored. This policy encourages seasonal employment and many spin-off industries.

CASE STUDY: *EUROPE'S SOUTHERN COASTLINE*
ADVANTAGES OF THE MEDITERRANEAN FOR TOURISM

1 Climate

▲ Fig. 6.7 Tourists on a beach in the Mediterranean

Over 80 per cent of tourists who visit the Mediterranean area do so because of its climatic advantages. The cool and wet summers of western and northern Europe as well as the unpredictability of its weather encourage people to seek sunshine, warmth and dry conditions elsewhere. The Mediterranean area has a predictable climate. It is hot (in the high twenties Celsius), with twelve hours of guaranteed sunshine every day, and very dry for the summer months of June, July, and August. The dry north-east trade winds blow across the area from the Eurasian landmass, bringing this distinctive weather cell over the region. Even in winter, temperatures rarely fall below 10°C. People with a limited holiday time are guaranteed ideal conditions during their summer holidays.

2 Accessibility

Developments in aircraft technology allowed for faster, more comfortable, cheaper and regular flights to holiday destinations. The creation of numerous airports along the Mediterranean coast near holiday centres ensures that a minimum of time is needed for journeys abroad. As airports were established, holiday centres became more developed, with modern facilities, which in turn increased the attraction of the area.

The improvement of roads throughout the EU has aided the development of the Mediterranean as a tourist destination. In 1985, 68 per cent of all holidays were undertaken by car, and a large percentage of these were to the Mediterranean region, many people availing of self-catering facilities or serviced campsites. In all, some 100 million tourists visit the region each year.

3 Prices

The price of holidaying in the Mediterranean area is low when compared with north-western Europe or the United States. The availability of package holidays to the Mediterranean also adds to its attraction. The cost of flight, accommodation and the journey to and from the airports is included, as well as insurance. All the stress of travel is carried by the tour operators, with the minimum of disturbance for the customer. Apartment accommodation with modern facilities, as well as chalets or villas, is also available if desired at a relatively low price. Many tour operators concentrate on 'family holidays' and offer a large range of holiday types and prices.

4 Cultural-Historical Tourism

▲ Fig. 6.8 Tourists in Venice

Civilisation spread across the Mediterranean area from east to west. Throughout this area the remains of the Greek and Roman civilisations attract millions of tourists each year. Rome has its Colosseum, while Athens has the Parthenon. The invasion of Spain by Arabs (the 'Moors') from North Africa in the Middle Ages has given a distinctive architecture to many cities in southern Spain. The Renaissance, especially in Italy, has added great character to many of its cities. Florence is a centre where the Medici family were patrons of the arts. Venice, a city in a delta, retains many of its original buildings, such as the Basilica of St Mark and the Doge's Palace.

Rome is Italy's capital city, and the Vatican City State is the centre of the Catholic Church. The Sistine Chapel is world-famous for its frescoes by Michelangelo. This historic background, together with the stunning landscape of the Plain of Lombardy, with its castles and cities, makes Italy a very popular tourist country.

ADVANTAGES OF TOURISM

1 Employment

Tourism is a labour-intensive service industry. The industry has a large direct employment content: jobs are provided in accommodation (hotels and guesthouses), catering (cafés and restaurants), entertainment (theatres and bars), and transport. Those who benefit indirectly include farmers who produce the food consumed by tourists, manufacturers who make souvenirs and sports equipment, and shopkeepers. In Switzerland

150,000 people are employed in the tourist trade, while 91,000 people are in full-time or part-time employment in Ireland.

Income earned is also generally higher than in the more traditional jobs that would be available in such areas. Tourism stimulates the construction industry (e.g. extensions to hotels, new family homes), and jobs can become more varied and less dependent on traditional employment, such as forestry and farming.

2 Revenue

Tourism is regarded as an invisible export. Foreign money is spent by tourists, and the higher incomes earned by local residents create a multiplier effect within a region. In Portugal in 1986 tourists spent $1,200 million. In Switzerland, 9 per cent of foreign currency earnings comes from tourism. In Ireland revenue from foreign tourists exceeds £1,000 million.

Profits made from tourism by businesses encourage the improvement of local facilities, such as health centres attached to hotels. These can often be used by the local community as well as tourists.

3 Social effects

Travel helps to promote international understanding and good will through contact between different peoples and cultures. Cultural contacts with foreigners can help to undermine the national stereotypes sometimes still held about people of certain countries. Fear of change can disappear, and this may lead to an improvement in the quality of life.

Tourists may add interest and activity for local people, especially in small communities, which in turn may create an incentive for some development for the people of the area.

4 Infrastructure

Government financing is attracted into these regions on a large scale. The demands for high standards in roads, telecommunications, sanitation and recreation facilities (e.g. promenades and marinas) by tourists cannot be met by local financing alone. Thus much of the west of Ireland has an excellent road network, while the road surface generally has a high standard. The roads of Cos. Clare and Mayo are envied by many inland counties that are not on the tourist trail (e.g. east Limerick, Cavan).

The counties of Kerry, Galway, Mayo and Donegal all have international airports, which help in the promotion of tourism. Local airports encourage emigrants to visit regularly.

DISADVANTAGES OF TOURISM

1 Seasonal Employment

Tourism is confined to a limited period, generally the months of June, July, and August. In fact 62 per cent of all holidays are taken during the months of July and August. There are a number of reasons for this, one of them being that many schools are open until the end of June, so families are unable to travel until early July. August is also the main month for industrial holidays throughout the EU. In France most people take their holiday at this time.

This means that the Mediterranean area is heavily populated during the summer, while in winter trade almost ceases. Many people are employed during this summer peak period, while in winter they are unemployed. Much employment is therefore part-time (e.g. waiting at table, cleaning). However, many Spanish resorts offer special packages to tourists, such as retired people, who can avail of the off-season times to take their holiday.

2 Environmental Problems

1. The excessive building of apartment blocks along a coastline may be completely out of character with the region. Many of these may be unsightly in their design. This takes away from the scenic quality of the area, which was the main factor in the creation of tourism for that place. In some regions these hotel complexes control the beach or coastal stretch and even access to and use of these areas. This creates problems for local people who may wish to gain access to beaches.
2. The disposal of waste regularly leads to pollution of the water. Rapid expansion of many of the Mediterranean resort towns has created a situation where 85 per cent of urban effluent is untreated. In Italy only 200 of the country's 8,000 towns have sewage treatment works. The estimated 100 million visitors to the Mediterranean area is expected to increase, which will undoubtedly lead to further problems.

3 Cost of Housing and Land

As tourist areas develop (e.g. Benidorm), the cost of land in and near these centres rises rapidly. Rural land uses are unable to justify these costs. So rural land is bought up by developers as landowners sell off their property.

Wealthy people are willing to pay high prices for summer homes. This puts the buying price of land and homes for local people well above what they can afford, and they are forced to live away from tourist centres. This has two main effects. The first is that local people have to commute long distances to work, as they can no longer afford to live in the resort towns. The second is that many farmers seek better-paid work in the tourist trade, causing outlying farms to be abandoned or reduced to part-time working.

4 Changes in Local Culture

The movement of large numbers of tourists to an area can lead to a change in local culture and traditions. Fishing villages get taken over, and the fishermen's way of life is diminished or wiped out completely. A sense of community and commitment to family life and traditional customs gets swept away by consumerism. So a conflict of interest may arise between those who desire jobs and higher living standards and those who respect a more traditional life-style or a different type of tourism (naturalists and anglers), which may not interfere as much with their environment.

Solutions: See the Blue Plan, page 209.

TRANSPORT SYSTEMS

AIR TRANSPORT

■ Advantages of Air Transport

1. As with water, air routes occur naturally, and route maintenance costs other than airport maintenance do not exist. Airport development, however, is costly, although once developed, maintenance is not unduly high. Airports may be built close to areas of high population density, such as London and New York. This allows easy access to departure and destination areas. Time is highly valued in modern society; air transport allows for the minimum of time loss and is the most efficient means of travel.

2. Air transport is most efficient for the transport of people and of cargo of low bulk and high value. Aircraft space is limited, and maximum use of available room is vital. Goods such as mail and newspapers, flowers, precision tools and high-technology equipment use this mode of transport. People are the greatest users of air transport. Millions of people each day fly to various destinations throughout the world. The density of traffic is greatest over the United States. The importance of air over other forms of travel is greatest in some of the remoter parts

of the world, such as the Australian 'outback' (e.g. for medical aid) or central South America, where alternative transport is absent or poorly developed, and distances are great.

3. The great advantage of air transport is its speed and frequency of flights. Today's supersonic aircraft, such as the Concorde, can fly faster than sound. Most travellers can cover thousands of kilometres in a few hours. Business people regularly have demanding schedules and avail of this transport mode. The frequency of flights is high, especially in industrialised countries. Every large city, even in Europe, has its own airport. Ireland alone has ten international airports.

   Access from cities to airports is generally easy, as they are connected either by motorway or dual carriageway. Tourists are regular users of air transport. This industry has created a demand for airports at holiday centres, such as resorts along the Mediterranean coast. The Spanish Costa Brava has developed numerous airports to accommodate increasing numbers of tourists.

■ Disadvantages of Air Transport

1. Cost is a major disadvantage. Aircraft are very expensive to purchase and maintain. They also have a very short life-span, which increases their cost relative to their potential income. Because of the limited size of aircraft, the unit cost of air transport is high. However, its flexibility in timetable, aircraft type and availability of destination outweighs cost disadvantages. It is therefore a fast-increasing mode of transport.

2. Aircraft are used for only a tiny portion of total world goods movement. Space is limited, and so costs are high. Suitable cargo is limited to light items, such as mail and newspapers, perishables, such as flowers, mushrooms, and seafood, and expensive goods, such as fashion clothing, gemstones, and precious metals.

3. Large tracts of level land are needed for runways, with approaches unobstructed by mountains or high buildings. The availability of such areas is limited, and they cannot easily be found in some regions, such as volcanic islands (e.g. Japan, Canary Islands). The increased size of aircraft and the excessive congestion and consequent delays at some of the largest airports make the extension and development of existing airports desirable; however, land adjoining airports is generally either limited or unavailable, and suitable tracts of new land can normally only be found at considerable distance from city centres. This increases access time and limits the usefulness of air transport for short-distance journeys.

4. Airports are particularly vulnerable to attack by terrorists, and all airports are regarded as areas of high security. Heathrow Airport in London was attacked by the IRA in 1994. Throughout the world most airports have their own airport police, many of them armed and trained against terrorism, to constantly monitor activity within the airport zone. Individual aeroplanes have been hijacked, while others have been subjected to bombing. Yet air traffic is still regarded as the safest mode of transport today.

WATER TRANSPORT

■ Advantages of Water Transport

1. Waterways, such as seas, lakes, and rivers, occur naturally, and so maintenance costs are for the most part non-existent, except perhaps for dredging. The oceans of the world are connected and are free for the use of all countries. Vessels have considerable freedom to roam, although most journeys are influenced by the availability of suitable harbours for berthing. Journeys follow the shortest routes, except where they deviate because of land obstructions or shallow water.

2. Water transport is most competitive when large loads are carried over long distances. Larger vessels have proportionately lower construction, fuel and labour costs. Larger oil tankers, called 'supertankers', are among the largest vessels afloat. They are specially designed to transport enormous quantities of petroleum from the Middle East or Alaska to consumer countries such as the EU, the United States, and Japan.

The North Atlantic is the busiest of the world's shipping routes. It is followed by the routes from western Europe to eastern Asia and to South America. Another major shipping route is that from North America to Japan.

3. Some countries, such as Norway and Greece, have a long seafaring tradition. Their ships continue to carry the trade of other countries, earning important foreign exchange. Industries such as iron

▲ Fig. 6.9 Container ships at Felixstowe Docks, England

and steel and shipbuilding employ large numbers of engineers, craft workers and electricians in the manufacture of ships and component parts. In the case of Norway, the sea is its lifeline, with much of its coastal population involved in fishing, merchant shipping, and other sea-related activities.

4. Canal transport was suited to areas where low watersheds existed between rivers, enabling them to be easily connected to a canal system. There was widespread canal construction in Ireland and in Britain in the second half of the eighteenth and the early nineteenth century. Canals were most competitive on the North European Plain, where there was a number of large rivers that could be connected by a canal system with limited expense. Foremost is the Rhine system, which is connected to the Seine, Elbe, Danube and Rhône waterways. The Panama and Suez Canals have greatly reduced some voyage distances, but such maritime canals are few, because of the increasing size of ocean vessels.

■ Disadvantages of Water Transport

1. Water transport usually involves transhipment at both ends of a journey. Each 'stopping off' adds to the transport cost of goods, especially over short journeys.
2. Water offers considerable resistance to fast movement, so that slowness is the great disadvantage of water transport. This is especially true of cargoes carried over short distances. Other types of transport can be more competitive and can give door-to-door delivery.
3. Ships and boats are usually designed to carry one commodity only. This especially applies to oil tankers, which are designed so that they cannot carry any cargo other than oil.
4. When a collision occurs at sea, especially of vessels carrying oil, great damage may be done to the environment. This has occurred on many occasions (e.g. the *Exxon Valdéz* in Alaska). Oil spills cover vast areas, and local ecosystems take many years to recover.

ROAD TRANSPORT

■ Advantages of Road Transport

1. Road transport is more competitive over short distances than any other form of travel. It is also being increasingly used for medium and long journeys in the carriage of relatively small consignments and valuable goods. Its competitiveness is due partly to short turn-around

time, reduced storage requirements, and loading and unloading installations that are less costly than other forms of transport.

2. Roll-on, roll-off (RORO) road haulage is dominated by three main types of trailer systems:
   (a) curtain-sided trailers
   (b) box-vans
   (c) flats.

   Curtain-sided trailers are generally used for partial loads on multi-stop journeys. This means that a full load sets out, and part of the load is delivered at different places. Goods are stacked on pallets, which can be unloaded from the side of the trailer by a fork-lift truck. **Box-vans**, on the other hand, are generally used for full loads to individual destinations. They are rigid steel-sided trailers that can only be loaded and unloaded from the rear. **Flats** are used for the movement of goods, such as machinery and plant equipment, that may vary in width and would not fit into a standard size. They are also used for the movement of containers to ports for delivery by sea or to individual destinations that are within short or medium distances of the factories. Containers offer an organised delivery system where packaged goods use space to a maximum, and they can be sealed for security. Such flexibility in delivery systems makes road transport very competitive with other forms of transport.

3. Road transport is supreme in passenger movements that are predominantly over short distances. Buses are more flexible than trains, and the frequency of service is greater. This is especially true within towns that have not got an underground rail transport system. The convenience, flexibility, speed and comfort of the private car has caused the number of vehicles to escalate throughout the world. However, the cost of cars is restrictive, and most motor vehicles are in the rich countries of the industrialised world.

▲ Fig. 6.10 Road transport

4. The density of roads is greater than that of any other means of travel. They operate over a much greater length of route than either railways or inland waterways. Route networks are especially dense over lowland areas that are attractive for human settlement, such as fertile plains. Roads also penetrate difficult terrain, such as mountainous areas. Valleys and mountain passes, such as cols and gaps, provide access, while the road gradient is reduced by the use of hairpin bends, mountain spurs, and valley sides.

5. In industrialised countries, such as the United States, Britain, and Germany, highways, motorways and autobahns provide fast road movement. This is aided by limited access from other roads, diminished gradients and curves, and **dual carriageways** (the separation of traffic moving in opposite directions). Small towns and villages are bypassed, while large and medium-sized towns are well served.

■ Disadvantages of Road Transport

1. Traffic congestion is a serious problem in built-up areas. This is especially true at peak travel hours. Commuters travelling to and from work in the early morning and in the evening compete for space on roads that serve urban centres. In cities like New York, queues may be many kilometres long. This has the added disadvantage that pollution levels increase because of exhaust.

2. Road transport is relatively dangerous. Traffic accidents are frequent, many of them fatal. High speeds on narrow and winding roads as well as dangerous driving give rise to collisions. In reality, cyclists and pedestrians have few if any rights on modern roads. In the Netherlands, however, special roads for cyclists are provided in some areas.

RAIL TRANSPORT

■ Advantages of Rail Transport

1. In the nineteenth century, railways provided a faster, cheaper and more flexible means of transport than inland waterways. Journeys that took days by barge were now completed in less than ten hours. Railways had fixed timetables and were punctual and reliable.

2. Today the main advantage of rail is speed. The journey from Dublin to Cork by train takes two-and-a-half hours, while the same journey by road takes four hours. On the Continent, electrification and double-

tracking allow for higher speeds as well as more comfortable travel. French National Railways operate the *Train à Grande Vitesse* (TGV), a very high-speed train. A world record of 380 km/h (236 miles per hour) was achieved during trials in February 1981. This system was designed entirely for passenger trains. There are no level crossings and no tunnels, and the line follows the land contours in the same way as a motorway.

3. Goods trains compete for bulky goods and container traffic. Railside cranes load and unload sealed containers for passage to Dublin city and port. Rail is second only to road in being the most competitive mode of transport over relatively short journeys, and is more competitive than road and air over long distances.

   An adaptation of containerisation developed in North America is the 'piggy-back'. In this system, truck trailers are carried on flat wagons between two distant points, are unloaded at the rail terminal, and are hitched to trucks that bring them to their final destination. The length of these goods trains is huge, some powered by three, four or even more locomotives. This piggy-back system combines the advantages of rail for long-distance movement with the door-to-door service of road transport.

4. Rail transport is a safe means of travel. Few accidents occur, as each train is confined to a specific time and route. Comfort is also important. Most trains contain dining carriages, while first-class accommodation offers meals served to the passenger's seat. Some Continental trains offer sleeping accommodation on overnight journeys. Commuter trains are attractive for people travelling to and from work. No congestion, short journey times and regular service make this a well-used system in the early morning and evening near large cities. The Dublin Transport Initiative intends to increase investment and provide improvements and upgrading of the urban rapid-transit system. At least two more rail systems are planned for before the end of the decade.

■ Disadvantages of Rail Transport

1. Rail transport is only competitive where population density is high. In many areas of the west of Ireland, rail tracks have been uprooted and railway stations closed, as the lines were not commercially viable because of depopulation. This has had an isolating effect on an entire region, and limits the area's potential for attracting industry. This calls

into question the viability of allowing some transport systems, such as rail transport, to be run on a profit-making basis. As transport is withdrawn, a community becomes deprived of a vital link in the ability to survive.

2. Railways link main towns only, while Dublin remains the hub of the system, with main lines radiating outwards to the other towns. People living in places not on these routes are therefore denied local access. Thus railways are selective in the areas they serve. Many areas in the midlands and west are not served at all by the rail system.

3. The greatest disadvantage of rail transport is the need for transhipment to road vehicles at each end of the journey. The shorter the journey, the greater is the disadvantage of transhipment. Loading and unloading of cargo increases the cost, and much valuable time may be lost in the delivery of some goods. This activity, however, is becoming more competitive with the mechanical loading and unloading of sealed containers, which are loaded with goods at the origin of the journey and not opened until their final destination.

ENERGY IN THE WORLD

■ Definitions

Finite: non-renewable; fuels such as oil, coal, natural gas and turf will no longer be available when supplies are burned. Once it is burned it cannot be used again.

Infinite: renewable; resources such as wind, waves and falling water can be used again and again.

Large quantities of energy are used by society today, in the following ways:

1. Domestic uses: television, heaters, cookers, lights (35 per cent)
2. Manufacturing: machines, lighting, welding, heating (30 per cent)
3. Transport: fuel for cars, buses, tractors, aeroplanes (20 per cent)
4. Commercial: shop lighting, heating, signs (15 per cent)

OIL SUPPLY AND DEMAND

■ Some Areas of High Energy Demand

1. **The United States** is one of the wealthiest countries in the world. With 257 million people, it has 5 per cent of the world's population, who use 25 per cent of the world's energy. Its high standard of

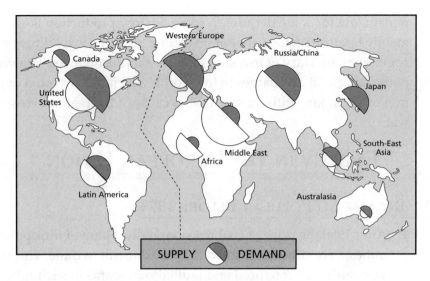

▲ Fig. 6.11 World oil supply and demand

housing, with all modern facilities, and air-conditioned offices and shopping centres all contribute to this demand. Transport in the United States uses large quantities of energy. Many cars have six-cylinder engines and may only produce 24 km (15 miles) per gallon. The conurbations, such as New York, Washington, and Los Angeles, demand huge amounts of energy for lighting and power.

2. **Western Europe** is one of the world's most technically advanced and wealthiest regions. A number of its countries have joined to form the European Union, which is destined to increase its membership still further. High standards of living and a large population (350 million) create a great demand for energy in the form of oil, coal, and nuclear power.

3. **Japan**, with a population of 123 million, is one of the most densely populated as well as technically advanced countries in the world. Its overdependence on oil was realised in 1973 with the oil crisis. Japan still imports huge amounts of oil, but it has become more efficient in its use, and has emphasised higher-value industries by giving greater attention to detail. Standards of living are high. Standards of cars are high; to ensure energy-efficiency, car engines are replaced after 25,000 km (15,000 miles).

ONE AREA OF LOW ENERGY DEMAND

Standards of living in Africa are generally low compared with the industrialised world. Because of drought, desertification, wars and spiralling national debts in many African countries, living standards will remain low for some decades to come. Energy production is also low, mainly because of government instability and civil wars. Energy companies are wary of investment in unstable economies. Chevron, one of the largest oil companies in the world, which had invested over $1,000 million in Sudan, withdrew in 1993 because of the region's ceaseless civil war.

ENERGY IN THE EUROPEAN UNION

WHY OIL BECAME SO POPULAR BEFORE 1973

1. After 1950 the price of coal rose markedly. Many of Europe's best coal mines were either exhausted or more difficult to mine. This difficulty was caused by fractured and faulted coal seams in such mining areas as the Sambre-Meuse Valley and the Nord. In other mines the best-quality coal and the easiest seams were exhausted. They had been in production since the Industrial Revolution in 1750. Oil was a desirable alternative, and it was in plentiful supply from the Middle East, Venezuela, and North Africa.

2. The EU is mostly an urban-industrial region. Standards of living are high, and energy consumption per capita is among the highest in the world. The popularity of private motor vehicles and the introduction of domestic central heating increased the demand for oil during the 1950s and 1960s. In addition, industrial expansion (e.g. petrochemicals) created an added demand for oil. Petroleum has many advantages over traditional fuels: it is clean, easy to use, easy to transport, and heat-efficient. It was also very cheap when compared with coal, and it had many uses as an industrial raw material (e.g. synthetic materials). Demand for oil therefore soared, and little or no attention was paid to the economic and strategic consequences if such a supply were not available. Therefore in the 1960s, governments in almost all western European countries decided on a policy of cheap energy.

3. Marine engineering allowed for the development of 'supertankers', which were specially built for the haulage of oil over long distances. Some measure

▲ Fig. 6.12 A 'supertanker' in Swansea, Wales

over 350 m long and 50 m wide and can carry more than 300,000 tonnes of oil. Such tankers reduced the cost of transporting oil, thus making it very competitive. Huge storage facilities were constructed at ports such as Rotterdam. Other oil depots were built at such deep-water bays as Bantry Bay in Co. Cork. All these developments encouraged governments to continue with oil as the main source of energy.

4. Oil pipelines were introduced as a competitive means of transporting oil. Pipelines are a comparatively cheap method of transporting bulk liquids over long distances, and they particularly benefited regions that up to then were regarded as isolated and that suffered from high energy costs (e.g. Bavaria in southern Germany). Three major pipelines were built across the Alps from the Mediterranean ports of Trieste, Genoa, and Venice, which provided raw material that has led to the creation of industrial regions such as that centred on Ingolstadt.

THE OIL CRISIS

What was the 1973 energy crisis? Who created it, and what were its consequences?

The main oil companies of the world were those of North America and western Europe. Companies such as Standard Oil of New Jersey (now called Exxon), Shell and British Petroleum drilled and produced oil for the markets of the world. Many of these wells were in the United States and South America, but the greatest reserves of oil were in the Middle East: in Iran, Saudi Arabia, Iraq, and the smaller states of the Persian Gulf. In 1973 the Arab-Israeli war brought about a limited unity among the Arab countries. After the war Kuwait, Saudi Arabia and a number of other oil-producing countries temporarily stopped oil shipments to the Netherlands and the United States and also to other countries that had supported Israel. This was partly to win support for the Arab side in the Arab-Israeli conflict. Their action caused serious oil shortages in western Europe, bringing with it the realisation of the long-term consequences of dependence on supply from the Middle East.

Also at this time the oil-producing countries formed a cartel called the Organisation of Petroleum-Exporting Countries (OPEC) to protect their reserves and to increase their revenue from oil sales. On 5 October 1973 the OPEC countries raised the price of crude oil from $3.65 to $17 a barrel and at the same time limited their annual output in order to conserve their energy supplies. At this time European countries were heavily dependent on oil as a source for their energy, and in 1973 they realised that they had no control over the energy market and were at the mercy of the oil cartel. In 1979 the price of oil was doubled from $17 to $34 a barrel. Again this encouraged the EC to continue with its new policy of alternative energy sources and its search for oil and gas within Europe (e.g. North Sea areas).

■ Consequences of the Oil Crisis

As a direct consequence of the oil crisis, the EC decided on a radical change in its energy policy. Overdependence on imported fuels was to end. Also the EC aimed to reduce the rate of energy consumption. These aims were to be achieved by the following means:

1. Member-states were encouraged to search for oil and natural gas within their own territories.
2. Alternative sources of energy were to be developed, such as wind, wave, solar and nuclear power.
3. Energy was to be conserved by increasing the efficiency of combustion methods. Houses were to be insulated to reduce heat loss.
4. Countries were to diversify their energy requirements by using a number of energy sources, such as natural gas and nuclear power, so that dependence on a single fuel no longer existed.
5. Coal mines were to be rationalised and production increased so that energy could be produced competitively.

ENERGY CASE STUDIES
HYDRO-ELECTRIC POWER

Hydro-electric power accounts for only 1 per cent of total energy consumed in the EU. However, it remains a very important source of energy in Italy, where the fast-flowing Alpine rivers (e.g. Ticino) provide cheap and plentiful supplies of energy for industries such as electrometallurgy, chemicals, and textiles. Most of the hydro-electric potential of western Europe lies outside the EU, in countries such as Norway and Sweden. However, these countries may wish to join the EU in the future.

NORWAY: A CASE STUDY

In Norway most of the hydro-electric power stations are in the south, because most of the country's population and industry is in this area. Production is therefore close to the area of greatest consumption, which reduces transmission costs.

Norway has many advantages for the large-scale production of hydro-electric power:

1. The prevailing onshore south-westerly winds that blow over the North Atlantic Ocean bring heavy rainfall to the southern Norwegian highland area. These rain-bearing winds are forced to rise over the Scandinavian highlands, thus cooling, condensing, and falling as relief rain. In the most elevated areas (e.g. Kjølen Mountains) precipitation falls as snow, which thaws in springtime, producing vast volumes of fast-flowing water to supplement normal surface run-off.

   The impermeable nature of the crystalline igneous rock that forms the Scandinavian Highlands prevents water seepage. This adds to the advantages of the area for the generation of hydro-electric power.

2. In Norway glaciation has produced vertical-sided glacial valleys and deep glacial lakes. Such features produce ideal conditions for the construction of dams and reservoirs. The steep gradient of Norwegian rivers and the constant water supply make Norway's west and south-west mountain slopes ideal for the production of hydro-electric power.

3. Norway's ability to produce large quantities of cheap electricity has been vital in establishing manufacturing industries in the country. Electrometallurgical industries, such as aluminium smelting, need large amounts of cheap electricity. Norway, with large energy supplies together with deep, sheltered **fjords** (drowned glaciated valleys), e.g. Sognefjord, provides ideal conditions for such industries. The largest aluminium smelter is at Ardal at the head of the Sognefjord.

NUCLEAR POWER

Dependence on nuclear power varies greatly throughout western Europe. No nuclear power is generated in Ireland, Denmark, Luxembourg, Norway, or Portugal. Some countries that had ambitious nuclear power programmes, such as Sweden, have now changed their policies, and nuclear power is being either reduced or phased out completely. Britain and France have continuing nuclear power programmes. Nuclear reactors in France are grouped in 'nuclear parks' along the coast near the Gironde estuary, along the English Channel, and along the principal rivers, the Seine, Loire, and Rhône.

Financial inducements to local communes help reduce opposition to nuclear facilities. However, there are many arguments that can be made against the development of nuclear power. Anti-nuclear groups such as Greenpeace, Earthwatch, the Campaign for Nuclear Disarmament (CND) and the Green Parties lobby against the development of nuclear power.

Nuclear waste is highly toxic and remains dangerous to life support systems for thousands of years. It causes cancer and other diseases, and its effects are not limited by national boundaries. The Chernobyl disaster in Ukraine led to many deaths near the nuclear plant and contamination in animals by 'fall-out' in areas as far west as Co. Donegal.

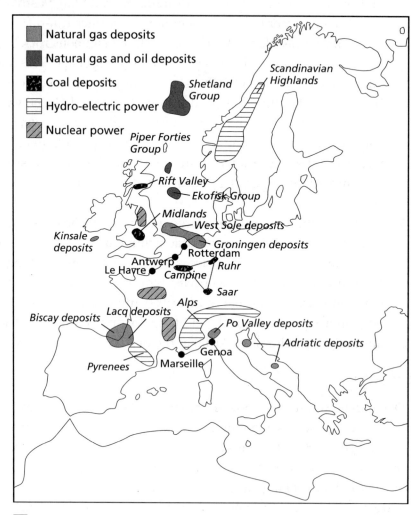

▲ Fig. 6.13 Energy deposits in western Europe

OIL AND GAS PRODUCTION IN WESTERN EUROPE

■ Norway: Oil and Gas

Oil was first found at Ekofisk in 1969. By 1985 Norway had become a major producer and exporter of oil and natural gas. The chance to increase its revenue and energy sources prompted Norway to search for hydrocarbons in the North Sea. In 1973 some 66 per cent of Norway's energy demands were met by hydro-electric power. Hydrocarbon deposits in the North Sea meant that oil and gas reserves could be conserved while at the same time limited exports could play an important role in developing Norway's economic and social life.

However, development of oil-based industries along the Norwegian coast was limited in the beginning, because of the presence of a deep offshore trench that prevented the oil and gas being brought ashore. Because of this, Norway exports much of its oil and almost all its gas directly from production platforms. Since 1986, Norway has succeeded in laying pipelines across this trench, and gas and oil can now be brought directly to the coast. This has been a boost for the oil-refining and petrochemical industries.

Norway has greatly benefited from onshore support industries for the oil and gas wells. Bergen and Stavanger have particularly benefited, as they are nearest to the hydrocarbon deposits. Norway has become a world leader in the production of drilling platforms, tankers, support vessels, and other essential equipment for offshore drilling. Concern with environmental pollution has encouraged Norway to limit its development of its hydrocarbon deposits. Oil spillage, gas rig explosions and other potential disasters make Norway aware of the dangers to its fishing industry. Existing deposits have been developed south of latitude 62° N. Extensive deposits are believed to exist to the north, but there has been a reluctance to develop these, as they could endanger the fishing resources of the area. Heavy seas, icy winds and regular storms are some of the limiting factors, as well as the fact that Norway at present does not need such resources, as it already has a surplus in its balance of trade, which will continue for some time to come.

■ Britain

Natural gas was discovered in commercial quantities off the Humber Estuary in 1965. Since then oil has been discovered in two major groups of oil-fields, the Forties Group and the Shetland Group (fig. 6.13). Britain has adopted a policy of high output over a short period. Britain has a large unemployed work force, and its ailing economy needed extra revenue to overcome its economic difficulties. Production of Britain's hydrocarbon deposits has had the following effects:

1. There has been a reduction in energy imports, which has benefited its balance of trade.
2. An impressive network of pipelines and hydrocarbon-related facilities has been developed in the North Sea.

3. Hydrocarbon-related industries, such as the manufacture of drilling rigs, production platforms and supply vessels and the manufacture of pipes provide a large number of jobs onshore along the east coast.
4. Peripheral regions, such as the north-east coast of Scotland and the north-eastern part of England, have developed new spin-off industries, which help their economies.
5. There have been huge revenue gains from sales (home and export) of hydrocarbons, as Britain demands a high rate of tax and royalty payments on North Sea oil and gas.
6. Britain's energy base has been diversified.

■ Netherlands: Natural Gas

A major discovery of natural gas occurred at Slochteren in the province of Groningen in 1959. It is the biggest gas field in the world. At first large-scale production of gas led to the development of industries such as aluminium, smelting and chemicals in an effort to industrialise this underdeveloped northern region of the country.

The large-scale production and exporting of gas gave rise to concern over the rate of depletion of the resource. Output is now limited, so that domestic supplies will last for quite some time. In the long term this is seen as a more beneficial way of using the resource.

■ Ireland

The first commercial hydrocarbon deposit was discovered off the Old Head of Kinsale in 1974. Production began in 1978, and the gas was piped ashore to Cork Harbour.

Before the discovery of gas at Kinsale, Ireland's energy profile underwent dramatic change. During the 1950s Ireland followed a protectionist policy. Home industry was protected by the imposition of tariffs on foreign products entering the country. This caused stagnation, and the economy declined. As Ireland was a rural society, there was little demand for energy. Unemployment was considerable, and there was mass emigration.

In the years of the Lemass government in the 1960s, an industrial policy devised by T. K. Whitaker attracted foreign companies to Ireland. Growth and confidence in the booming economy of the 1960s created a huge demand for energy, and oil imports rose sharply to accommodate this demand. By the time Ireland joined the EC in 1973, oil supplied 75 per cent of the energy market.

The discovery of natural gas at Kinsale changed this trend. Gas replaced oil at two electricity generating stations, at Marina, Cork, and Ringsend, Dublin. A third generating station using gas was built at Aghada in Cork Harbour. As a result, by 1988 dependence on energy imports had fallen to 62 per cent.

Kinsale gas has been responsible for the development of Cork Harbour as an industrial zone, with industries such as Pfizer, ICI and Sandoz established in the bay.

COAL

By 1950 coal still accounted for 90 per cent of European energy needs. The main areas of production were the British midlands and the industrial triangle of the Ruhr, Saar and Nord regions. Steel production coincides with these areas, as coal is used in its manufacture.
In 1951 the European Coal and Steel Community (ECSC) was formed to co-ordinate the development of these industries and encourage efficient production. Output was to come from the most economic coalfields. However, coal production failed to satisfy energy needs. From 1960, output of coal in all EC countries declined, and the last colliery in the Netherlands was closed in 1975.

Because of ECSC policy, individual countries concentrated output on their most economic coalfields. Thus Belgium produced most of its coal from the Campine, while Germany concentrated on the Ruhr. This caused mass unemployment in the old coal-mining areas, such as the Sambre-Meuse valley and many of the British coal-mining regions. In Britain at present only 40,000 miners are employed at 50 pits, whereas 718,000 miners were employed at 958 collieries when the coal industry was nationalised in 1947. Britain intends to further reduce the number of coal-miners to 11,000 in the near future.

However, the 1973 oil crisis gave a new lease of life to the coal industry. The rise in the cost of oil and the change of EC policy to diversify sources of energy changed the fortunes of the coal industry until the 1980s. Recently the drop in oil prices and the import of foreign coal (Poland, United States, and Russia) has been disappointing for the coal industry. Coal-mining regions, such as those in the British midlands, are facing a bleak future. Entire regions are economically, socially and culturally tied to the coalfields. When large-scale closures occur, communities are devastated, and it is difficult to attract alternative industries to the areas because of the scarred and sometimes peripheral locations.

FIELDWORK TIPS

It may help to limit a fieldwork exercise to an area within a few minutes' walking distance of the school, so that
- facts can be rechecked
- the area can be visited a number of times if needed
- class time is gainfully used to a maximum
- students can develop a sense of responsibility towards working without supervision, earning trust, and learning the importance of time management.

■ Title of Survey

Choose a title that gives a clear idea of the work to be carried out. This will help you to focus on the key ideas of the fieldwork, and it will help to clearly outline the type of information that is required for completion of the survey.

■ Aims of Fieldwork

Give at least five aims, e.g.
- to identify land uses in …
- to record data accurately
- to learn to work with maps of various scales in the field and in the classroom – orient, update, amend and colour, etc.

■ Careful Gathering of Information

- What steps were taken in the classroom to gather the information before the exercise and during the fieldwork?
- State how it was to be gathered, e.g. orientation of map, key for land uses, how the key was to be applied during the fieldwork; questionnaire: its layout, who was to be asked and why, how this was to be carried out during the exercise.
- Two groups should do the same section, to compare for accuracy of each group.
- Each group should give a description of how their various tasks were to be gathered carefully.

■ Careful Recording of Information

- Box options for questionnaire; give sketch.
- Letters used instead of colours for land uses; give sketch of method.

◆ Cross-section, e.g. of beach material – measurement and material at various measured intervals; give sketch.

◆ Photographs – explain why they were needed.

◆ Sketches, e.g. of building types and characteristic features.

■ Results

What were the fieldwork findings? – discovered facts, e.g.

◆ How many people live in the settlement?

◆ How many derelict houses in the settlement?

◆ Numbers of vehicles and types in the traffic survey.

◆ Fall or slope of the beach.

◆ State the facts of the gathered information.

■ Conclusions

What conclusions were drawn from the facts mentioned above? Develop each conclusion fully and in detail.

■ Presentation of Findings

Draw sketches of facts, using various charts, e.g. pie charts, bar charts, line graphs, to display clearly. **Use colour** where possible.

Coloured Ordnance Survey maps with colour key marked in.

Freehand sketches, photographic material.

Headings and written script on display board.

Group plenary session.

EXAMINATION PREPARATION TIPS

◆ Limit final account so that it can be handwritten within forty minutes (higher level) or thirty minutes (ordinary level) in an exam.

◆ Write neatly.

◆ Lay out your survey under the headings given in the previous Leaving Certificate examination, and for each heading –

   (a) give a written account in sufficient detail to gain maximum marks

   (b) use sketches and diagrams when possible to explain points made

   (c) practise this many times within the allocated time, and compare it with your own fieldwork account to see if any important item was omitted.

7

WESTERN EUROPE

POLICIES OF THE EUROPEAN UNION

1. COMMON AGRICULTURAL POLICY

■ **Purpose of Policy**

1. To improve the living standards of farmers.
2. To raise the output and productivity of agriculture.

These aims were to be achieved by a system of price support, which operated as follows.

1 Target Price

A target price for products is fixed at the beginning of each season. This acts as a guide for farmers planning their crops for the coming year.

2 Intervention Price

The intervention price is a minimum price a farmer can expect for his or her product. In the past, oversupply of produce caused prices to fall dramatically. Intervention eliminated this unpredictability. If the market price falls below 5–7 per cent of the target price, the EU intervenes with a minimum price that is guaranteed regardless of how much oversupply exists. High target prices, annual price increases and tariff protection from non-EU countries have combined to stimulate productivity and raise living standards.

■ **Farm Modernisation**

The main objective of this scheme is to provide viable farm units that give farmers a reasonable standard of living. This is achieved in the following way:

1. Encouraging farmers to purchase neighbouring farms to increase their holdings.
2. Encouraging elderly farmers to retire and to pass on the farms to their heirs.

RESULTS OF THE COMMON AGRICULTURAL POLICY

■ Positive Effects

1. Farming has become more specialised and mechanised. This has been achieved through improvements in farming methods and the amalgamation of farms. Larger fields allow for the easy use of machinery for tillage, while the clearance of field fences has added land to many farms.
2. Education in advanced farming methods has led to improved productivity, while the quality of produce has also been raised by competition on European markets. Also, higher standards are demanded by co-operatives.
3. Living standards have risen for those who have remained in farming.
4. There are guaranteed minimum prices for farm produce.

■ Negative Effects

1. Huge surpluses of farm produce have been created in the EU. The cost of storing such products is high. Intervention storage also creates an embarrassing social situation, as shortages continue to cause starvation in some underdeveloped countries, such as Sudan.
2. There have been large sales of butter and beef at low prices to countries such as Russia to avoid flooding the EU markets.
3. The benefits of the policy have tended to flow towards the richer countries. Many Continental countries were already advanced in farming methods and productivity before the introduction of the quota system. This system has allowed them to retain this advantage, while it restricts farming economies in countries such as Ireland.
4. As large farm units are needed to maintain existing living standards, many smaller farmers are forced to sell their holdings. This has drastically reduced the permanent farming population, especially in peripheral areas, such as the west of Ireland.

3 Common Regional Policy

The purpose of the common regional policy was to reduce the gap between the richer core areas and the poorer peripheral areas. The creation of the EC increased the attraction of the core region for manufacturing industry. This has had negative effects on peripheral areas, such as the west of Ireland, Scotland, and southern Italy. Under the Common Regional Policy, the European Regional and Development Fund and the European Social Fund were introduced to help in the promotion and development of these regions. Since the signing of the Single European Act in 1986, such funds greatly help to improve **infrastructure** (e.g. roads), job creation and small industries in the disadvantaged areas. However, some of these funds have been used on occasions for political or private gains.

4 Common Energy Policy

Following the 1973 oil crisis, the EC was determined to end overdependence on imported fuels, especially oil. Also, the EC aimed to reduce the rate of energy consumption. These aims were to be achieved in the following ways.

1. Countries of the EC were encouraged to search for fossil fuels, such as oil and natural gas, within their own territories.
2. Alternative sources of energy were to be developed, such as wind, nuclear, solar and biomass power.
3. Energy was to be conserved by increasing the efficiency of combustion methods. Also houses were to use insulation methods to prevent heat loss.
4. Countries were to diversify their energy requirements by using a number of energy sources, so that dependence on a single fuel no longer existed.

5 Common Fisheries Policy

See p. 138.

ADVANTAGES OF THE CORE AREA FOR MANUFACTURING INDUSTRY

1. COAL SUPPLIES

Since the Industrial Revolution of 1750, coal has formed the basis of manufacturing industry in western Europe. The transport of coal – a low-value, bulky commodity – was expensive. Factories were therefore established on the coalfields. The core of western Europe has many coalfields, for example the Ruhr, the Saar, the Campine, the British midlands, and the Yorkshire coalfields.

Centred on these coalfields are many large industrial centres, such as Lille in the Nord, Liège and Namur in the Sambre-Meuse, and Dortmund

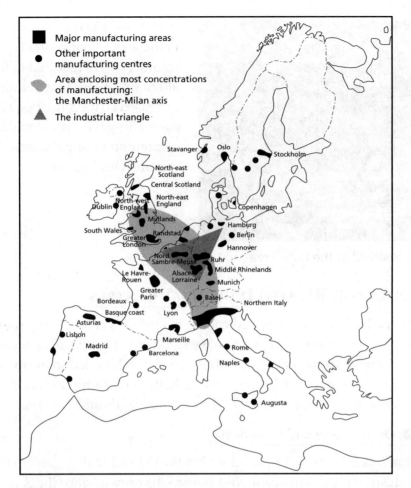

Major manufacturing areas

● Other important
manufacturing centres

Area enclosing most concentrations
of manufacturing:
the Manchester-Milan axis

▲ The industrial triangle

▲ Fig. 7.1 Industrial areas of western Europe

and Duisburg in the Ruhr area. These cities grew rapidly in the last century, offering much employment. The long-established industrial tradition of these regions provides a highly skilled work force. Dominant industries, such as iron and steel, engineering, and chemicals, give these regions their distinctiveness.

In Germany, industrial development has spread outwards from the Ruhr coalfield into the larger Rhine-Ruhr conurbation. The advantages of this region, such as vast coal supplies (sufficient for another 300 years at the present rate of extraction), industrial tradition, and the presence of the Rhine waterway system, make it the most important industrial region within the core. Some of its specialised industrial areas are Solingen and Remscheid (special steels, cutlery, and precision instruments), Wuppertal and Krefeld (textiles), and Leverkusen (chemicals).

The oil crisis of 1973 and 1979 brought welcome change to the coalfield areas. Europe needed to diversify its energy requirements, as imported oil

dominated the energy market. Because of a change in EC policy, countries were required to find alternative fuels. One solution was increased coal production within the core. This gave a boost to the mining communities, bringing stability and creating employment.

▲ Fig. 7.2 A coalfield in the Ruhr area

2. Oil Supplies and Related Industrial Centres

By the 1960s oil had replaced coal as the region's chief energy source, and its abundance and availability have resulted in significant changes in industrial location patterns. Within the core, oil has led to the expansion of most core industrial areas, such as Rotterdam-Europoort, and the creation of others, such as the Middle Rhinelands and Bavaria.

■ Oil Refining and Chemicals

Rotterdam is centrally placed within the EU and with respect to the major industrial centres of north-west Europe. Its growth since the Second World War has been due to oil. It is the main oil port of western Europe, and pipelines distribute crude oil to many inland refineries, mainly in Germany. Expansion was carried out westwards along the left bank of the new waterway to meet demands for berthing facilities, industry, oil storage, and container storage. Initially Pernis and Botlek were developed as oil and chemical complexes. Europoort was developed in the 1960s to accommodate supertankers of up to 300,000 tonnes. In 1974 Maasvlakte was developed, with greater storage and berthing areas and industrial sites.

Other oil-refining centres along the coast near Rotterdam are Antwerp in Belgium and Le Havre in France. Large industrial areas are associated with these ports.

■ The Middle Rhinelands and Bavaria

Oil refining was promoted in Bavaria and Baden-Württemberg in Germany. This region prospered as a major chemical region because of a number of factors. The Rhine was a deep, wide canalised river with the ability to provide bulk transport facilities for importing raw materials. The region was centrally placed within western Europe, where a large demand for chemicals existed. Three pipelines – the Trans-Alpine from Trieste, the Central European from Genoa, and the South European from Marseille – supply this southern region with energy and raw materials. Ingolstadt and Karlsruhe were selected as large-scale industrial centres. Two large industrial companies, BASF and Hoechst, are based at Ludwigshafen and Frankfurt, respectively. The BASF plant employs 45,000 people.

In Bavaria, Ingolstadt and Bergshausen are large industrial centres, based mainly on the pipelines from Italy. However, small local gas and oil supplies at Bergshausen encouraged industrial development, such as oil refining and chemicals.

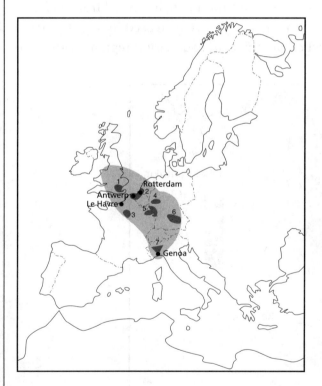

Core region

1. Greater London: general manufacturing
2. Antwerp-Randstad: oil refining, chemicals, diamond cutting
3. Paris: car manufacture
4. Ruhr: engineering, precision instruments
5. Alsace-Middle Rhinelands: light engineering and car manufacture
6. Bavaria: chemicals and oil refining
7. Industrial triangle (Milan-Turin-Genoa): car manufacture, ship-building, chemicals

◀ Fig. 7.3 Major industrial areas in the core region

3. LARGE URBAN MARKETS AND MANUFACTURING CENTRES IN THE CORE

The EU has a total population of almost 340 million. The greater proportion of these people are in the core area of the 'Manchester-Milan axis'. Some of the more populated areas are the Randstad, Greater

London, Paris, and the Rhine cities from Cologne to Stuttgart. All these urban centres create a demand for consumer goods, which can be satisfied by manufacturing nearby. For example, in the past, demand for motor vehicles led to the growth of vehicle manufacture within the core. Access to a prosperous and growing market, a large, skilled work force, good transport networks (motorways and the Rhine) and access to component suppliers led to the success of BMW, Mercedes-Benz, Opel, Audi, Volkswagen, Citroën, Renault, Peugeot, and Fiat.

The industrial triangle of northern Italy includes the three main cities of Milan, Turin, and Genoa. Fiat employs 140,000 people in its twenty-three factories around Turin. This is the richest and most urbanised region of Italy. Genoa, with its oil refining, chemicals, and shipbuilding industry, is a major oil-importing centre. Within this industrial triangle, centrally placed factories are supplied with component parts from other factories, while some raw materials, such as aluminium, are imported from as far afield as Japan. Production and efficiency have increased in recent years, making this one of the most competitive and successful regions within the core of the EU.

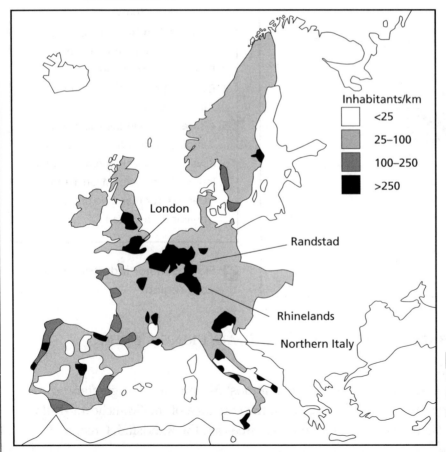

◀ Fig. 7.4 Population density in western Europe

THE SAMBRE-MEUSE:
A PROBLEM REGION IN THE CORE

■ Problem no. 1

The Sambre-Meuse coalfields in Belgium are an extension of the Nord coalfield of northern France and stretch for a distance of 150 km along the Sambre-Meuse Valley. Borinage, Centre, Charleroi and Liège are the main coalfields in the valley. Mining has continued in the valley for some 150 years, and most of the best seams are exhausted. In addition, difficult mining conditions – faulted, fractured and thin seams – added to the high cost of production. In the increasingly competitive energy market after 1960, this coalfield region experienced rapid and continuous decline.

The European Coal and Steel Community (ECSC) emphasised production in the most efficient coalfields. This meant a downgrading of Belgium's coalfields, while imports of lignite and coking coal from the Ruhr were encouraged. Imports of cheap American and Polish coal were also available. After 1986 the Belgian coal industry collapsed, and deep mining of coal in effect ceased in this region as the last colliery was closed. The region owed its initial prosperity to coal-mining and a limited range of related heavy industries: steel, engineering, and chemicals. Decline of coal as a basic raw material has therefore had repercussions throughout the area.

■ Problem no. 2

By the twentieth century, Belgium's growth industries, such as textiles, had become outdated. The canals, roads, railway system and working-class housing of Wallonia (French-speaking southern Belgium) were all out of date. Furthermore, the landscape of the coalfields, its nineteenth-century expansion and uncontrolled development resulted in much pollution from colliery waste heaps and an urban environment that is drab in appearance, overcrowded, and in need of renovation. With the decline of the industries, environmental problems were worsened by the many derelict buildings, collieries and railway sidings that dotted the landscape. Such an environment deters modern industry, and yet modern industry had to be encouraged into the region.

■ Problem no. 3

The coalfield towns of Liège, Namur and Charleroi were the centres of Walloon culture. The loss of employment and low living standards were causing a decline in the population as people migrated to such growth centres as Antwerp and Brussels. The Walloon population was outnumbered by that of Flanders (Dutch-speaking northern Belgium), and was actually declining, since Wallonia did not share in the population boom that occurred in Flanders, France and the Netherlands immediately after the war. It relied on immigrants to fill the gaps in its work force.

It seemed to the Walloons that they had been outpaced by their Flemish neighbours. Flanders became the new growth region. It had a large, young work force ready for industrial work, while Wallonia had a work force on strike because of rationalisation of its outdated industries. Flanders had plenty of new sites for factories and ports, such as Antwerp, which guaranteed deep-water access for ocean-going vessels. These characteristics were quite different from the cramped, outdated factory areas in the land-locked south and the demand for higher wages from an aging Walloon work force.

SOME SOLUTIONS FOR THE SAMBRE-MEUSE PROBLEM REGION

1 Rationalisation of Coal-Mines

The opening of the Albert Canal has allowed access to the North Sea. This has allowed the importing of iron ore from Sweden and coal from the Campine to revitalise the iron and steel industry in the Sambre-Meuse. As a result, the steel industry survives and produces a substantial proportion of Belgium's steel, because of tradition and industrial inertia (reputation for local product, cost factors). However, steel making today is concentrated in fewer, larger integrated plants at Liège and Charleroi, because they are more cost-effective locations. Uneconomic industries were closed, allowing more funds to be concentrated in more profitable areas, such as along the North Sea coast.

2 Revitalisation: Encouraging New Growth

Huge amounts of ECSC and Belgian government funds have been invested in Wallonia to retrain unemployed miners, encourage native and foreign investment, and attract new industries. Many new factories have been built, with the emphasis on clean growth industries: telecommunications, electronics, consumer goods, and light industry. A number of industrial estates have been established throughout the region and have provided a much-needed diversity and variety in Wallonia's industrial revitalisation.

The basic infrastructure is notable in transport, where modern motorways have been built or improved, and has contributed to a healthier economic outlook.

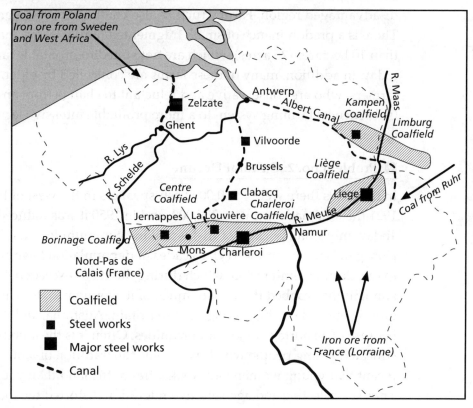

▲ Fig. 7.5 Major coalfields and steelworks in Belgium

THE WEST OF IRELAND: A PROBLEM REGION IN THE PERIPHERY

■ Problem no. 1: Relief and Agriculture

The west of Ireland is on the extreme edge of western Europe. As a result it gets the full force of the elements from the North Atlantic Ocean. Rain-bearing depressions that travel across the North Atlantic bring heavy rainfall (2,000 mm a year), while gales gust up to 130 km/h along the west coast in winter. The landscape of the west is rugged, with mountains such as Macgillycuddy's Reeks, the Connemara mountains, Nephin and the Donegal mountains covering much of the area. The soils are mainly acidic, because of the heavy rainfall, which leaches minerals to the subsoil. Much of the land is covered with blanket bog.

This marginal landscape limits the ability of the farming community to compete with the eastern part of Ireland, and so their output is low. The EU recognised the difficulties for this region when it designated it a disadvantaged region. Farm structure also contributes to the problem. There is a predominance of small, fragmented family farms, many of less than 10 hectares (25 acres), which are not suited to profitable farming today. In addition, many of these farms are controlled by older, single farmers, who are conservative and reluctant to change from an extensive (subsistence) farming system to a more profitable intensive farming system.

■ **Problem no. 2: Cultural Decline**

In the 1850s there were 1,500,000 Irish-speakers in the west of Ireland. By 1921 the total had shrunk to 250,000, and in 1950 it was reduced to 70,000. Today only small pockets of Irish-speaking communities exist (e.g. in Cos. Donegal, Galway, and Kerry). Decades of depopulation have contributed to this decline. Emigration, which during the 1980s exceeded 40,000 annually, has robbed the west of much of its young people. This active group (aged 18–30) have emigrated to Britain, Australia, and America, because of a shortage of job opportunities. Often it is the ambitious and educated young people who leave, while the tradition of land inheritance meant that young women had weaker ties to the land than young men. Thus sex-selective and age-selective migration distorted the local population, creating a cycle of rural depopulation. This emigration of young adults meant that birth rates fell, reducing the population still further and leading to a consequent loss of local services.

Migration losses are most severe in really isolated areas (e.g. Belmullet peninsula) than in settlements that provide some basic living standards. Despite these problems, dependence on farming remains high. Attachment to the land is strong, and those who wish to remain in farming realise that to survive they must raise their living standards.

■ **Problem no. 3: Industry**

The west of Ireland has few raw materials with which to generate manufacturing industry. Agricultural output is mainly confined to beef and the rearing of sheep on lower and sheltered slopes. Much of the rural work force is unskilled in industrial practices.

The west of Ireland is isolated from the economic core of the EU. Distance from this core industrial region puts it at a disadvantage for the manufacturing, transport and marketing of products. Extra cost is incurred in the haulage of raw materials to the west, while its western location on an island country on the edge of Europe increases the cost of products on the Continental market.

In the west, unemployment rates and dependence on primary activities are higher than in the east, while income levels, access to services and living standards are lower. In addition, the recent ending of the compulsory Shannon stop-over will add to the isolation of the west. Tourists who at one time were required to stop at Shannon and thereby possibly visit the west may now continue to Dublin to spend most of their time in the east. Viable tourist revenue could not be sustained or justified by exerting pressure on tourists to visit the west.

SOME SOLUTIONS TO PROBLEMS IN THE WEST OF IRELAND

1 Regional Planning

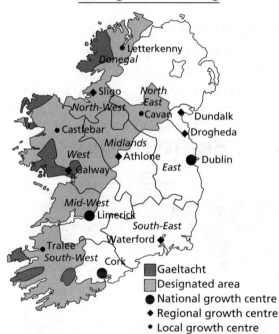

The Buchanan Report (1968) advised the Government to adopt a 'growth centre' policy. According to the plan, industrial development should be encouraged in selected towns, such as Castlebar and Sligo, in each of the planning regions. The Industrial Development Authority opted for a greater dispersal of industry. The IDA also attracted many foreign companies to the area. However, many of these have since closed, because of a world recession, and the IDA has changed its policy to favour a greater development of native industrial projects (e.g. craft industries, textiles, cheesemaking).

▲ Fig. 7.6 Planning regions, designated areas, the Gaeltacht, and Buchanan's proposed growth centres

2 Encouragement of Small Irish Industry

Support for the development of local craft industries is now seen to complement the tourist industry. Knitwear and the manufacture of pottery are two such craft industries. Generous incentives and advice are given to people in starting their enterprises. By the mid-1980s over 2,500 small industries employed more than 30,000 people. These small industries are well suited to rural communities and are more likely to succeed in improving conditions in the west than multinational companies, which have no loyalties to the local area.

3 Natural Resources

Better use of the region's natural resources is to be promoted. Developments in the fish processing industry are to be encouraged. This enables fishing villages to survive and grow into prosperous communities, such as Killybegs in Co. Donegal. The development of mariculture in places such as Killary Harbour in Cos. Mayo and Galway has provided extra jobs. However, this industry has many disadvantages for areas such as the west of Ireland (e.g. it has been blamed for the loss of sea-trout runs, which in turn has almost wiped out angling tourism in the area).

The development of the timber industry is encouraged. Local sawmills can supply timber products at competitive prices, while at the same time reducing the import bill and helping with the balance of payments. This is due mainly to the huge increase in land devoted to reafforestation over the past twenty years.

THE IMPORTANCE OF THE SEA TO NORWAY

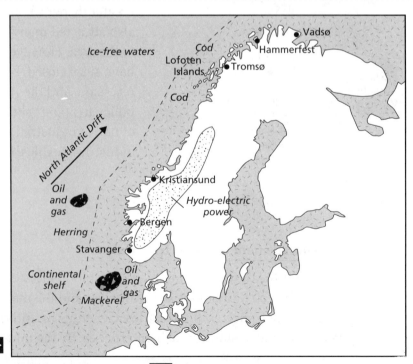

Fig. 7.7 ▶

ADVANTAGES OF THE SEA AREA TO NORWAY

1 Alternative Livelihood

Norway is the leading fishing country of Europe. Because of its high latitude, the harsh climate and rugged mountainous terrain make farming difficult. This, together with the absence of extensive mineral and forest resources, has caused Norway to turn to the sea.

Cod and herring fishing dominate Norway's fishing industry. Whaling in the Antarctic is also important. The numerous fjords provide excellent sheltered fishing areas and ports. The fjord coastline provides the main herring fishery, based on rich feeding and spawning grounds. In spring, huge shoals of cod migrate from the Arctic waters to their spawning grounds in the coastal waters around the Lofoten Islands. This fishery attracts large numbers of fishing boats from the south of Norway, as well as providing a rich harvest for northern fishermen. More than half of Norway's boats are registered in northern Norway and are engaged in cod fishing along the coast. Northern Norway's climate is most severe in this area, and the numbers of fishermen here reflect the attractive alternative that the sea offers. The main fishing ports are Hammerfest, Tromsø, and Vadsø. Co-operatives and quality control are playing an increasing role in providing a ready outlet for fish caught, some 90 per cent of which is exported. Norway's main markets are the United States, Britain, and Sweden.

2 Ice-Free Waters

The North Atlantic Drift is also directly responsible for the year-round fishing season. Because of its warm waters, the eastern North Atlantic is ice-free throughout the year, even within the Arctic Circle and as far north as Hammerfest in Norway. Waters in similar latitudes in other parts of the Atlantic, such as along the Labrador coast and the St Lawrence Estuary in eastern Canada, are frozen for up to three months of the year.

These ice-free waters off western Europe allow owner-skippers to constantly provide cash flow to meet heavy repayments on their fishing vessels. The number of larger vessels has increased in recent years, as has the use of expensive equipment to track and catch the fish (e.g. echo sounders and sonar). As fishing has become a specialist occupation and as levels of efficiency have increased, a large financial investment in trawlers is necessary. Therefore a steady cash flow is necessary, which can only be achieved in ice-free and sheltered fishing grounds. So the north-east Atlantic is a major fishing area.

3 Hydro-Electric Power

The prevailing onshore south-westerly winds that blow over the North Atlantic Ocean bring heavy rainfall to the southern Norwegian highland area. These rain-bearing winds are forced to rise over the Scandinavian highlands, thus cooling, condensing, and falling as relief rain. In the most elevated areas (e.g. Kjølen Mountains) precipitation falls as snow, which thaws in springtime, producing vast volumes of fast-flowing water to supplement normal surface run-off.

The impermeable nature of the crystalline igneous rock that forms the Scandinavian Highlands prevents water seepage. This adds to the advantages of the area for the generation of hydro-electric power.

4 Hydrocarbon Deposits

Oil was first found at Ekofisk in 1969. By 1985 Norway had become a major producer and exporter of oil and natural gas. The chance to increase its revenue and energy sources prompted Norway to search for hydrocarbons in the North Sea. In 1973 some 66 per cent of Norway's energy demands were met by hydro-electric power. Hydrocarbon deposits in the North Sea meant that oil and gas reserves could be conserved while at the same time limited exports could play an important role in developing Norway's economic and social life.

However, development of oil-based industries along the Norwegian coast was limited in the beginning, because of the presence of a deep offshore trench that prevented the oil and gas being brought ashore. Because of this, Norway has exported much of its oil and almost all its gas directly from production platforms. Since 1986, Norway has succeeded in laying pipelines across this trench, and gas and oil can now be brought directly to the coast. This has been a boost for the oil-refining and petrochemical industries.

Norway has greatly benefited from onshore support industries for the oil and gas wells. Bergen and Stavanger have particularly benefited, as they are nearest to the hydrocarbon deposits. Norway has become a world leader in the production of drilling platforms, tankers, support vessels, and other essential equipment for offshore drilling. Concern with environmental pollution has encouraged Norway to limit the development of its hydrocarbon deposits. Oil spillage, gas rig explosions and other potential disasters make Norway aware of the dangers to its fishing industry. Existing deposits have been developed south of latitude 62° N. Extensive deposits are believed to exist to the north, but there has been a reluctance to develop these, as they could endanger the fishing resources of the area. Heavy seas, icy winds and regular storms are some of the limiting factors, as well as the fact that Norway at present does not need such resources, as it already has a surplus in its balance of trade, which will continue for some time to come.

REGIONAL DIVISIONS – CASE STUDIES

Q. In the case of one European country that you have studied, draw a sketch map to divide it into regions. Explain your divisions, giving *three* reasons.

SUGGESTED LAYOUT

◆ Name of country: France
◆ Map showing physical regions

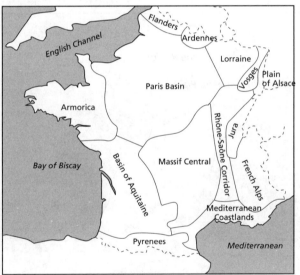

◀ Fig. 7.8

Choose any three regions above (unless otherwise stated), and for each region –

■ choose any three of the following headings and develop each one fully:
   Climate
   Relief and soils
   Agriculture or primary activity
   Industry or secondary and tertiary activities

You may join some headings, as below:
   Climate
   Relief and Soils
   Agriculture and Industry

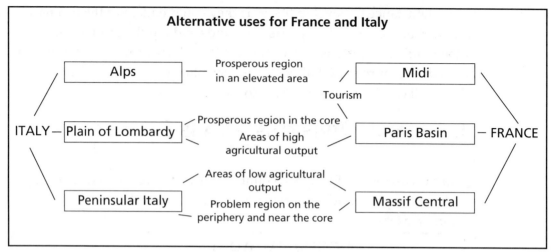

Alternative uses for France and Italy

Alps	Prosperous region in an elevated area	Midi
	Tourism	
Plain of Lombardy	Prosperous region in the core	Paris Basin
	Areas of high agricultural output	
	Areas of low agricultural output	
Peninsular Italy	Problem region on the periphery and near the core	Massif Central

ITALY — FRANCE

CASE STUDY

ITALY: A REGIONAL DIVISION

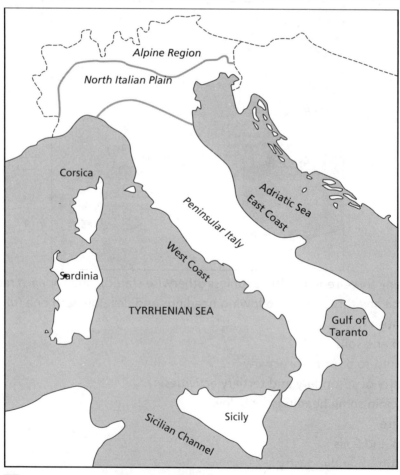

▲ Fig. 7.9 Physical regions of Italy

THE ALPS

■ Climate

In the Alpine region the climate varies according to altitude and aspect. Areas near the lakes (Maggiore and Como) experience mild winters, because of the influence of their warm waters. The mountains are snow-covered in winter, with temperatures a few degrees below freezing point. Summer temperatures reach a maximum of 25°C. Sheltered south-facing villages have a less severe winter, as clear skies ensure a high proportion of sunshine hours. Temperatures change with altitude by 1°C for every 150 m. The highest peaks and **benches** (less steep slopes above the valley sides) are snow-covered throughout the year, while the snow line varies from season to season. Avalanches sometimes occur in spring, because of snow-melt as **overhangs** (large masses of snow) becoming unstable. In winter, westward-moving depressions across the Mediterranean draw cold air from the Alpine region. These icy and violent winds, called the Mistral (Maestrale) and the Bora, can have a damaging effect on fruit blossoms if they occur in early spring. Precipitation is high in the Alps and is greater in summer than winter. No season is dry. Como has an annual precipitation of 1,650 mm.

■ Agriculture

Most of the valley slopes are forested. As the valleys widen near the Plain of Lombardy, the woods are deciduous. As one moves up towards the head of the valleys the vegetation changes to coniferous trees because of the effect of altitude.

Agriculture is carried out on the valley floors. Crops at various stages of maturity form a mosaic pattern on the flat valley floors. In these lower and open valleys cereals, maize and root crops are grown. Because of the milder winters near the central lakes, crops of peaches, apricots and olives are produced. Lemons are particularly susceptible to frost, and protective measures are taken when temperatures are low.

Transhumance is carried on in the higher valleys, where cattle are carried to the higher mountain pastures in summer and stall-fed during the long winter months. Fodder crops, potatoes, rye and barley are the main crops in these valleys.

■ Relief and Soils

The Alps curve in a crescent shape from the Gulf of Genoa to the Gulf of Venice. Their crest-line forms the frontier between France, Switzerland

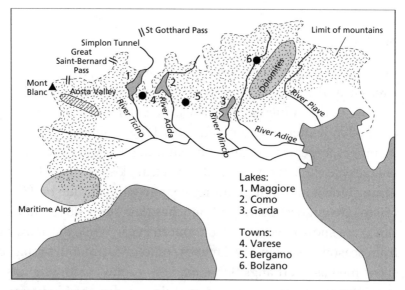

St Gotthard Pass

Limit of mountains

Simplon Tunnel
Great
Saint-Bernard
Pass

6

Mont
Blanc

Dolomites

Aosta Valley

River Piave

1

2

River Ticino

River Adda

4

5

River Mincio

3

River Adige

Maritime Alps

Lakes:
1. Maggiore
2. Como
3. Garda

Towns:
4. Varese
5. Bergamo
6. Bolzano

▲ Fig. 7.10 The Alps

and Austria for much of their length. The southern slopes of the Alps lie mostly in Italy, and they are drained by fast-flowing streams either to the Po or directly to the Adriatic Sea. Some valleys are blocked at their southern ends by moraine enclosing Lakes Maggiore, Como, and Garda (moraine-dammed lakes).

Apart from the boundary ridges, several groups of mountains lie within Italy, including the Bergamo Alps in the centre and the Dolomites in the east. The Dolomites consist of dolomite limestone (magnesium carbonate) and form towering pinnacles rising steeply above the pinewoods and meadows of the lower slopes and the valley floors. The high Alps are breached in places by mountain passes, such as the St Gotthard, the Splügen and the Simplon passes. Soils are generally stony, with higher valley floors covered in gravel. However, lower valley floors are level, with large areas of well-drained soil used for tillage.

■ Industry

The fast-flowing streams from the Alps, such as the Adige, Piave, and Ticino, have been harnessed to develop hydro-electric power, and electricity is transmitted by grid to the manufacturing towns of the valleys (e.g. Varese and the North Italian Plain, Turin, and Milan). Throughout the valleys of the Alps these streams as well as mountain torrents are used to their full potential. Huge pipes carry water from the mountain benches down to the hydro-electric stations at their base. These high heads of water are ideal for electricity generation. Factories concerned with electrometallurgical, chemical and textile industries are built near the power stations. The Ticino valley has many industries, and the valley is also served by many small airports, which increase access to this mountain area.

In the upper valley of the Ticino as well as the Aosta valley numerous quarries excavate gravel from the valley floor, and this is used in construction. The Alps are a major tourist region and attract people throughout the year. In winter, sports such as skiing dominate the season's activities, with powder snow falling in abundance. In summer the Alpine valleys with their attractive south-facing villages attract thousands of tourists from the North Italian Plain. Especially attractive are Lakes Como, Garda, and Maggiore. Their steep mountain slopes are dotted with holiday houses and apartments that look out across the lakes.

THE PLAIN OF LOMBARDY

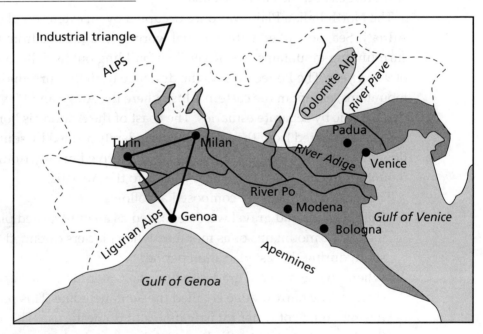

▲ Fig 7.11 The Plain of Lombardy

■ Climate

The Plain of Lombardy has a sub-continental climate. This suggests that the Northern Plain has a climate of extremes. These extremes are generated by the influence of the surrounding mountains and the land-locked nature of the plain, which limit the influence of, and form a barrier to, the mild anti-trade winds, which blow especially during the winter.

The large expanse of the North Italian Plain reduces the influence of the Mediterranean (distance from the sea and influence of ocean winds).

The Plain of Lombardy has cool winters and hot summers. Rain, which falls mainly in summer, decreases from west (750 mm) to east (500 mm) and from north to south. However, all places get a minimum of 500 mm.

Relief and soils

Winters are short but severe, especially when cold air drains from the Alps and settles in hollows. January temperatures at Milan are 0°C; at Venice, sea influences allow 4°C. July temperatures are everywhere about 24°C.

The Plain of Lombardy is bordered on three sides: to the north there are the Alps, to the west the Dolomite and Venetian Alps, and to the south the Ligurian Alps and the Apennines. The eastern end opens to the Adriatic Sea and the Gulf of Genoa.

The North Italian Plain was once occupied by an extension of the Adriatic Sea, now filled with material worn by the streams from the surrounding mountains. The River Po is building out its delta at the rate of 9 m a year. The Po receives all the drainage from the surrounding mountains, except in the eastern Alps, where the Adige and Piave reach the Adriatic by separate estuaries. The coast of the Adriatic is bordered by lagoons separated from the sea by long sandspits formed by south-flowing currents. These marine deposits are derived mainly from the mountain rivers, which carry heavy loads to the Adriatic.

The soils of the plain are composed as follows:

1. Glacial sands and gravel were deposited as an out-washed plain at the foot of the mountains or as moraine, when glaciers extended further south during the last glaciation period.
2. Where coarse material grades to fine, the water-table reaches the surface. The narrow zone is called the Fontanelli line. This provides a reliable source of water for irrigation and domestic use. The annual flooding of the plain by the Po and Adige has also built up great alluvial deposits, which make this the richest expanse of soil in the country.
3. Finer sands and silts were carried to the centre of the plain.

Agriculture

The rich alluvial soils of the North Italian Plain allow intensive farming, both in tillage and dairying. The main dairying areas are to the north of the River Po. Here stall feeding and the intensive production of fodder crops (i.e. silage and grain) allow high yields. The lowland relief, fertile alluvial soils, sunshine and all-year supplies of water ensure high yields in cereal production. Wheat is still the most important crop, although maize and rice are grown. Maize is used as fodder. Here farming is large-scale, and highly mechanised methods of cereal production characterise the region. Market gardening is carried out in the vicinity of towns and cities. There is a great demand for vegetables from the towns, and the high value of the crops enables this form of agriculture to compete for valuable land near the cities of Milan, Turin, and Genoa.

■ Industry

To the north of the Po, because of growth in industry, towns such as Verona and Padua have shared in the development of modern food processing, textiles, and engineering works. Large natural gas and petroleum supplies in the plain are used as raw materials in the chemical industry and as fuel for industrial and domestic purposes. The Plain of Lombardy is connected to the Central European Pipeline and the Transalpine Pipeline. Genoa and Venice are terminals for oil tanker routes from the Middle East to western Europe. Large quantities of fuel and raw materials have therefore boosted industry at these ports as well as the establishment of foot-loose industries throughout the plain.

The industrial triangle of Turin, Milan and Genoa dominates the economic life of Italy. Milan is the focus of road and rail routes across the plain and Alps. It is the commercial, financial and industrial capital of Italy. In Milan and its hinterland there are approx. 100,000 small to medium-sized manufacturing units. The province of Lombardy, with Milan as its capital, accounts for 40 per cent of Italian exports. Turin is the second industrial city. It is situated at the confluence of the Dora Ripira and the four rivers. It controls the passes and roads through the Alps to France and Switzerland and the southern route to Genoa. The Fiat and Lancia factories dominate the city, making it the capital of the car industry. Fiat employs 200,000 people. Olivetti, the office equipment manufacturer, has its main works here. Genoa has a deep, sheltered harbour that can accommodate large tankers, accounting for 90 per cent of its total imports. Oil is the chief item, and so this is a major European oil port. It has steel works and shipyards as well as refineries and petrochemical industries.

PENINSULAR ITALY

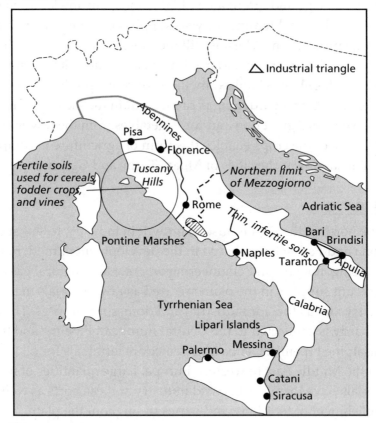

▲ Fig. 7.12 Peninsular Italy

■ Climate

A Mediterranean climate dominates peninsular Italy. In summer it is hot and dry, and winters are mild and wet. However, there are considerable differences between the north and south of the peninsula. The January temperature for Livorno is 7.5°C. From Naples southwards January temperatures are high, usually over 8°C. Coastlands west of the Apennines come under the influence of depressions during the winter. These are blown by the south-west anti-trade winds and travel over the North Atlantic; they are therefore wet winds, bringing annual rainfall to 890 mm. At this time the Adriatic coastlands are in the rain shadow of the Apennines, thus giving a reduced annual rainfall of 480 mm.

The Adriatic coastlands are also open to cold north-east winds from eastern Europe. In summer the peninsula comes under the influence of the north-east trade winds from the European continent. Because they come from a land area they are warm and dry, bringing drought at this time of year. Summer temperatures are hot: Livorno 24.5°C, Naples 24°C. Sicily is affected in summer by the Sirocco (a dry, sand-laden wind from the Sahara), which results in scorchingly hot days.

■ Relief and Soils

Peninsular Italy is dominated by the Apennines. Composed mainly of limestone, these mountains are high and karst-like. Although rainfall, especially in winter, is high, there is little surface water except in depressions in valleys. In the north, coastal plains such as the Plain of Tuscany are wide, but level land is in short supply as one travels south towards Calabria. Deep, well-drained soils are found in the Plain of Tuscany. Apulia on the eastern side of the Apennines has a thin cover of marine clays and sands.

In some places the underlying limestone has rotted and its residual deposits have formed a thick, impermeable layer below the surface, producing malarial swamps. In other places the limestone is porous, making irrigation difficult. Generally, the steep slopes of the Apennines have a thin, infertile soil cover producing rough grasses and scrub, the mountains are rugged, and the terrain is difficult.

■ Agriculture

Productive agriculture in peninsular Italy is limited to the northern part around Tuscany. The Plain of Tuscany (i.e. lower Arno) is intensely cultivated with wheat, maize, sugar-beet, and fodder crops. Dairy cattle are reared in the middle of the plain, and all the hill slopes are covered with vineyards and olive groves. The Chianti hills in the east are famous for their wines. South of the Arno Plain the hills and valleys of Tuscany and Umbria are covered with farms, even at the tops of the hills. Everywhere cereals, peaches and apricots are grown.

In the lower Tiber basin there were malarial swamps and marshes. Today these marshes have been drained and are occupied by wheat fields, dairy farms, and vineyards. The reclamation of the Pontine Marshes, south of the Tiber delta, was part of this scheme.

The area to the south of Naples known as the Mezzogiorno has been classed as a problem region. Fertile farming is confined to small fertile plains formed by rivers from the mountains. The bare limestone (karst landscape) and crystalline rock produce an absence of surface water and a rugged landscape where farming is difficult.

■ Industry

The economy of southern Italy contrasts strongly with the prosperity of the Italian Plain. This has occurred for a number of reasons:

1. The south possessed few raw material resources and energy supplies for industrial development.
2. There was an inadequate development of communication systems to compensate for the peripheral location.
3. The labour force was unskilled and largely illiterate.
4. The Mezzogiorno provided only a poor market, because of the low standards of living and high unemployment rates in the region.
5. It had a poor agricultural base on which to establish a food-processing industry.
6. As a result of poverty and unemployment, 6 million people migrated from the region between 1950 and 1970.

■ Establishing Industry

In 1975 it was first recognised that industry had to be directly encouraged in the Mezzogiorno, and capital allocations for industry were made (e.g. positive attractions for development in the 1960s):

1. Cheap labour.
2. A more productive agricultural sector based on modern intensive farming with the use of irrigation.
3. Natural gas deposits.
4. Deep-water port facilities for the import of raw materials and the export of finished goods. A new motorway network also made the region less isolated from the north.
5. Most importantly of all, a law introduced in the early 1960s forced state-controlled industries to place 60 per cent of all new investments in the Mezzogiorno. Much of Italian heavy industry is state-controlled (e.g. the Taranto steel works, the Alfa-Romeo car plant at Naples, Fiat at Palermo, and petrochemicals at Brindisi and Siracusa-Augusta).
6. In the late 1960s a 'growth centre' policy was adopted to encourage industrial development. It was hoped that better facilities at such centres would attract industries and that development would be extended in the surrounding areas. The three most important centres were Naples, the Bari-Brindisi-Taranto triangle, and eastern Sicily.
7. Tourism has been encouraged in this southern region. Areas such as Florence, Rome, Naples and Sorrento are important tourist destinations. However, tourism is absent from many of the rural areas in the south, such as Calabria.

FRANCE: A REGIONAL DIVISION

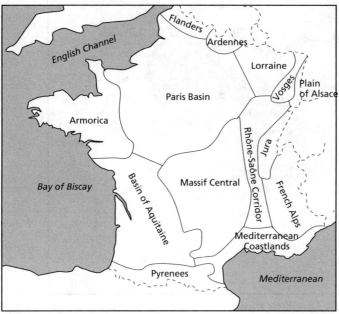

▲ Fig. 7.13 Regions of France

PARIS BASIN

■ Relief and Soil

The Paris Basin occupies 25 per cent of France and so by itself is larger than Ireland. Structurally it is a broad, shallow **downfold** (depression) consisting of layers of sedimentary rock, one inside the other, and might be described as a series of stacked saucers. In the centre are sandstones and limestones, which are surrounded by belts of chalk, clay, and boulder limestone. In the east and south-east the edges of the chalk and limestone stand out prominently. Erosion has exposed the sedimentary rocks and has produced a landscape of alternate scarps (Côte de Meuse, Côte Moselle) and vales (Dry and Wet Champagne).

Paris is at the centre of the Île de France, which has a covering of **limon**, a wind-blown soil deposited here after the Ice Age. Limon soils are fine-grained, rich in minerals, and level. Champagne Pouilleuse (Dry Champagne) is named after the permeable nature of the chalk. East of this again is an outcrop of clay, once an area of marsh, shallow lakes, and damp soils, called Champagne Humide (Wet Champagne). There has been much reclamation, and some small lakes have survived in the area.

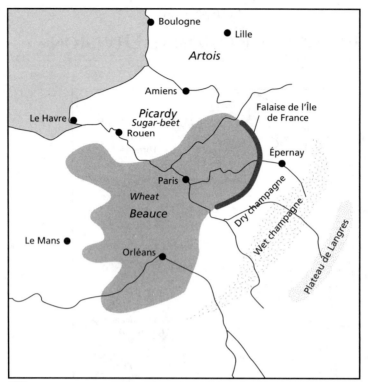

▲ Fig. 7.14 The Paris Basin

The Paris Basin is drained by the Seine and its many tributaries (e.g. Oise, Marne, Aube, and Yonne).

■ Climate: Two Types

The Paris Basin incorporates two types of climate.

1. Along the English Channel (coastal strip) there is a maritime climate. South-west anti-trade winds blowing over the English Channel and the North Atlantic Ocean bring rain throughout the year. These warm, moist winds keep the climate mild in winter and warm in summer.

2. But because the Paris Basin forms part of continental Europe, its summer temperatures are higher than average for its 49° latitude. Inland, towards Paris and the scarplands, a transitional type of climate is experienced. This means that it forms a buffer zone between the maritime climate on the coast and the continental type in central Europe. Thus Paris has average temperatures of 2.5°C in January and 18.6°C in July. Its annual rainfall is 570 mm. Therefore it has a cool, dry winter and hot summers, with a rainfall maximum in spring and summer.

Agriculture

The rolling expanses of loamy soils grow wheat and sugar-beet on the Île de France. In Beauce, large farms and level, open landscape allow intensive mechanised cultivation of cereals: wheat, barley, and sugar-beet. Many farms exceed 80 hectares (200 acres) and have large fields where a high degree of mechanisation is achieved. It is called the granary of France.

Falaise de l'Île de France, a limestone scarp, extends in a great semi-circle from the River Oise to the River Seine. It marks the northern limit of the vines in France. The scarp slopes are sheltered and sunny. This is a region of vineyards famous for champagne, a sparkling white wine. Reims and Épernay are market centres of the wine industry.

Mixed farming is carried on in the Dry Champagne with cereals such as wheat and animal farming. In Wet Champagne dairy farming is practised on the valley floor. Surrounding Paris, market gardening is practised on an intensive scale to supply the conurbation with a large variety of vegetables. The population of Paris is approx. 10 million.

Industry

Paris is a focus of routes – air, water, road, and rail – on a bridging point on the River Seine. It is a centre of an important inland waterway system, and is connected by canal and canalised rivers to the Plain of Alsace, the Rhine, the Loire, and the Saône, and to the sea at Le Havre. Although 160 km from the sea, it is an extremely busy inland port. Products from the Nord and the Paris Basin and imports are stored on the quays upriver from Le Havre and Rouen.

Paris has 20 per cent of the national work force and a highly diversified economy: craft industries, such as perfumes and fashion clothing, vehicle assembly, oil refining, and chemicals. Industry in Paris has been successful because

(a) it is in the centre of a rich agricultural hinterland with processing such as milling and canning

(b) it is near major iron ore deposits in Lorraine and coal deposits in the north-east (Nord), which provide the basis for iron and steel industries and heavy engineering in Paris

(c) it is built on a wide and deep river, the Seine, and has excellent dock facilities for the export of products and the import of raw materials.

Le Havre is an important port at the estuary of the Seine. It has many industries, such as oil refining and chemicals, which occupy a large area on the northern bank of the river. Ship repairs and maintenance are also important in Le Havre. Rouen on the River Seine is an inland port with large oil-refining and chemical industries.

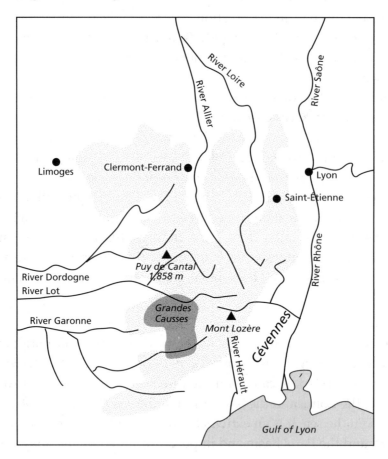

▲ Fig. 7.15 The Massif Central

MASSIF CENTRAL : A PROBLEM REGION NEAR THE CORE

■ Climate

The climate of the Massif Central is varied, partly because of the high relief (Puy de Cantal 1,858 m) and partly because the upland lies between Atlantic, Mediterranean and continental influences and so has a transitional climate.

The high uplands (e.g. Puy de Cantal, Puy de Dôme, and Cévennes) are cold and snow-covered in winter and receive over 2,000 mm of rain annually. Some areas are too damp and bleak for anything but moorland, especially to the north. Here Atlantic depressions bring rain for much of the year at this altitude.

Other areas in the south are too dry and sun-scorched in the summer because of continental influences and the north-east trade winds. **Garrigue** (poor scrub) is common in this southerly region. Rainfall decreases from north to south as one approaches the Mediterranean coast, and drought is common in some areas.

■ Relief and Soils

The Massif Central is an upland area of ancient crystalline rock and is deeply dissected by rivers and streams, such as head streams of the Loire and the Allier, the Dordogne, and the Garonne. Because of the earth movements that formed the Alps, the plateau was tilted so that its general fall of elevation is to the north-west, and so most rivers flow in that direction. Surrounding the Massif Central is limestone rock, which in the south rises to form extensive plateaus called the Grandes Causses. Many of the upland peaks of this region are small volcanic cones of ash and cinders. So the Massif Central has a fragmented and difficult terrain. Lowland areas are limited to river valleys and small river basins. Weathering of the crystalline rock has provided a poor soil cover, and therefore fertile areas are only found in valleys. The Cévennes form the southern crescentic edge of the Massif Central.

■ Agriculture

Throughout the Massif Central farming is difficult. This is due to the thin and/or acidic soil. In the south, for instance, limestone rock allows surface water to pass quickly downwards, limiting available moisture for plant growth. So in places to the south, such as the Causses and the Cévennes regions, Mediterranean and summer drought emerge as a restricting influence on farming, limiting animals to sheep and goats.

The high altitude causes winter temperatures to be very low, and precipitation falls as snow. Cattle have to be housed and stall-fed in winter, which adds to the costs for marginal farmers.

Farm structure increased the difficulty of farming in the Massif Central. Over the centuries farm holdings have been subdivided among farmers' families, and this has produced fragmented and small holdings. Individual holdings comprise scattered fields some distance apart, creating loss of time and inefficiency for the owner, and output is therefore low. Many of the farmers are elderly and conservative, and young people tend to move out of the area towards urban and industrialised zones (e.g. Paris and Marseille).

However, planning agencies have helped to improve the poor structure of agriculture. Rural depopulation and the poor state of agriculture allowed land to be purchased cheaply for redistribution to increase farm size. In addition, the planning agencies helped irrigation projects in the Allier valley and promoted livestock breeding to give a better return to farmers. Today, beef farming forms an important part of farming activity in the northern region.

■ Industry

The Massif Central contains several important industrial centres (e.g. Saint-Étienne, based on its coalfields). Rivers used for centuries to work mill wheels have now been harnessed by modern schemes such as barrages, necessary to hold up water in summer when the river flow reduces. They have been built in the Dordogne, Lot and Truyère valleys to supply power stations linked into the grid system, providing a quarter of French output of hydro-electricity.

Several centres of iron and steel production were based on the coalfields, some of which are now closed. Pig iron from Lorraine is used, and specialised articles often of high-grade steel are produced (e.g. at Saint-Étienne). The armaments industry is based on such steel products. Other industries include the production of chemicals in the coalfields, and tyres of the Michelin works (France's biggest company) in Clermont-Ferrand. In recent years roads and therefore transport links to cities and towns have improved. This will reduce the isolation of the Massif Central and encourage industry to be more competitive within the European market.

THE MIDI: MEDITERRANEAN COASTLANDS

■ Relief and Soils

The coastline of France between the Italian and Spanish frontiers is a region known as the Midi. In the centre a great expanse of sand and mud forms the ever-growing delta of the River Rhône, between whose two main outlets are the lagoons and salt marshes of the Camargue. To the west of the Rhône is the region known as Languedoc. This is a flat region with coastal sand dunes backed by lagoons and salt marshes and bordered to the north by the Cévennes limestone uplands. Soils in this area are generally of limestone and well drained.

To the east of the Rhône is Provence. Here the crystalline uplands of Maures near Toulon and the limestone ridges of the Southern French Alps

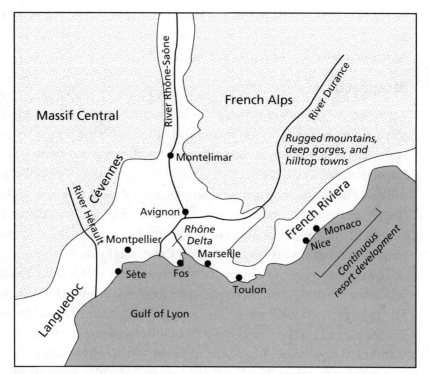

Fig. 7.16 The Midi

reach the coast to form cliffs and headlands with pocket beaches and coves along the Mediterranean in the region known as the French Riviera. In places roadways are perched on cliff edges and run like a contour, with sheer drops to the sea. On a higher level and using tunnels through the Maritime Alps is a motorway system, which helps the free flow of heavy traffic between Italy and France.

The Midi Climate

The Midi experiences a Mediterranean climate. During the winter this coastal region comes under the influence of the south-west anti-trade winds from the Atlantic. Coming from the south, they are warm, and the Atlantic influence increases their moisture content, bringing mild, moist weather at this time of the year. Mean January temperatures at Montpellier are 5°C. For the south they are higher.

In summer when 'the sun moves north' the Mediterranean coast comes under the influence of the north-east trade winds. As they blow from the continent of Europe, they are hot and dry, thus providing constant high pressure and permanent sunshine for up to twelve hours a day during June, July, and August. In the Provence and Languedoc regions, summer drought is made worse by the widespread distribution of limestone and gravel, producing the dry scrub known as *garrigue*. Summer temperatures are 23°C in July. Perpignan has experienced the highest shade temperatures ever recorded in France: 42°C.

■ Agriculture

Agriculture consists of typical Mediterranean crops: wheat, vine, and olive, using terraces of better soil and alluvial plains where irrigation water is available. Much agriculture is small-scale but varied. Some farmers may have a piece of irrigated land growing vegetables near a village. Further up the terraced slopes are patches of wheat and maize, then fruit trees (e.g. peaches, succeeded by vines and, on the upper slopes, groves of olives and sweet chestnut). Large-scale reclamation and irrigation schemes are completed on the coastal plain.

The eastern part of Languedoc is irrigated by water from the Rhône, while the western area receives water from the Aude, Hérault, and Orb. The area planted with vines has been greatly reduced, and the emphasis is now placed on the production of quality wine rather than the traditional low-value, high-output *vin ordinaire*. High-value crops such as *primeurs* (early vegetables) and fruit crops have also been produced. Thus specialisation and intensive irrigated farming have replaced a more subsistence economy.

In Provence the mild winters and springs encourage the growth of early vegetables, flowers, and fruit, both for rapid transport northwards by rail to Paris and to supply local towns and resorts. Recently growers have organised into co-operatives for processing and marketing. This part of the south is protected from the Mistral by the east-west ridges, which run parallel to the coastline.

INDUSTRY

■ Tourism

Sun, sea and sand are synonymous with southern France. The hot, dry summers attract millions of tourists to France each year. Beaches such as Saint-Tropez and cities such as Nice and Cannes and nearby Monte Carlo are famous tourist centres. Summer tourist migration to the Midi causes huge population increases, creating an inflow of money, and so tourism becomes a vital export industry and earner of foreign currency.

■ Industry

East of the Rhône is Marseille, the third-largest city in France and the largest port. As a port it has three major physical advantages:

1. It is a port city sited on a coastal plain around a sheltered bay.
2. It is at the southern outlet of the Rhône-Saône corridor, with canal links to the Rhine, Switzerland, and the Danube.
3. The opening of the Suez Canal in 1869 increased Mediterranean trade, so the port became important for France's colonies.

Recently deep-water berths and industrial sites developed around the Étang de Bère and a new port and industrial complex have been developed at Fos, accommodating bulk tankers of over 250,000 tonnes. Industries here include iron, steel, petrochemicals, and vehicle assembly. In 1960 Marseille was designated a growth centre to counterbalance Paris. Oil accounts for 80 per cent of port transport at Fos.

ENVIRONMENTAL PROBLEMS IN WESTERN EUROPE: AIR, LAND, AND WATER

1. GREENHOUSE EFFECT – AIR

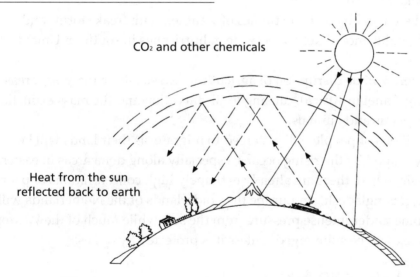

CO$_2$ and other chemicals

Heat from the sun reflected back to earth

▲ Fig. 7.17 The greenhouse effect

'Greenhouse gases' allow the sun's ultraviolet light to pass through our atmosphere to heat the earth's surface. These gases in their natural state trap the radiant heat that is reflected from the earth's surface. Without these gases we could not survive, as the earth would be a lot colder – on average –18°C. However, because of a rapid rise in population, there is an increasing and potentially catastrophic build-up of greenhouse gases. These extra amounts of gases are trapping too much heat and are causing a gradual rise in global temperatures.

■ Main Causes of Greenhouse Gases

1. The combustion of fossil fuels – turf, oil, coal, and gas – for heating, transport, industry and power is releasing huge amounts of carbon dioxide and nitrous oxides into the atmosphere.
2. A greatly increased use of fertiliser, huge herds of cattle and large areas of rice paddy are releasing extra methane gas.
3. The use of chlorofluorocarbons (CFCs) in aerosols, fridges, foams and solvents causes about 14 per cent of global warming.
4. Deforestation (e.g. Amazon rain-forest) and the burning of trees also give off greenhouse gases, while the absence of trees reduces the earth's ability to soak up these gases.

■ Effects of Greenhouse Gases

1. If trends continue, predictions indicate that sea levels will rise by 0.2–1.4 m through thermal expansion and the melting of ice at the polar ice-caps.
2. There will be greater extremes of weather, with freak storms and droughts more likely to occur (e.g. hurricanes in southern United States).
3. There will be disruption of agriculture, especially in marginal areas (e.g. Sahel in Africa), causing local starvation and the mass extinction of plants and animals.
4. Millions of people will be forced to migrate, as their lands will be swamped by the rising oceans, especially along delta areas in eastern Asia, where there are already extremely high concentrations of people (e.g. Bangladesh). In Europe the polderlands of the Netherlands will come under intense pressure from the sea, while much of the Wexford coast will be submerged, unless it is protected by dykes.

2. ACID RAIN – LAND AND AIR

■ Main Causes of Acid Rain

Acid precipitation (acid rain) is the term used to describe polluted rainfall. When water vapour from the oceans and the land rises into the atmosphere it is non-acid (neutral in reaction). In the atmosphere it mixes with naturally occurring carbon dioxide and sulphur and forms very weak acids, such as carbonic acid. However, in the industrialised countries of western Europe, such as Britain and Germany, the heavy combustion of fossil fuels (oil and coal) results in the emission of sulphur

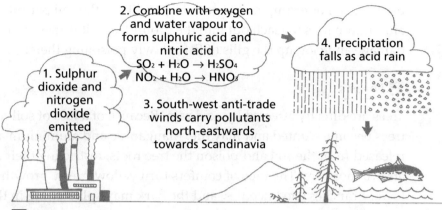

1. Sulphur dioxide and nitrogen dioxide emitted

2. Combine with oxygen and water vapour to form sulphuric acid and nitric acid
$$SO_2 + H_2O \rightarrow H_2SO_4$$
$$NO_2 + H_2O \rightarrow HNO_3$$

3. South-west anti-trade winds carry pollutants north-eastwards towards Scandinavia

4. Precipitation falls as acid rain

▲ Fig. 7.18 Acid rain

dioxide and nitrogen oxide into the atmosphere. These gases combine with water vapour in the atmosphere and form sulphuric acid and nitric acid. This artificial acidification of the cloud water results in an increase in the acidity of the rainfall.

Acid rain has a number of negative effects on the environment.

■ Effects of Acid Rain

1 The Soil

Acid rain penetrates the soil, and essential minerals, such as calcium and potassium, are leached out of the soil at a rapid rate. Soil productivity declines. Regions with acid soils overlying granite rocks (such as Scandinavia) or heavily weathered sandy soils are more easily affected. In addition, such areas have a covering of coniferous trees, whose needles increase acidity. Thus Scandinavia suffers from a problem that it never created, because the prevailing south-west winds of western Europe blow towards the region.

2 Water Pollution

Acid rain, surface run-off and ground-water flow into rivers and lakes. In Scandinavia, much precipitation falls as acid snow. This accumulates during the winter on the mountains and lowlands of Norway, Sweden, and Finland. In spring, melting snows release huge volumes of acid water to river courses. This concentration of acid water kills fish spawn and aquatic life. As a result, most of Finland's lakes are dead, with no aquatic life whatsoever.

Acid water and acid rain release dangerous metals into the water, which can build up in lake water to levels that are toxic to fish and other organisms. For example, this growing acidity of the soil permits aluminium ions to leach out into the ground, and it is these ions that damage and clog up the gills of fish, slowly poisoning them.

3 Forests

Trees are directly affected by acid rain. Because of a loss of soil nutrients, trees become stunted and may die. Manganese and aluminium are released from the soil and poison the tree roots, restricting their ability to absorb moisture. The tops of conifers turn yellow-green, growth stops, the lower branches shed needles, and the bark may split, letting in the cold winds in winter and the bark beetle in summer. Over half of the trees in the Black Forest in Germany are affected.

4 Buildings

Ancient monuments, such as the Celtic high crosses of Ireland, have suffered severely in recent decades from acid rain. As a result, many have been moved indoors to museums while replicas have replaced the originals in the monastic graveyards.

Buildings made of limestone, such as the Parthenon in Greece, are particularly vulnerable to acid rain erosion. The limestone is easily dissolved even by mild acids, such as carbonic acid. Thus the sulphuric and nitric acids of acid rain have a particularly damaging effect.

REDUCING ACID RAIN AND THE GREENHOUSE EFFECT

■ Control of Gas Emissions from Burning Fossil Fuels

There are now a number of techniques available for reducing emissions of sulphur dioxide and oxides of nitrogen.

1. Before the fuel is burnt, a decision can be taken to change from using a fuel with a high sulphur content to one that contains less sulphur. The sulphur content of coal, for example, can vary from as much as 5 per cent to as little as 0.5 per cent. Natural gas contains almost no sulphur, and North Sea oil is also a low-sulphur fuel. Fuels may be blended to produce a medium-sulphur fuel from a mix of high and low-sulphur fuels. The sulphur can also be removed from the fuel before it is burnt, although coal washing offers only very limited scope for the removal of sulphur before combustion.
2. It is possible to reduce the eventual emissions of sulphur dioxide by special methods of burning. Coal can be mixed with finely ground limestone and burnt in suspension in a process called **fluidised-bed**

combustion. Limestone finely ground can also be injected into a special burner that helps to **neutralise** (make safe) the sulphur in the fuel.

3. After burning, gases can be **scrubbed** or **desulphurised** by mixing a chemical absorbent, such as lime or limestone, with the chimney gas to remove the sulphur dioxide. This method is widely used in Japan, the United States, and Germany.

4. For reducing oxides of nitrogen (NO_x) there are developments such as low-NO_x burners and catalytic conversion with ammonia. In the longer term, pressurised fluidised-bed combustors and fuel gasification offer the prospect of simultaneous reduction of both sulphur and nitrogen oxides within the combustion process, in combination with improvements in fuel efficiency.

5. Governments must establish strict controls on the emission of dangerous gases and severe penalties for abuses of set limits. Governments must be willing to introduce such changes even though public expense may be involved, which may be politically damaging.

▼ Fig. 7.19 A change of atmosphere in the United States – where the burdens fall

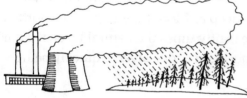

Acid rain
Sulphur dioxide emissions will be cut in half by 2000, to 10 million tonnes annually, and nitrogen oxides reduced by 33 per cent, to 4 million tonnes annually, starting in 1992. Coal-burning utilities will have to spend $3,000 million a year to burn low-sulphur fuel or install scrubbers.

Car exhaust
Passenger cars will have to emit 60 per cent less nitrogen oxide and 40 per cent less hydrocarbon waste by 2003, and pollution control equipment must last ten years. Cleaner-burning petrol will be required in the most polluted cities, and 1 million vehicles using cleaner fuel or equipped with special emission-reducing exhaust pipes must be available in California by 2000.

Petrol and car companies will have to develop new products. Consumers will pay 1–1.5p per litre more for petrol by 2000, and by 2003 an average of £400 more for a new car.

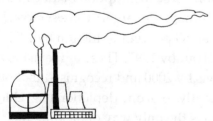

Toxic emissions
By 2003 there must be a 90 per cent reduction in the output of 189 toxic and cancer-causing chemicals.

Most large manufacturers and public services and many small businesses will have to invest heavily in new pollution control equipment, and this will raise the retail price on things as diverse as bread and dry cleaning.

Ozone depletion
Chlorofluorocarbons (CFCs) and most other ozone-destroying chemicals will be phased out by 2000. Refrigerator and air-conditioner manufacturers , users of industrial solvents and makers of foam insulation – all heavily dependent on the regulated chemicals – will have to pay more for substitutes. Ultimately, costs will be passed on to the consumer.

3. OZONE DEPLETION – AIR

■ Causes of Ozone Depletion

Ozone is most dense in the stratosphere at a level of 20–25 km above the earth. But it is scattered very thinly. This ozone layer absorbs most of the harmful ultraviolet rays of the sun and thus prevents serious damage to life on earth. Ozone is a form of oxygen, O_3, that has three atoms instead of the normal two in each molecule. At ground level ozone can be dangerous to humans, but high up in the atmosphere the maintenance of a thin layer of ozone is essential for human, animal and plant life.

In modern times, human activity has introduced chemicals that destroy this ozone layer. The most destructive chemicals contain chlorine (e.g. CFCs) and bromine (e.g. halons). Chlorine and bromine steal oxygen atoms from the ozone molecule and change it into ordinary oxygen. Each chlorine and bromine atom can do this many thousands of times.

Chlorofluorocarbons (CFCs) were developed as cooling agents for fridges and air-conditioning systems. Since the 1950s they have been used as propellants in aerosol cans. They are also used to blow foam for furniture, packaging, and insulation, and to clean delicate computer circuits. Today there is a hole in the ozone layer above Antarctica; it is as large as the United States and as deep as Mount Everest. In the northern hemisphere over the Arctic there is fifty times the natural level of chlorine monoxide. This means that the northern ozone layer is quickly being destroyed.

■ Solutions

In 1985 a convention was concluded under the supervision of the United Nations Environment Programme (UNEP). This led to a meeting at which countries agreed that the production and consumption of all CFCs should be phased out by the year 2000. Intermediate targets were set to achieve a 50 per cent reduction by 1995 and an 85 per cent reduction by 1997. The EU countries intend to phase CFCs out by 1997. These agreements also supported the phasing out of halons by 2000 and recognised that other substances that contribute significantly to ozone depletion (e.g. chlorine) should be controlled. Global action is the only way of tackling the depletion of the ozone layer.

4. SMOG – AIR

■ Causes of Smog

Smog is a combination of smoke and fog. The word accurately describes that canopy of air pollution that hangs over a densely built-up area in winter under certain atmospheric conditions. This is when there is an **air inversion**, with cold, still air near ground level trapped by warmer air above. And because there is no wind to blow it away, the smoke belching out of chimneys and car exhausts builds up in the air.

Smoke is the most visible pollutant; but it may conceal a range of dangerous chemicals, such as sulphur dioxide and nitrous oxides as well as a variety of gases from industrial plants. Above a certain level of concentration, smog causes a deterioration in health, especially among those already suffering from respiratory complaints, such as asthma or bronchitis. Old people, young children and those who already have lung disease are the most vulnerable.

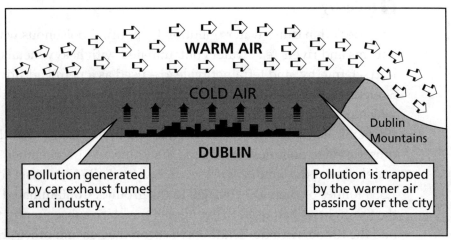

▲ Fig. 7.20 Smog in Dublin

5. WATER POLLUTION

■ Main Causes of Water Pollution

1 Farming

Polluting wastes can arise from a range of farm wastes, including livestock manure, silage effluents, dairy waste, and vegetable washing water, and may have the following consequences:

1. When organic matter (e.g. farm wastes and some pesticides) enters a stream, river, or lake, particularly the soluble constituents, it can lead to **deoxygenation** of water as organic compounds are broken down by

oxygen-using micro-organisms. This can result in the death of fish and aquatic plants, the growth of slime-producing micro-organisms, the blackening of plants, and unpleasant smells.

2. **Eutrophication** of water with plant nutrients (fertilisers), particularly nitrogen and phosphorus, washed from the soil by rain, is an important factor contributing to the excessive growth of plants and algae in still or slow-moving waters. They choke the river, and when they die the material reduces the oxygen in the water still further and the animal life dies. Most pollution of surface waters by farm wastes is caused by the discharge of effluents from around yards and buildings.

3. The addition of nitrates and/or phosphates (eutrophication) to the sea may cause excessive blooms of phytoplankton, which lower the depth to which sunlight can penetrate. Photosynthesis is prevented and the oxygen may be used up, so that fish die and only anaerobic bacteria and a few other species can survive.

2 Industry

Factories often cause water pollution by pouring poisonous wastes into streams and rivers (e.g. water contaminated with heavy metals, organic lead – tetraethyl and tetramethyl lead – used as a petrol additive, etc.). Sometimes these wastes turn the river into a smelly, poisonous drain in which nothing can live.

Chemical accidents at the Ciba-Geigy plant in Basel, Switzerland, have caused severe pollution damage to the Rhine. On 1 November 1986 a warehouse at the Sandoz works in Schweizerhalle near Basel containing 1,350 tonnes of chemicals burned to the ground. Contaminated water that the fire-fighters had used to extinguish the blaze subsequently flowed into the Rhine, with devastating effects on the fish and other organisms in the river.

Unforeseen pollution can occur. For instance, harmful chemicals are sometimes dumped in the wrong place; when rain falls, they are washed into the soil and eventually into a river or watercourse. Motorists illegally empty dirty oil from their cars into surface drains; oil tanker lorries spill oil. A factory accident can allow harmful substances to escape into the drains or watercourses.

3 Urban Sewage

Raw sewage is composed of industrial, household, agricultural and hospital waste. Particularly nasty components include **pathogens** (agents capable of producing disease), parasites, detergents, disinfectants, pesticides, heavy metals, and toxic metals. Sewage contains bacterial and viral pathogens. These cause mild infections resulting in vomiting, diarrhoea, headaches, fever, and skin infections; other, more serious diseases include hepatitis, typhoid fever, and polio, to which unvaccinated swimmers, especially young children, are most at risk.

Fishing and aquaculture are especially at risk through the accumulation of toxins and pathogens by many commercial fish and shellfish (e.g. oysters and mussels). This renders them unfit for human consumption. Non-degradable wastes can ruin the scenic value of an area and are a threat to the tourist industry.

Many of our cities and towns emit millions of litres of untreated and semi-treated sewage into waterways. Cities continue to grow and so does their sewage discharge. Municipal sewage sludge dumped off Howth Head has more than doubled since 1980. In addition, all city sewage effluent contains toxic heavy metals and chemicals from industrial wastes. These make it impossible to use sewage as agricultural fertiliser. Sewage solids are often deposited on beaches along our coast. For example, the treatment plant at Ringsend in Dublin has difficulty in coping with sewage from an expanding capital city. In 1990 vast quantities of untreated sewage were pumped untreated into Dublin Bay. Much of this was deposited at Dollymount Strand, causing a serious health risk in the area. Deposits such as these become a health hazard when used syringes, condoms and other artefacts are associated with the deposits. In Germany many cities, such as Cologne, Bonn, Koblenz, and Düsseldorf, are on the Rhine. Many of these cities emit raw sewage into the river, and thus justify the river's title, 'the Sewer of Europe'.

POLLUTION IN THE MEDITERRANEAN SEA

■ Causes of Pollution in the Mediterranean

The Mediterranean Sea is virtually enclosed and tideless. The enclosed nature of the sea means that it takes up to a hundred years for its waters to turn over naturally. So the Mediterranean is not cleansed naturally by the tide, and pollutants are trapped within the basin. Evaporation is also high, and this creates an increased concentration of pollutants in the sea. The main causes of pollution are as follows:

1. An estimated 350 million people live in the eighteen countries that border the Mediterranean, and 90 per cent of the sewage from this population enters the sea untreated. In addition, 100 million people

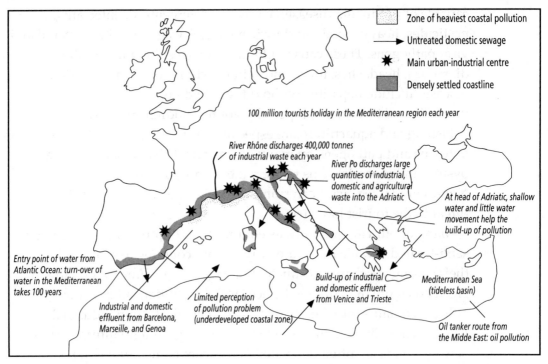

Fig. 7.21 Pollution and the Mediterranean Basin

visit the area during the summer months, and this figure is likely to increase in the future.

2. Industrialisation, especially in the north-western areas (i.e. southern France near Marseille and northern Italy near Genoa and Venice), has seen the construction of oil refineries, coking plants, steel works, and chemical plants, all of which tend to dump their wastes back into the sea. The Rhône, Po and Ebro discharge waste from inland industrial areas into the Mediterranean.

3. In 1980, 500,000 tonnes of oil found its way (mostly through accidents) into the Mediterranean Sea; 470,000 tonnes of that was the result of collisions at sea or direct spillage. This occurs because the Mediterranean is on the major tanker route from the Middle East and North Africa to Europe. In the past, lack of co-operation, especially between the richer countries of Europe and the poorer countries of North Africa, led to a disregard of precautions and consequent pollution of the basin.

4. Less fresh water enters the Mediterranean Sea as rivers become polluted. Also, rivers such as the Nile are dammed to store water for irrigation instead of, as previously, being allowed to flow into the sea.

■ A Solution: the 'Blue Plan'

In 1972 the UN environmental organisation, UNEP, met to discuss the problems of the Mediterranean. Four years later the eighteen countries that met produced the 'Blue Plan', and an agreement was signed in 1979. The purpose of the plan is to improve the environment of the Mediterranean Sea.

They agreed to end chemical dumping and to plan united action to prevent possible oil spillages. New sewage treatment plants were to be constructed for urban areas along the coast and on inland rivers. Pollution problems were to be reported and remedial action taken by governments (and responsible parties) to remedy the effects.

However, some difficulties have been encountered. Estimates suggest that a minimum of £2,500 million is needed just to solve the untreated sewage problem. The poorer countries cannot finance such schemes. Despite the ban on chemical dumping, a 'grey list' has been drawn up of chemicals that a country can dump provided it obtains a special permit. The practical difficulties of co-operation between countries in western Europe, eastern Europe, the Middle East and North Africa are huge. The richer countries, which have largely been responsible for the pollution, now wish to clean up their beaches as tourism increases. The poorer countries, which need to become more industrialised and create jobs, see the protection of the environment as secondary to the creation of new industries.

8

LOCATION GEOGRAPHY
AND EXAMINATION PAPERS

■ **Main Mountain Areas of the World**

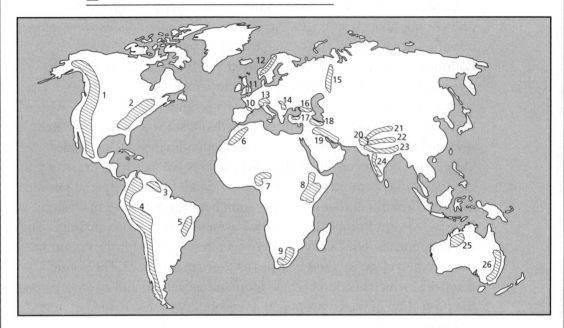

Use the spaces to name the mountain areas:

1.	2.	3.	4.
5.	6.	7.	8.
9.	10.	11.	12.
13.	14.	15.	16.
17.	18.	19.	20.
21.	22.	23.	24.
25.	26.		

■ Main Rivers of the World

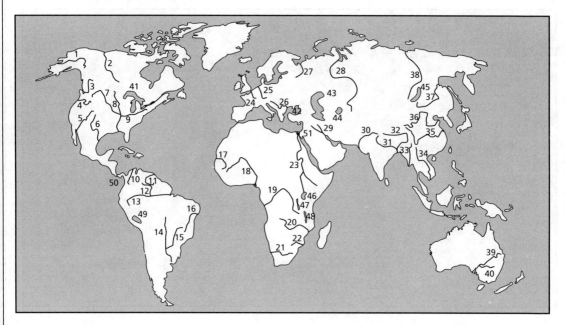

Use the spaces to name the following:
Rivers (1–40)
Inland seas and lakes (41–49)
Canals (50–51)

1.	2.	3.	4.
5.	6.	7.	8.
9.	10.	11.	12.
13.	14.	15.	16.
17.	18.	19.	20.
21.	22.	23.	24.
25.	26.	27.	28.
29.	30.	31.	32.
33.	34.	35.	36.
37.	38.	39.	40.
41.	42.	43.	44.
45.	46.	47.	48.
49.	50.	51.	

■ Main Sea Areas of the World

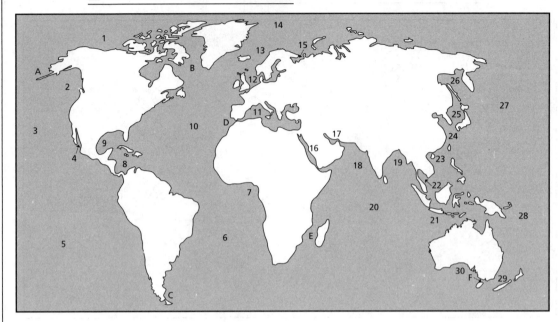

Use the spaces to name the following:
Sea areas (1–31)
Straits (A–F)

1.	2.	3.	4.
5.	6.	7.	8.
9.	10.	11.	12.
13.	14.	15.	16.
17.	18.	19.	20.
21.	22.	23.	24.
25.	26.	27.	28.
29.	30.	31.	
A.	B.	C.	D.
E.	F.		

■ Main Islands and Island Groups of the World

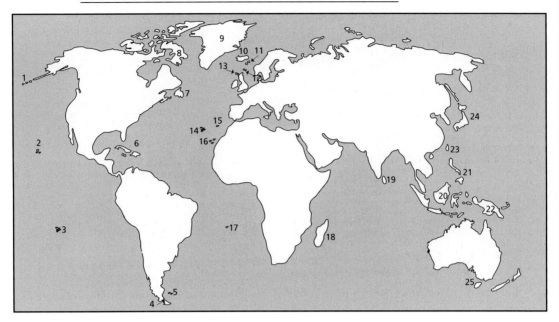

Use the spaces to name the islands and island groups:

1.	2.	3.	4.
5.	6.	7.	8.
9.	10.	11.	12.
13.	14.	15.	16.
17.	18.	19.	20.
21.	22.	23.	24.
25.			

■ Main Cities of the World

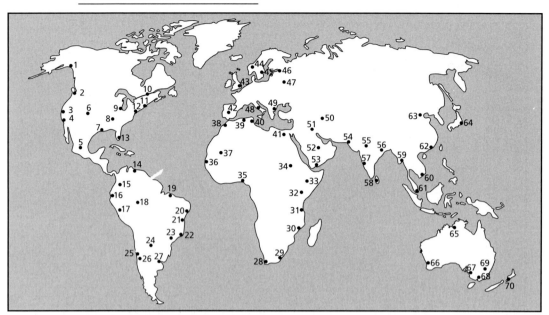

Use the spaces to name the cities:

1.	2.	3.	4.
5.	6.	7.	8.
9.	10.	11.	12.
13.	14.	15.	16.
17.	18.	19.	20.
21.	22.	23.	24.
25.	26.	27.	28.
29.	30.	31.	32.
33.	34.	35.	36.
37.	38.	39.	40.
41.	42.	43.	44.
45.	46.	47.	48.
49.	50.	51.	52.
53.	54.	55.	56.
57.	58.	59.	60.
61.	62.	63.	64.
65.	66.	67.	68.
69.	70.		

■ Main Deserts and Natural Regions of the World

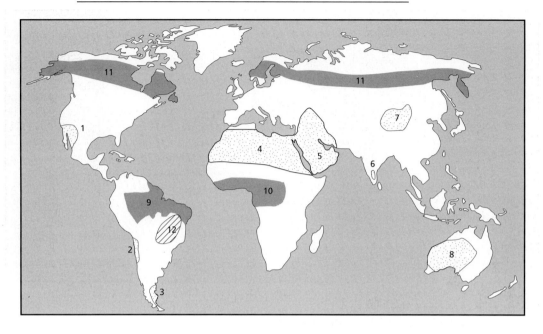

Use the spaces to name the following:

Deserts (1–8)

Natural regions (9–12)

1.	2.	3.	4.
5.	6.	7.	8.
9.	10.	11.	12.

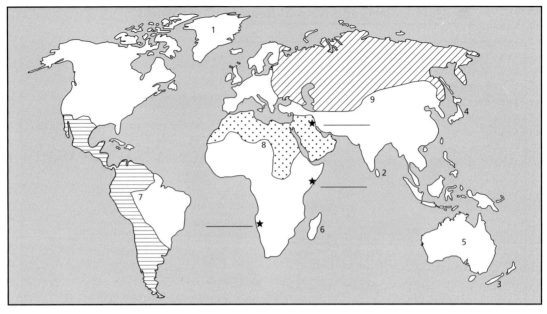

1993

■ **Question 6**

Examine the map of the world that accompanies this question and answer the following questions:

(i) Identify, in the spaces provided, the features numbered as follows: countries 1–4; continent 5; island 6. [12 marks]

(ii) In the remaining spaces, identify which of the following is the main language spoken in areas 7, 8 and 9: Arabic, Russian, Spanish. [9 marks]

(iii) The three regions marked with stars on the map have all suffered serious conflict in recent times. Using the spaces provided, name these regions. [9 marks]

(iv) Select *two* of the regions, and for *each* one you choose, describe and explain the causes of the conflict. [50 marks]

1.	2.	3.
4.	5.	6.
7.	8.	9.

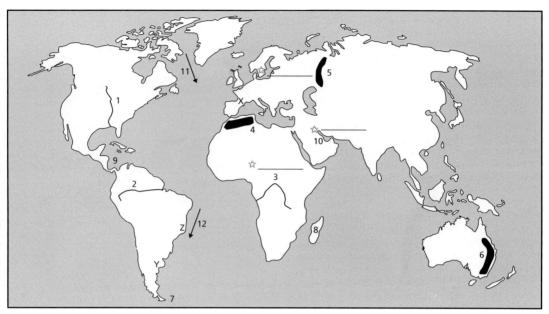

1992

■ **Question 6**

Examine the world map that accompanies this question and answer the following:

(i) Name, in the spaces provided, the features numbered as follows: rivers 1, 2, 3; mountains 4, 5, 6; islands 7, 8; sea areas 9, 10; ocean currents 11, 12. [24 marks]

(ii) Study the three areas marked X, Y and Z on the map. In the spaces provided, say which of the following descriptions best applies to *each* of these three areas:

    A: An area where cereals are produced on a large scale.

    B: An area where the vine is grown extensively.

    C: An area where coffee is produced. [12 marks]

(iii) Study the three areas marked with a star on the map. Each of these areas has recently suffered from particular environmental problems. In the space provided beside *each* star, name the particular problem involved. [12 marks]

(iv) Select *one* of the areas in part (iii) of this question and explain the causes of its particular environmental problems. [32 marks]

1.	2.	3.	4.
5.	6.	7.	8.
9.	10.	11.	12.
X.	Y.	Z.	

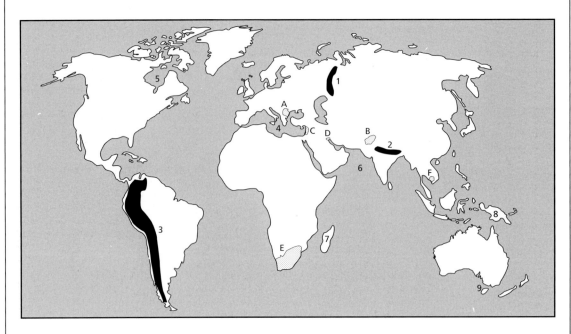

1991

■ Question 6

Examine the world map that accompanies this question and answer the following:

(i) Identify, in the spaces provided, the features numbered as follows: mountains 1, 2, 3; sea areas 4, 5, 6; islands 7, 8, 9.   [18 marks]

(ii) The following areas of the world have all experienced political conflict in recent times: Kuwait, South Africa, Israel, Kampuchea, Afghanistan, Romania. In the spaces A, B, C, D, E, and F, associate *each* of these areas with the appropriate letter used to identify it on the map.   [18 marks]

(iii) Select *two* of these areas, and for *each* one explain some of the main causes of its political conflict.   [44 marks]

1.	2.	3.	4.
5.	6.	7.	8.
9.	A.	B.	C.
D.	E.	F.	

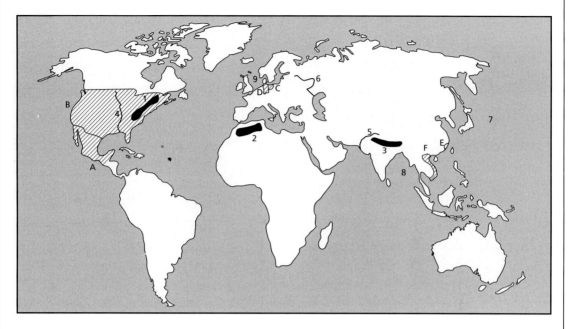

1990

■ Question 6

Examine the world map that accompanies this paper and answer the questions that follow:

(i) Name, in the spaces provided, the features numbered as follows: mountain areas 1, 2, 3; rivers 4, 5, 6; sea areas 7, 8, 9. [18 marks]

(ii) The following states are shown on the map, marked with the letters A, B, C, D, E, and F: West Germany, Viet Nam, United States, Hong Kong, Mexico, East Germany. Associate the states with the correct letters, using the spaces provided. [18 marks]

(iii) The states identified in (ii) above can be grouped in pairs (i.e. A and B; C and D; E and F) in order to study international migration problems in recent times. Select any *two* of the pairs. For *each* pair you choose, explain some of the principal causes of their migration problem. [44 marks]

1.	2.	3.	4.
5.	6.	7.	8.
9.	A.	B.	C.
D.	E.	F.	

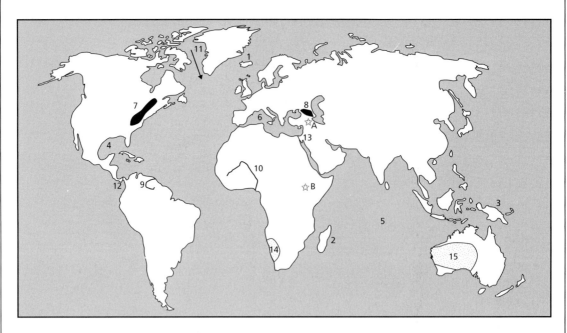

1989

■ Question 6

Examine the world map that accompanies this question, and answer the following:

(i)   Identify, in the spaces provided, the features numbered as follows: islands 1, 2, 3; sea areas, 4, 5, 6; mountains 7, 8; rivers 9, 10; ocean current 11; canals 12, 13; hot deserts 14, 15.   [30 marks]

(ii) The areas marked A and B on the map have each experienced serious emergencies in recent times, caused by natural environmental hazards. Identify the areas and the hazards in the correct order in the spaces provided.   [12 marks]

(iii) Select *one* of the areas mentioned in part (ii) above and explain briefly why the hazard occurred there and how the international community responded to the situation.   [38 marks]

1.	2.	3.	4.
5.	6.	7.	8.
9.	10.	11.	12.
13.	14.	15.	
A area		A hazard	
B area		B hazard	

EXAMINATION PAPERS

LEAVING CERTIFICATE EXAMINATION, 2000

GEOGRAPHY – ORDINARY LEVEL

MONDAY, 12 JUNE – AFTERNOON, 2.00 to 5.20

INSTRUCTIONS TO CANDIDATES

Question 1 concerns the Ordnance Survey map and is compulsory.

The other questions, from 2 to 18, are laid out in **FOUR** sections. These are Physical Geography, Social Geography, Economic Geography, Regional and World Geography.

Five questions must be answered but **not more than two questions** may be answered from any one section. Candidates must attempt:

● Question 1;

● One Regional and World Geography question [from Questions 14–18];

● Three other questions from 2–18;

The choice of questions from 2 to 18 is subject to the restriction, specified above, that **not more than two questions** may be answered from any one section.

PLEASE MAKE SURE YOU HAVE AN ORDNANCE SURVEY MAP AND AN AERIAL PHOTOGRAPH BEFORE ATTEMPTING THIS PAPER.

THIS QUESTION <u>MUST</u> BE ANSWERED

<u>QUESTION 1.</u>   <u>ORDNANCE SURVEY</u>

(i) Draw a sketch map of the area covered by the Ordnance Survey Map supplied with this paper.
Mark on and identify:
● The Coastline
● A Nature Reserve
● A Railway Line
● A **named** Ancient Monument
● An area of Mixed Woodland
● A **named** River   **(30 Marks)**
[Note: The sketch map should <u>not</u> be a tracing.]

(ii) Drumcliff and Sligo Town are attractive places for tourists to visit.
Give **TWO** pieces of evidence that these settlements attract tourists. You must refer to **both** settlements in your answer. **(30 Marks)**

(iii) Using map evidence only, describe **ONE** way in which you know that coastal deposition is evident. **(20 Marks)**

PHYSICAL GEOGRAPHY

Questions 2–5

<u>QUESTION 2.</u>   <u>RIVERS</u>

Delta, Meander, Ox-Bow lake, Flood Plain and V-Shaped Valley

(i) Select <u>**THREE**</u> of the above River Features and, with the aid of a diagram, explain how they were formed. **(60 marks)**

(ii) 'Rivers can have both advantages and disadvantages to people.'

Explain one advantage <u>**AND**</u> one disadvantage to people. **(20 marks)**

<u>QUESTION 3.</u>   <u>THE SEA</u>

(i) Name <u>**THREE**</u> features formed by Coastal erosion <u>or</u> deposition. Explain, with the aid of a diagram, how <u>**EACH**</u> feature was formed. **(60 marks)**

(ii) Select any <u>**ONE**</u> feature from part (i) above and show how it could be of economic benefit to people. **(20 marks)**

<u>QUESTION 4.</u>   <u>KARST LANDSCAPE</u>

Stalactites, Limestone Pavements, Swallow Holes and Pillars.

(i) State which of the above are <u>overground features</u> and which are <u>underground features</u>. **(20 marks)**

(ii) Select any <u>**THREE**</u> of the features from part (i) above and for <u>**EACH**</u> one you select:-
describe and explain, with the aid of a diagram, how it is formed. **(60 marks)**

QUESTION 5.   THE PHYSICAL WORLD

Explain **TWO** of the following statements in some detail:

(i)   Irish weather is influenced by many factors.   **(40 marks)**

(ii)   Glacial action has resulted in distinctive landscape features in Ireland.

(40 marks)

(iii) Major earthquakes are associated with certain regions of the world.   **(40 marks)**

(iv) The Greenhouse Effect will have a great impact on the environment in the future.   **(40 marks)**

SOCIAL GEOGRAPHY

Questions 6–9

QUESTION 6.   AERIAL PHOTOGRAPH

NOTE: This is an oblique photograph (taken at an angle).
         Refer to left foreground, right background etc. when locating features.

(i)   Draw a sketch map (not a tracing) of the area covered by the aerial photograph of Sligo supplied with this paper.

   Mark on and identify:
   • Two connecting streets
   • A housing area
   • A building of historic interest
   • An off-street car park
   • A bridge   **(30 marks)**

(ii)   As a geography student you have been asked to suggest a suitable site for a Tourist Office on the area covered by the Photograph.

   Choose a location for the Tourist Office and give **THREE** reasons for your choice.   **(30 marks)**

(iii) Suggest **TWO** locations on the Photograph where there are likely to be traffic problems at peak times.

   Explain your choice in each case.   **(20 marks)**

QUESTION 7.   DEVELOPMENT AID

(i)   'The Government has in recent years increased the Irish Aid budget.'

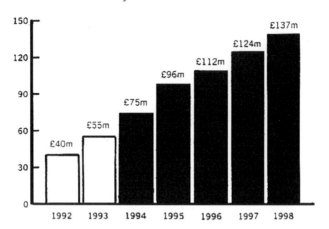

Examine the data in the chart above on the Irish Aid Budget and explain how the Aid Budget has increased.   **(20 marks)**

(ii) Below are some of the types of aid given to the Developing World.

- Bilateral Aid
- Multilateral Aid
- Emergency Aid
- Voluntary Aid

Describe and explain what is meant by any **TWO** of the above types of aid.

(60 marks)

QUESTION 8.   POPULATION STUDIES

(i)   'Push and pull factors are responsible for most of the world's population being concentrated in large cities.'

Explain what is meant by the terms Push and Pull factors. In your answer refer to examples you have studied.   **(60 marks)**

(ii) 'Forced Migration is a problem that has affected Europe in recent times.'

Explain any **TWO** problems caused by this type of Migration.   **(20 marks)**

QUESTION 9.   SOCIAL GEOGRAPHY ISSUES

Explain **TWO** of the following statements in some detail:

(i)   Birth rates and Death rates influence population change.   **(40 marks)**

(ii) Many parts of rural Ireland have had problems caused by de-population.

(40 marks)

(iii) One of the major problems facing Irish Towns and Cities is traffic.   **(40 marks)**

(iv) The role of women in society is changing rapidly.   **(40 marks)**

ECONOMIC GEOGRAPHY

Questions 10–13

QUESTION 10.   FORESTRY

(i)   'Preserving the Rain Forest will be one of the great challenges of the new millennium.'

Describe any **ONE** reason why the area of Rain Forest is declining and any **ONE** reason why Rain Forests should be preserved.   **(40 marks)**

(ii)   Explain **TWO** advantages that forestry brings to the Irish Economy.   **(40 marks)**

QUESTION 11.   ENERGY

(i)   Describe and explain **TWO** renewable sources of energy.   **(40 marks)**

(ii)   Explain **ONE** advantage and **ONE** disadvantage of coal as a source of energy.   **(40 marks)**

QUESTION 12.   ECONOMIC GEOGRAPHY ISSUES

Explain **TWO** of the following statements in some detail:

(i)   Farming can have both positive and negative effects on the environment.   **(40 marks)**

(ii)   Markets are an important influence on the location of manufacturing industries.   **(40 marks)**

(iii)   Fish farming brings both advantages and disadvantages to coastal communities.   **(40 marks)**

(iv)   Pollution of the environment is a major concern in the world today.   **(40 marks)**

QUESTION 13.   FIELDWORK

With reference to **ANY** fieldwork exercise that you have completed in Geography:

(i)   State the **title** and **aims** of the exercise.   **(8 marks)**

(ii)   Describe how **you prepared** for the exercise.   **(16 marks)**

(iii)   Describe the **methods you used to gather** the information.   **(24 marks)**

(iv)   Describe the **results** of the fieldwork.   **(12 marks)**

(v)   Explain the **methods you used to present** your results.   **(12 marks)**

(vi)   Explain **ONE** problem you encountered during the fieldwork exercise. **(8 marks)**

REGIONAL AND WORLD GEOGRAPHY

Questions 14–18

QUESTION 14.   TOURISM

Tourist regions and areas of outstanding beauty

(i) Describe and explain **TWO** reasons why tourism has grown rapidly in the Republic of Ireland in recent years.   **(40 marks)**

(ii) 'Large numbers of tourists can bring many problems to tourist regions.'

Explain any **TWO** of these problems. In your answer refer to **ANY** tourist area you have studied in Europe.   **(40 marks)**

QUESTION 15.   COUNTRIES AND THEIR REGIONS

Spain, Germany, Switzerland, Italy, Belgium and Denmark

In the case of **ANY ONE** of the above countries you have studied:

(i) Draw a sketch map to show how you would divide the whole country into **TWO OR MORE REGIONS**.   **(20 marks)**

(ii) Select **TWO** of these regions and, in the case of each, describe the development of the region using the following headings:

- Physical Geography
- Agriculture
- Manufacturing **or** Services   **(60 marks)**

QUESTION 16.   REGIONS IN EUROPE

Paris Basin, West of Ireland, South East England, North Italian Plain and The Scottish Highlands.

From the list above select **ONE** core and **ONE** peripheral region and describe the regions under the following headings:

- Physical Geography
- Climate
- Agriculture
- Manufacturing Industry   **(80 marks)**

QUESTION 17.   STATEMENTS ON EUROPE

Select any **TWO** of the following statements and discuss them in detail:

(i)   Irish agriculture has benefited greatly from our membership of the European Union.   **(40 marks)**

(ii) The enlargement of the European Union will bring benefits and problems to member countries.   **(40 marks)**

(iii) The Rhine-Ruhr area is one of Europe's largest industrial regions.   **(40 marks)**

(iv) The Irish fishing industry is facing enormous difficulties.   **(40 marks)**

(v)   The Netherlands is a very densely populated country.   **(40 marks)**

QUESTION 18.   WORLD GEOGRAPHY

Examine the map of the world below.

(i) Name the items numbered 1–8 **in your answerbook**.

Countries 1 and 2; Cities 3 and 4; Country 5 and Island 6; Mountain Range 7; Bay 8.   **(16 marks)**

*Note: The world map is on the examination paper rather than on a separate sheet.

(ii) The following areas have made world headlines in recent years.

- Kosovo
- East Timor
- Northern Ireland

Select **ONE** of the above areas and describe the issues involved.   **(40 marks)**

(iii) 'Racism is a problem in many countries of the world.'

Explain **TWO** reasons why this is so.   **(24 marks)**

GEOGRAPHY – HIGHER LEVEL

Four questions to be answered, namely Question 1, Question 5 and two questions from Section B (questions 2, 3, 4).

In discussion-type answers it is better to treat three or four aspects of the main theme in some detail rather than give a superficial treatment of a large number of points.

SECTION A — MAP WORK
Answer ALL of Question 1

---

1. Look at the 1 : 50 000 Ordnance Survey extract and Legend supplied and answer the following questions.

    (a) 'This region has a long history of human settlement'. With reference to the map extract, examine in detail the evidence in favour of this statement.

    (40 marks)

    (b) 'The Sligo region is served by a variety of modes of transport'. Examine this statement, with a sketch map to illustrate your answer. **(30 marks)**

    (c) Both the map extract and the aerial photograph provide useful evidence to support an analysis of the road infrastructure of Sligo Town. Examine how they differ in providing such evidence. **(30 marks)**

SECTION B — PHYSICAL, SOCIAL AND ECONOMIC GEOGRAPHY
Answer TWO Questions

---

2. **PHYSICAL GEOGRAPHY: Answer 2(a) or 2(b) or 2(c) or 2(d).**

    (a) (i) With reference to processes of erosion **and** to processes of deposition, examine **three** ways in which rivers shape the Irish landscape.

    (75 marks)

    (ii) Examine briefly **two** ways in which human societies attempt to manage rivers. **(25 marks)**

(b) **(i)** With reference to <u>two</u> characteristic landforms, examine how marine processes shape coastlines. **(60 marks)**

(ii) Briefly examine how <u>each</u> of the following can affect the rate at which a stretch of coastline is eroded:

- rock type
- human activity. **(40 marks)**

(c) **(i)** Using diagrams to illustrate your answer, describe the development of mid-latitude frontal depressions. **(40 marks)**

(ii) Examine in detail the sequence of weather associated with the passage of an Atlantic depression over Ireland.

In your answer, refer to:

- atmospheric pressure and wind
- cloud amount and type
- temperature
- precipitation **(40 marks)**

(iii) Outline briefly the impact which Modern Technologies have had on weather forecasting. **(20 marks)**

(d) 'The scale of human activities has increased to the point that we may be witnessing irreversible changes in the Earth's natural systems.'

Analyse this statement referring to:

- atmosphere
- soils
- forests
- waters **(100 marks)**

3. **SOCIAL GEOGRAPHY: Answer 3(a) or 3(b) or 3(c) or 3(d).**

(a) **Examine the colour aerial photograph of Sligo town supplied.**

(i) 'The influence of the river on the development of Sligo town is very evident from the photograph.'

Discuss this statement. **(40 marks)**

(ii) 'The part of Sligo town shown on the photograph is heavily populated.'

Discuss <u>two</u> pieces of evidence from the photograph which support this statement. **(30 marks)**

(iii) 'The map-maker selects what features to include on a map. The photographer includes everything within the view of the camera.'

Illustrate this difference with reference to the map **and** the photograph supplied. **(30 marks)**

(b) (i) Describe and explain any **two** examples of large-scale international human migration in the twentieth century. **(50 marks)**

(ii) Analyse **one** positive **and one** negative effect which such large-scale migrations may have on a destination or receiving area. **(50 marks)**

(c) **The Growth of Cities 1970–2010**

'Cities grow because of their efficiency in delivering a variety of services and their ability to fulfil a large number of functions for their inhabitants. A critical stage is reached, however, when this urban dream becomes a nightmare for many city dwellers.'

Los Angeles	+65%
Cairo	+153%
Tokyo	+90%
Rio de Janeiro	+127%
Mexico City	+97%

Analyse this statement with reference to the data given in the table above. In your answer, you should refer to the social and economic contrasts between different countries. **(100 marks)**

(d) (i) Among the factors which hinder development in the world's poorer countries are:

- the physical environment
- military spending
- rapid population growth
- unfair trade
- foreign debt

Examine with reference to examples how any **three** of these factors have hindered the economic development of developing countries. **(75 marks)**

(ii) Analyse briefly the relative merits of **two** types of aid for developing countries. **(25 marks)**

4.   **ECONOMIC GEOGRAPHY: Answer 4(a) or 4(b) or 4(c) or 4(d)**

(a)   **Key Urban Trends**

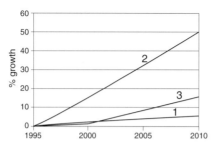
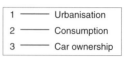

Economic development in Western economies is reflected in increasing levels of:

(i)   urbanisation;

(ii)   consumption;

(iii)   car ownership.

Discuss this statement with reference to any **two** of the above.   **(100 marks)**

(b)   (i)   'The factors affecting the location of manufacturing industry have changed over time.' Examine the validity of this statement, referring to examples which you have studied.   **(70 marks)**

(ii)   'Recycling should be central to economic planning — local, national and international — in the 21st century.'

Outline **two** arguments in favour of recycling, referring to examples which you have studied.   **(30 marks)**

(c)   The following economic forces have a major influence on modern agriculture:

*   Demand and supply in farm products;
*   The role of public policy;
*   Technology and rising costs;
*   Labour force reduction;
*   Enlargement of farms;
*   Farm incomes;

Select **three** of the above factors and examine the influence of **each** on modern agriculture.   **(100 marks)**

(d)   With reference to any exercise in geographical fieldwork which you have completed:

(i)   Give the title and aims of the fieldwork.   **(10 marks)**

(ii)   Explain how you prepared for the fieldwork.   **(20 marks)**

(iii) Describe how you carried out the work in the field.　　　**(30 marks)**

(iv) Explain how you presented your findings and outline your conclusions.　　　**(30 marks)**

(v) Describe **one** aspect of your findings which would merit further investigation.　　　**(10 marks)**

SECTION C
Answer Question 5

5. **Regional Geography: Answer 5(a) or 5(b) or 5(c) or 5(d).**

(a) With reference to Ireland **and** to **one** other maritime country in Western Europe, compare and contrast the factors which have influenced the development of their fishing industries.　　　**(100 marks)**

(b) Republic of Ireland, France, Germany, Sweden, Spain.

Select **one** of the above countries and, with the aid of a sketch-map, suggest and justify its division into **three** or more geographical regions. **(100 marks)**

(c) **(i)** Analyse the reasons for the successful development of the tourist industry in **two** contrasting countries in Western Europe.　　　**(40 marks)**

(ii) Examine the economic importance of the tourist industry in **one** of the countries which you identified in part (i) above.　　　**(30 marks)**

(iii) Briefly describe **two** ways in which mass tourism can have serious negative effects on a region.　　　**(30 marks)**

(d) Analyse the major factors which have influenced the development of **either** agriculture **or** manufacturing industry in a Scandinavian country of your choice.　　　**(100 marks)**

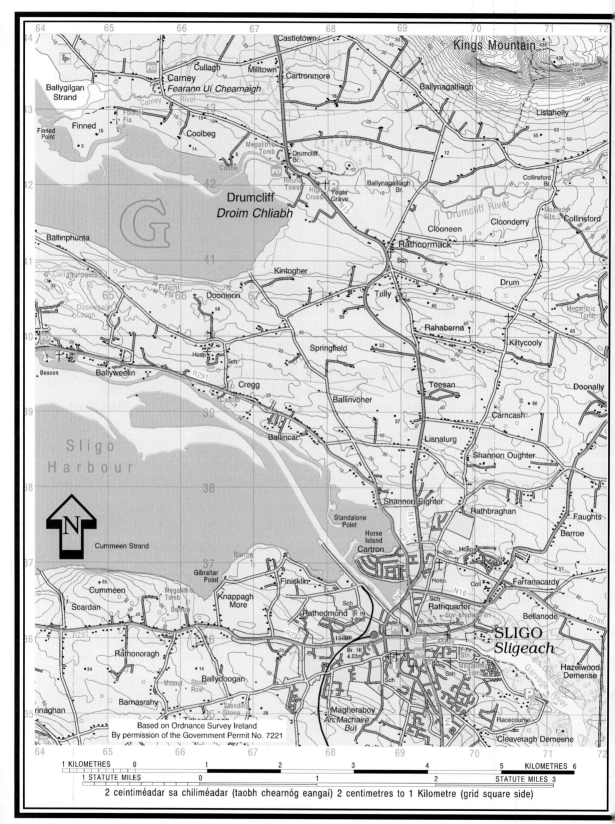

64   65   66   67   68   69   70   71   72

Castletown

Kings Mountain 438

436

Cullagh   Milltown   Cartronmore

Carney   Ballynagalliagh

Ballygilgan   Fearann Uí Chearnaigh
Strand

Lislahelly

Carney   River   43

Fulacht   15   Collinsford
Fia   Br.

Finned   Coolbeg

Finned   14   Megalithic   Drumcliff
Point   5   Tomb   Br.   12

Castle   Collinsford

Round   Ballynagalliagh   Clooneen   Cloonderry   Moated   Collinsford
Tower   Br.   Site

Drumcliff   High   Yeats'
Cross   Grave

Droim Chliabh   Rathcormack

Ballinphunta   Sch   Drum

41

Kintogher   Tully

Curraghnagap   Fulacht   Rahaberna
Fia   66   Doonierin   67

Doonweelin   58   Kiltycooly
Lough   50

PO   Springfield   53   Teesan   Doonally

Beacon   Hosp   Sch   Carncash

Ballyweelin   Cregg   Ballinvoher   Lisnalurg

Castle   Shannon Oughter

39   Ballincar

Sligo   Shannon Eighter   Rathbraghan

Harbour   Standalone   Faughts
Point   Barroe

38   Horse
Island   Rathquarter

N   Cartron   Farranacardy

Standalone   Hosp
Point   Coll   Bellanode

Cummeen Strand   Barrow   Hosp.   N16

Gibraltar   Finisklin   Rathedmond   SLIGO
Point   Br Ht
Cummeen   Megalithic   Knappagh   3·89m   Sligeach
Tomb   More
Scardan   Barrow   134MP   Hazelwood
Br. Ht   Demense
R292   Rathonoragh   R292   4·03m

Ballydoogan   Mound   Stone   Standing   Racecourse
Row   Stone

Barnasrahy   29   Cleaveragh Demense

rinaghan   Based on Ordnance Survey Ireland   Magheraboy
By permission of the Government Permit No. 7221   An Machaire
Buí

64   65   66   67   68   69   70   71   72

1 KILOMETRES   0   1   2   3   4   5   KILOMETRES 6

1 STATUTE MILES   0   1   2   STATUTE MILES 3

2 ceintiméadar sa chiliméadar (taobh chearnóg eangaí) 2 centimetres to 1 Kilometre (grid square side)

© Ordnance Survey Ireland

Ordnance Survey of Ireland
Suirbhéireacht Ordánais na hÉireann
DISCOVERY SERIES · SRAITH EOLAIS

Legend | Eochair

Eolas Turasóireachta / Tourist Information

- Láithreán carbhán (idirthurais) / Caravan site (transit)
- Brú An Óige / Neamhspleách / Hostel An Óige / Independent
- Ionad pairceála / Parking
- Láithreán picnicí / Picnic site
- Teileafón Poiblí / Public Telephone
- Láithreán campála / Camping site
- **i** Ionad eolais turasóireachta (ar oscailt ar feadh na bliana) / Tourist Information centre (regular opening)
- **i** Ionad eolais turasóireachta (ar oscailt le linn an tséasúir) / Tourist Information centre (restricted opening)
- Ionad dearctha / Viewpoint
- **A T** An Taisce / National Trust
- Tearmann Dúlra / Nature Reserve
- Galfchúrsa, machaire gailf / Golf Course or Links

Bóithre / Roads

- M 1 / 1 Mótarbhealach / Motorway (Junction number)
- N 11 Bóthar príomha náisiúnta / National Primary Road
- N 71 Bóthar tánaisteach náisiúnta / National Secondary Road
- Carrbhealach dúbailte / Dual Carriageway
- Bóthar príomha /tánaisteach náisiúnta beartaithe / Proposed Nat. Primary / Secondary Road
- R 574 Bóthar Réigiúnach / Regional Road
- 4 metres min / 4 metres max — Bóthar den tríú grád / Third Class Road
- Boithre de chineál eile / Other Roads
- Bealach / Track

Gnéithe ginearálta / General features

- Foirgnimh le hais a chéile / Built up Area
- Aerfort / Airport
- Aerpháirc / Airfield
- Oifig phoist / Post office
- Garda Síochána / Police
- Stáisiún cumhachta (uisce) / Power Station (Hydro)
- Stáisiún cumhachta (breosla iontaiseach) / Power Station (Fossil)
- Líne tarchurtha leictreachais / Electricity Transmission Line
- Crann / Mast
- Eaglais no séipéal / Church or Chapel
- Ardeaglais / Cathedral
- Cuaille triantánachta / Triangulation Pillar
- Trasnú cliathráin / Graticule Intersection
- Siúlbhealach le comharthaí; gan comharthaí / Waymarked Walks; Unmarked
- Ferry V Bád fartha (feithiclí) / Ferry (Vehicle)
- Ferry P Bád fartha (paisinéirí) / Ferry (Passenger)

Teorainneacha / Boundaries

- Teorainn idirnáisiúnta / International Boundary
- Teorainn chontae / County Boundary
- Páirc Náisiúnta / National Park
- Páirc Foraoise / Forest Park
- Seilbh de chuid an Aire Chosanta / Dept. of Defence Property
- Foraois bhuaircíneach / Coniferous Plantation
- Coill nádúrtha / Natural Woodland
- Foraois mheasctha / Mixed Woodland

Séadchomhartha / Antiquities

- Séadchomhartha Ainmnithe / Named Antiquities
- Clós, m.sh. Ráth nó Lios / Enclosure, e.g. Ringfort
- Láthair Chatha (le dáta) / Battlefield (with date)

Relíf / Relief

- Céim imlíne comhairde 10m / 10m Contour Interval
- Céim imlíne comhairde 50m / 50m Contour Interval
- 123 · Spota airde / Spot Height

Gnéithe uiscí / Water features

- Loch / Lake
- Canáil, canáil (thirim) / Canal, Canal (dry)
- Abhainn nó sruthán / River or Stream
- Teach Solais in úsáid / as úsáid / Lighthouse in use / disuse
- Bádóireacht / Boating activities
- Líne bharr láin / High Water Mark
- Líne lag trá / Low Water Mark
- shingle,mud sand or loose rock
- Trá / Beach

Iarnróid / Railways

- Iarnróid / Railways
- Iarnród tionscalaíoch / Industrial Line
- Tollán / Tunnel
- LC Crosaire comhréidh / Level Crossing
- Stáisiún traenach / Railway Station

IRISH NATIONAL GRID

	A	B	C	D	E
	F	G	H	J	K
	L	M	N	O	P
	Q	R	S	T	U
	V	W	X	Y	Z

SAMPLE GRID REFERENCE ONLY

NOTE: THESE GRID REFERENCES ARE **SAMPLE REFERENCES ONLY!** AND THE PLACES NAMED ARE NOT FOUND ON THIS MAP EXTRACT.

FROM :-

DISCOVERY SERIES SHEET 2
RATHMULLAN C 295 275

DISCOVERY SERIES SHEET 2
JACOBS BRIDGE C 347 323

©GOVERNMENT OF IRELAND
RIALTAS na hEIREANN 1996

EXAMINATION PAPERS

AN ROINN OIDEACHAIS AGUS EOLAÍOCHTA

LEAVING CERTIFICATE EXAMINATION, 2001

GEOGRAPHY – ORDINARY LEVEL

MONDAY, 11 JUNE – AFTERNOON, 1.30 to 4.50

INSTRUCTIONS TO CANDIDATES

Question 1 concerns the Ordnance Survey map and is compulsory.

The other questions, from 2 to 18, are laid out in **FOUR** sections. These are Physical Geography, Social Geography, Economic Geography, Regional and World Geography.

Five questions must be answered but **not more than two questions** may be answered from any one section. Candidates must attempt:

● Question 1;

● One Regional and World Geography question [from Questions 14–18];

● Three other questions from 2–18;

  The choice of questions from 2 to 18 is subject to the restriction, specified above, that **not more than two questions** may be answered from any one section.

PLEASE MAKE SURE YOU HAVE AN ORDNANCE SURVEY MAP AND AN AERIAL PHOTOGRAPH BEFORE ATTEMPTING THIS PAPER.

THIS QUESTION <u>MUST</u> BE ANSWERED

<u>QUESTION 1.</u>   <u>ORDNANCE SURVEY</u>

Examine the 1:50 000 Ordnance Survey Map and legend supplied with this paper.

(i) Draw a sketch map of the area covered by the Ordnance Survey Map. On the sketch map, show and name the following:

  • A Named River   • A Golf Course
  • An Electricity Transmission Line • A County Boundary
  • The Built up area of Ardee   • A National Secondary Route   **(30 marks)**

  [Note: The sketch map should <u>not</u> be a tracing.]

(ii) Using evidence from the Ordnance Survey Map only, suggest <u>**THREE**</u> reasons why the town of Ardee grew up at this location.   (30 marks)

(iii) "The area shown on the map has a long history of settlement." Identify **THREE** different types of information from the map that support this statement.

(20 marks)

PHYSICAL GEOGRAPHY

Questions 2–5

QUESTION 2.   **GLACIAL LANDFORMS**

Hanging Valley, Corrie (Cirque), Glaciated Valley, Drumlin, Esker and Outwash Plain.

(i) Select **THREE** of the above glacial features and, using a diagram, describe how each of them was formed. **(60 marks)**

(ii) Give **TWO** reasons why glaciated landscapes are very attractive to tourists.

(20 marks)

QUESTION 3.   **RIVERS**

(i) Name **TWO** features formed by river erosion and **TWO** features formed by river deposition. **(20 marks)**

(ii) Explain, with the aid of a diagram or diagrams, how any **THREE** of the features you have named in part (i) were formed. **(60 marks)**

QUESTION 4.   **THE SEA**

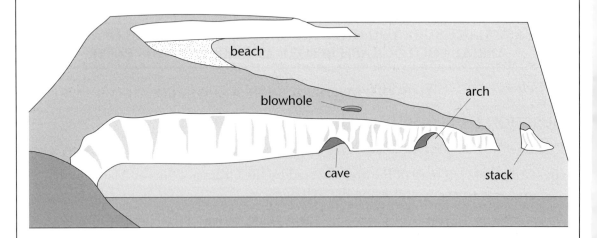

(i) Sea Stack, Sea Arch, Sea Cave, Blowhole and Beach.

Select any **THREE** of the features above and in the case of **EACH**:

- Describe and explain, with the aid of a diagram, how it was formed.

(60 marks)

ii) The sea is eroding the coastline in many places.

Explain any **TWO** ways to limit this erosion. **(20 marks)**

QUESTION 5.   THE PHYSICAL WORLD

Explain **TWO** of the following statements in some detail:

(i) Rocks have many economic uses. **(40 marks)**

(ii) Many occupations depend on accurate weather forecasts. **(40 marks)**

(iii) Soil erosion continues to be a major problem in many parts of the world.

(40 marks)

(iv) Name and briefly describe **ONE** cause and **TWO** consequences (results) of earthquakes. **(40 marks)**

SOCIAL GEOGRAPHY

Questions 6–9

QUESTION 6.   AERIAL PHOTOGRAPH

Draw a sketch map (not a tracing) of the area covered by the aerial photograph of Ardee supplied with this paper.

(i) On the sketch map name and identify:

- A church and graveyard
- A modern housing development
- A timber storage yard
- An area of agricultural land use
- The main shopping area **(30 marks)**

(ii) Identify and name **THREE** town functions in the town of Ardee. Give evidence from the map and the photograph in support of your answer. **(30 marks)**

(iii) Suggest a suitable location for a supermarket in the area covered by the photograph. State the location, with reference to foreground, background etc. and explain **ONE** advantage and **ONE** disadvantage of using evidence from the photograph only. **(20 marks)**

QUESTION 7.   FOREIGN DEBT

(i) "Each year Developing Countries pay the Developed World much more in debt repayments than they receive in grants."

Explain **TWO** effects this debt has on the countries in the Developing World.

(40 marks)

(ii) What measures can the Developed World take to reduce debt repayments from the Developing World? **(40 marks)**

Source – Trócaire: "Taking Action on Debt."

QUESTION 8. POPULATION STUDIES

(i) A number of problems are made worse by high population densities in cities or towns; some are listed below:

- Overcrowding
- Traffic congestion
- Poor health conditions
- Pollution
- Unemployment

Select any **THREE** of the above problems and explain them with reference to any **ONE** city or town you have studied. **(60 marks)**

(ii) The Irish Government plans to move some government departments out of Dublin to other parts of the country. Explain **TWO** of the effects this will have on

- Dublin
- Other parts of the country **(20 marks)**

QUESTION 9. SOCIAL GEOGRAPHY ISSUES

Explain **TWO** of the following statements in some detail:

(i) Families are usually larger in the Developing World. **(40 marks)**

(ii) Civil war is a major problem for countries in Africa. **(40 marks)**

(iii) Finding enough land for housing development is becoming a serious problem in some cities. **(40 marks)**

(iv) Labour shortages are now a major issue in many parts of Ireland. **(40 marks)**

ECONOMIC GEOGRAPHY

Questions 10–13

QUESTION 10.   **ENERGY**

Solar Power   Hydroelectric Power   Tidal Power   Wind Power

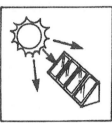 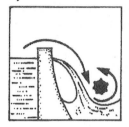  

(i)   Describe and explain any **THREE** of the above types of renewable energy
sources.   **(60 marks)**

(ii) Explain **TWO** ways in which people can save energy in the home.   **(20 marks)**

QUESTION 11.   **AGRICULTURE**

(i)   Agriculture is a system with **INPUTS**, **PROCESSES** and **OUTPUTS**.

Explain this system with reference to agriculture in any country you have
studied.   **(60 marks)**

(ii) Why are so many farmers leaving agriculture in the **Developed World**?

(20 marks)

QUESTION 12.   **ECONOMIC GEOGRAPHY ISSUES**

Explain **TWO** of the following statements in some detail:

(i)   Pollution control has economic consequences.   **(40 marks)**

(ii) Ireland is a world leader in computer manufacturing.   **(40 marks)**

(iii) Public transport provision is now a major concern in urban areas.   **(40 marks)**

(iv) Rising oil prices are a growing concern in the world today.   **(40 marks)**

QUESTION 13.   **FIELDWORK**

With reference to **ANY** fieldwork exercise that you have completed in Geography:

(i)   State the **title** and **aims** of the exercise.   **(8 marks)**

(ii) Describe how **you prepared** for the exercise.   **(16 marks)**

(iii) Describe the **methods you used to gather** the information.   **(24 marks)**

(iv) Describe the **results** of the fieldwork.   **(12 marks)**

(v)   Explain the **methods you used to present** your results.   **(12 marks)**

(vi) Did your fieldwork exercise **help you to understand** the practical value of Geography? **(8 marks)**

REGIONAL AND WORLD GEOGRAPHY

Questions 14–18

• **You must attempt at least One Question from Regional and World Geography <u>but</u> you may not attempt more than Two Questions.**

QUESTION 14.   TYPES OF REGIONS

- **Core/Developed Regions**
- **Peripheral/Underdeveloped Regions**
- **Depressed/Resource Declining Regions**

Select any **<u>TWO</u>** of these three types of regions and for **<u>EACH</u>**:

(i) Name **<u>ONE</u>** example of each type in Europe.   **(10 marks)**

(ii) Describe and explain some of the main characteristics of the **<u>TWO</u>** regions chosen.   **(70 marks)**

QUESTION 15.   COUNTRIES AND THEIR REGIONS

Ireland, Switzerland, Germany, Spain, Belgium and France.

In the case of **<u>ANY ONE</u>** of the above countries you have studied:

(i) Draw a sketch map to show how you would divide the whole country into **TWO OR MORE REGIONS**.   **(20 marks)**

(ii) Select **<u>TWO</u>** of these regions and, in the case of each, describe the development of the region using the following headings:

- Physical Geography
- Agriculture
- Manufacturing <u>or</u> Services   **(60 marks)**

QUESTION 16.   INDUSTRY IN IRELAND

Number of workers employed in Irish Industry 1987 to 1997:

(i) Explain **<u>THREE</u>** reasons why the number of industrial workers has increased so rapidly in Ireland. Refer to the graph above in your answer.   **(50 marks)**

(ii) The vast majority of Irish industries are concentrated in Dublin and other cities.

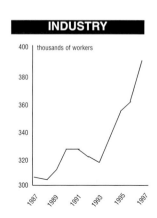

INDUSTRY

Explain **TWO** ways that industry can be attracted to other areas in Ireland.

(30 marks)

QUESTION 17. STATEMENTS ON EUROPE

Select any **TWO** of the following statements and discuss them in detail:

(i) Irish agriculture is facing many challenges in the future. (40 marks)

(ii) Norway is one of Europe's largest fishing nations. (40 marks)

(iii) Italy has many attractions for tourists. (40 marks)

(iv) The Ruhr in Germany is one of Europe's leading industrial regions. (40 marks)

QUESTION 18. WORLD GEOGRAPHY

Examine the map of the world above.

(i) **In your answerbook**, name the items numbered 1–10.

Countries 1, 2 and 3; Islands 4 and 5; Mountain Range 6; Capital Cities 7 and 8; Sea Areas 9 and 10. (20 marks)

* Note the world map is on the examination paper rather than on a separate sheet.

(ii) The following areas have made world headlines in recent years.

• Yugoslavia and its neighbours   • Middle East   • Northern Ireland

Select **ONE** of the above areas and describe the issues involved. (40 marks)

(iii) "The movement of refugees and asylum seekers across borders is becoming a major feature of the world today."

Discuss this statement by referring to any **ONE** area you have studied.

(20 marks)

AN ROINN OIDEACHAIS AGUS EOLAÍOCHTA

LEAVING CERTIFICATE EXAMINATION, 2001

GEOGRAPHY – HIGHER LEVEL

MONDAY, 11 JUNE – AFTERNOON, 1.30 TO 4.50

Four questions to be answered, namely Question 1, Question 5 and two questions from Section B (questions 2, 3, 4).

In discussion-type answers it is better to treat three or four aspects of the main theme in some detail rather than give a superficial treatment of a large number of points.

SECTION A — MAP WORK
Answer ALL of Question 1

---

1. **Make sure you have an Ordnance Survey map and an Aerial Photograph.**

    (a) Describe **three** key factors affecting the evolution of the town of Ardee.

    Make detailed reference to map evidence in your answer. **(30 marks)**

    (b) "Much of the historic settlement in the area covered by the map is rural settlement."

    Comment on the validity of this statement using map evidence only.

    (30 marks)

    (c) Suggest a suitable site for a new hotel/conference centre complex.

    Justify your selection with detailed evidence from both the map **and** the photograph supplied. **(40 marks)**

SECTION B — PHYSICAL, SOCIAL AND ECONOMIC GEOGRAPHY
Answer TWO Questions

---

2. **PHYSICAL GEOGRAPHY: Answer 2(a) or 2(b) or 2(c) or 2(d).**

    (a) <u>River Studies</u>

(i) Explain the processes involved in the formation of **three** landforms found along the course of a river.   **(75 marks)**

(ii) "River flooding cannot be totally avoided but it must be controlled."

Assess the validity of this statement in the light of examples you have studied.   **(25 marks)**

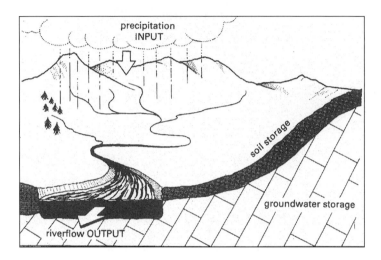

(b) Plate Tectonics, Earthquakes and Volcanoes

(i) Explain the relationship between Plate Movements and the occurrence of volcanoes **and** earthquakes.   **(75 marks)**

(ii) Discuss, with reference to examples, **two** negative effects of volcanic action.   **(25 marks)**

(c) Types of Weathering

(i) Describe and explain **one** example of CHEMICAL WEATHERING and **one** example of PHYSICAL **or** MECHANICAL WEATHERING.

(60 marks)

(ii) Examine the causes **and** effects of ACID RAIN.   **(40 marks)**

(d) Rainfall in Ireland and Climatic Change

(i) "The amount of rainfall in Ireland varies from place to place."
Comment on this statement by outlining **three** of the factors affecting this variation.
Use examples from the map below to illustrate your answer.

(60 marks)

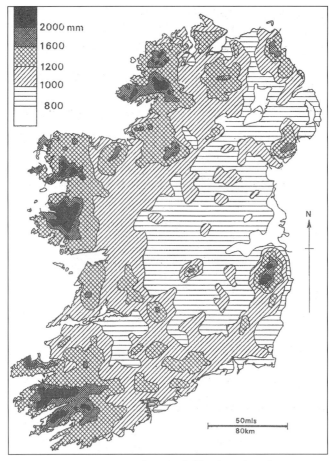

| 2000 mm |
| 1600 |
| 1200 |
| 1000 |
| 800 |

N

50mls
80km

Annual Rainfall of Ireland

(ii) "Climatic change and the human contributions to that change are major issues facing humankind." Explain this statement. **(40 marks)**

3. **SOCIAL GEOGRAPHY: Answer 3(a) or 3(b) or 3(c) or 3(d).**

(a) **Examine the colour aerial photograph of Ardee supplied.**

(i) Draw a sketch map of the area of Ardee covered by the aerial photograph.
Identify and name on your map **four** different land uses evident on the photograph. **(40 marks)**

(ii) "Traffic congestion is likely to be a problem in Ardee."
Using evidence from **both** the Ordnance Survey **and** the aerial photograph supplied, comment on the validity of this statement.
In your answer identify **two** places where traffic congestion is likely to be at its worst. **(30 marks)**

(iii) Imagine that the timber yard in the centre foreground of the aerial photograph is about to close.

Suggest **one** private and **one** public use of this site that would benefit the town of Ardee. **(30 marks)**

(b) Famines in Africa

(i) "In recent years we have again witnessed the tragedy of famine in Africa."
Examine **three** causes of such famines using examples from Africa that you have studied. **(60 marks)**

(ii) Discuss **two** courses of action which could be taken to address the problem. **(40 marks)**

(c) Urbanisation and Development

"The growth in the percentage of population in urban areas has brought advantages **and** problems to both developed and developing countries."

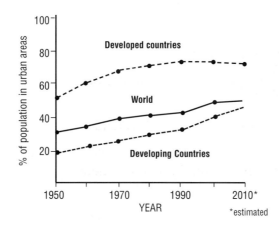

Examine this statement with reference to the graph above and to examples you have studied. **(100 marks)**

(d) Migration

(i) "The influx of refugees, migrant workers and asylum seekers presents opportunities and difficulties for receiving countries."
Examine some of the opportunities **and** difficulties referred to in this statement. **(70 marks)**

(ii) Outline **three** ways in which the Irish Government might respond to the challenges outlined in Part (i). **(30 marks)**

4. **ECONOMIC GEOGRAPHY: Answer 4(a) or 4(b) or 4(c) or 4(d).**

   (a) Uses of Energy

   (i) Examine some of the arguments in favour of **and** some of the arguments against the continued use of Nuclear Power in the economies of Western Europe. **(60 marks)**

   (ii) Assess the merits of any **two** renewable energy sources you have studied. **(40 marks)**

   (b) Industrial Location

   (i) "Labour and markets are now more important than the availability of raw materials as factors affecting the location of modern industries." Discuss this statement with reference to examples you have studied. **(60 marks)**

   (ii) "In spite of changes in the factors affecting industrial location, ocean ports continue to be attractive to manufacturing industries." Examine this statement, referring in your answer to examples you have studied. **(40 marks)**

   (c) Agriculture

   Examine, with reference to specific examples, the importance of **each** of the following in the development of Agriculture:
   • Physical conditions
   • Distance from markets
   • Political factors. **(100 marks)**

   (d) Fieldwork

   In relation to **any** geographical fieldwork which you have completed:
   (i) State the title and aims of the exercise. **(10 marks)**
   (ii) Explain how you prepared for the fieldwork. **(15 marks)**
   (iii) Describe how you gathered and recorded data in the field. **(30 marks)**
   (iv) Explain the main results and conclusions. **(30 marks)**
   (v) What Geographical Skills did you use in conducting your fieldwork Project? **(15 marks)**

SECTION C
Answer Question 5

---

5. **REGIONAL GEOGRAPHY: Answer 5(a) or 5(b) or 5(c) or 5(d).**

   (a) Ireland's Economic Expansion

(i) Ireland's economic growth over the past decade has been very impressive.
Examine any **three** factors which account for this development.

(80 marks)

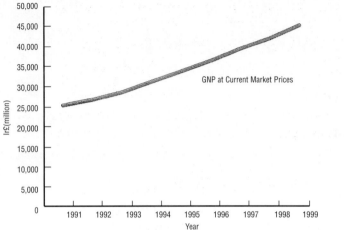

GNP at Current Market Prices

Republic of Ireland's

Gross National Product

(ii) Discuss **one** negative impact of such rapid economic expansion.

(20 marks)

(b) Natural Resources

"Natural Resources play a major role in the economic development of countries."
Discuss this statement with detailed reference to any **one** of the following countries

– Switzerland, Netherlands, Norway, Sweden, Britain, Spain, Ireland.

(100 marks)

(c) Core and Periphery areas

(i) Examine, with reference to two examples from your study of Western Europe, three characteristics of a CORE region. **(60 marks)**

(ii) Suggest and justify **two** policies to adjust imbalances between CORE and PERIPHERAL regions in Europe. **(40 marks)**

(d) The Role of the Sea in Western Europe

Examine, with reference to at least **two** countries, the role of the sea in the economy of Western Europe. **(100 marks)**

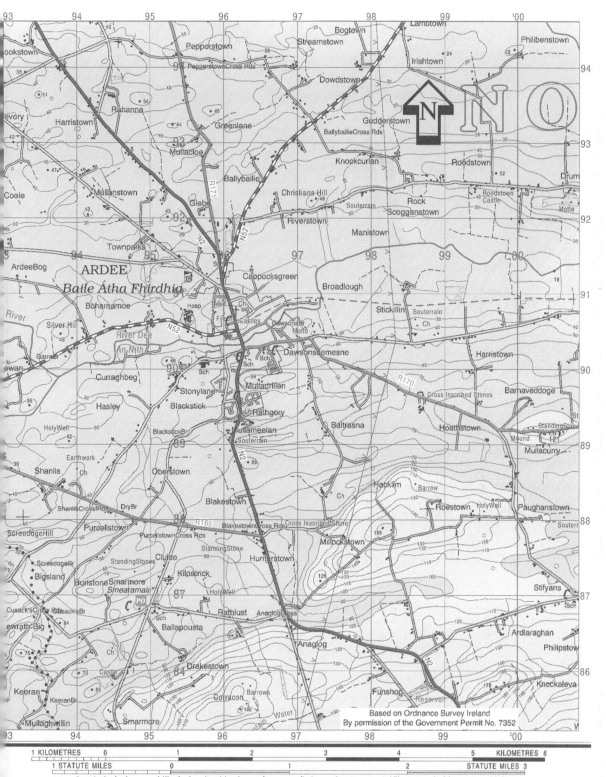

1 KILOMETRES 0 1 2 3 4 5 KILOMETRES 6

1 STATUTE MILES 0 1 2 STATUTE MILES 3

2 ceintiméadar sa chiliméadar (taobh chearnóg eangaí) 2 centimetres to 1 Kilometre (grid square side)

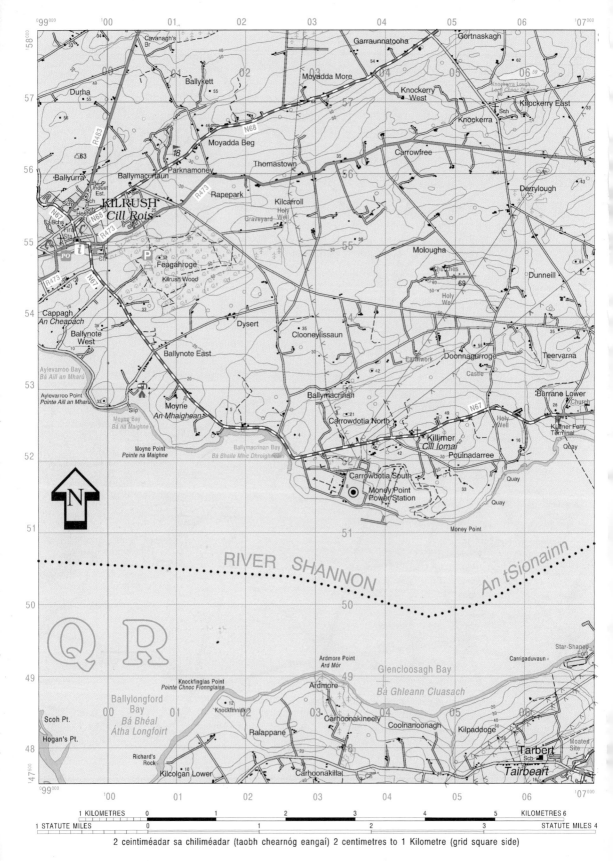

© Ordnance Survey Ireland